The CHIANTI RAIDERS

The Extraordinary Story of the
Italian Air Force in the Battle of Britain

Other Second World War titles by Peter Haining and published by Robson Books:

The Jail That Went To Sea: An Untold Story of the Battle
of the Atlantic
The Mystery of Rommel's Gold: The Search for the
Legendary Nazi Treasure
Where The Eagle Landed: The Mystery of the German
Invasion of Britain, 1940

The
CHIANTI
RAIDERS

The Extraordinary Story of the
Italian Air Force
in the Battle of Britain

PETER HAINING

ROBSON BOOKS

First published in Great Britain in 2005 by Robson Books,
The Chrysalis Building, Bramley Road, London W10 6SP

An imprint of **Chrysalis** Books Group plc

British Library Cataloguing in Publication Data
A catalogue record for this title is available from the British Library.

ISBN 1 86105 829 2

All photographs © The Peter Haining Collection and the W. O. G. Lofts Archive
Index created by Indexing Specialists (UK) Ltd
Printed by Creative Print & Design (Wales), Ebbw Vale

For Robert and Rachel Haining –
my Italian connection

Indications that Italian aircraft now in Belgium may soon operate over South East England. Types include BR.20 bombers, G.50 fighters and CR.42 fighters. Small number of Cant Z1007 long range bombers also believed to be in Belgium.

Air Intelligence Report
20 October 1940

CONTENTS

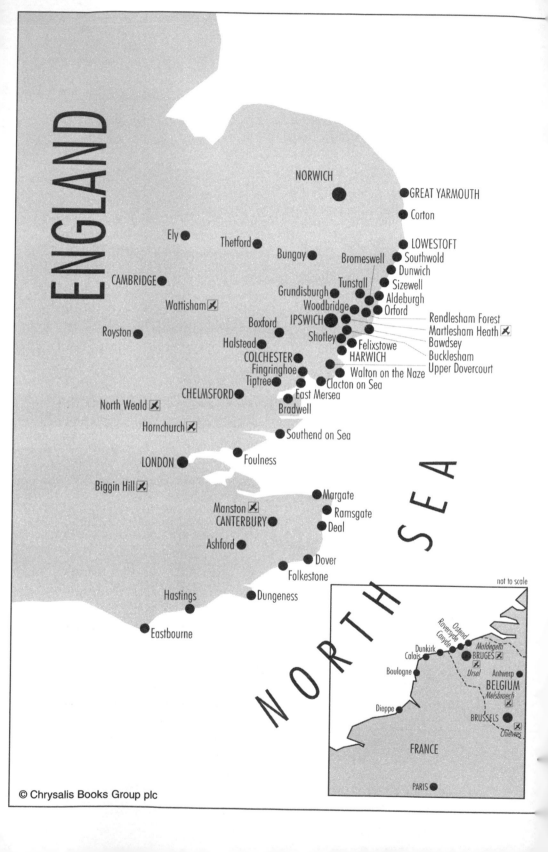

ENGLAND

NORWICH

● GREAT YARMOUTH
● Corton

Ely ●   Thetford ●   ● LOWESTOFT
                        Bungay ●   Bromeswell ●   ● Southwold
CAMBRIDGE ●   ● Dunwich
                              Tunstall ●   Sizewell
Wattisham ✈   Grundisburgh ●   ● Aldeburgh
                         Woodbridge ●   ● Orford
           Boxford ● IPSWICH ●   Rendlesham Forest
Royston ●   Shotley ●   Martlesham Heath ✈
        Halstead ●   Bawdsey
              COLCHESTER ●   ● Felixstowe   Bucklesham
        Fingringhoe ●   HARWICH   Upper Dovercourt
         Tiptree ●   Clacton on Sea
                              ● Walton on the Naze
North Weald ✈   CHELMSFORD ● ● East Mersea
                              Bradwell
Hornchurch ✈
                      ● Southend on Sea
LONDON ●   ● Foulness

Biggin Hill ✈
                                    ● Margate
           Manston ✈   ● Ramsgate
           CANTERBURY ●   ● Deal
       Ashford ●
                              ● Dover
                         Folkestone
   Hastings ●   ● Dungeness

● Eastbourne

NORTH SEA

not to scale

Ostend
Raversyde
Coxyde
Dunkirk   Maldegem
Calais   BRUGES ✈
Boulogne   ✈
            Ursel   Antwerp ●
                     BELGIUM
                     Melsbroech ✈
Dieppe ●
                     BRUSSELS ●
                          Chièvres ✈
FRANCE

PARIS ●

FOREWORD

Sixty-five years ago, on the night of 5 November 1940, the stillness that enveloped the Suffolk village of Boxford as completely as the darkness was suddenly shattered by the noise of an exploding bomb. Although the small community nestling in a fold of East Anglian countryside is today well known for its annual firework celebrations on Guy Fawkes Night, there was no mistaking the explosion in that second year of the war as anything other than a reminder of the dangerous threshold on which the whole nation stood. Throughout the summer, what had become known as 'The Battle of Britain' had been fought out overhead – and with winter approaching, there seemed to many people little likelihood of a let-up. Yet, on this particular evening, *something* about the raid was to prove very different from those attacks that had gone before.

Like everyone else in Britain at this time, the people of Boxford went about their daily lives as best they could – many of them offering silent prayers for the fathers, sons and daughters who had been called away by the demands of the war. There was, though, an ever-present reminder on their doorstep: less than a mile away from the village stood an RAF airfield. Or what *seemed* like an airfield, complete with a landing strip, operational buildings and a number of aircraft that any schoolboy could have identified as Wellington Bombers. By day and night, the site bustled with the activity of RAF personnel as they operated the station, serviced the aircraft and kept a constant watch for enemy aircraft overhead.

Yet the Boxford airfield was a dummy, a decoy site, known in official jargon as a 'K', possibly for 'Konky', site. It had been built in collaboration between RAF electricians and engineers, and technicians from the British film industry. Their collective skills – in particular the art of make-believe, courtesy of the men from Shepperton Studios, in the design of such sites and the creation of authentic-looking dummy aircraft – were all part of the British Air Ministry's strategy to defeat German bombing by deception. Already, almost 500 of these sites had been built across the country as part of a campaign of illusion that probably did more to protect the nation's forces and civilians from the Nazi threat than they ever knew – at the time, at least.

Of course, it was impossible to keep the truth of such places from the local population. But the consistency with which the sites were bombed – 440 hits during the Battle of Britain alone – demonstrated that this was one secret that fooled the Germans. And others, too, in the winter days and nights that followed.

The 'Decoy Men' who ran these sites had the unique distinction of being probably the only servicemen deliberately trying to *make* the *Luftwaffe* bomb them. One of their number was 20-year-old Corporal Doug Patrick, an engineer from Middlesbrough, who had been posted to the 'K' site at Boxford in early 1940 and survived numerous raids. While there, he met a local girl, Peggy, and remained to make his home in the village, where he still lives. An engaging man, he talks modestly about his experiences in the art of deception – at the same time providing another piece of the jigsaw in an almost forgotten episode of the war:

> It was our job to fool Jerry into bombing us. If they hit our 'K' site then it would save a real airfield and show we were doing a good job. We weren't supposed to talk about what we did to anyone then – just say we were in the Air Force and leave it at that.

When Doug joined the RAF at the start of the war he was posted to Weston-super-Mare for training and then on to the Bomber Command station at Wattisham, to the south-west of Ipswich. In order to try and protect the airfield from enemy attack, the Air Ministry decided to erect the decoy site at Boxford, only a few miles away. Doug and a dozen other men under the command of Sergeant 'Chappie' Chapman were sent to build an airfield identical to Wattisham on farmer Bill Peake's acres of agricultural land.

Over the next few hectic weeks, the RAF crew assembled the wooden framework Wellington Bombers that arrived from Shepperton complete with the same squadron markings as those at the parent aerodrome. They painted old lorries to look like a fire tender, an ambulance and transport vehicles, and built a dummy hangar, a petrol store, ammunition dump, gun pit and even piles of bombs good enough to fool any raider passing overhead. An RAF roundel was inscribed on the door of Bean's Barn, which served as home to the airmen – as well as to a voracious colony of rats that proved to be just one of the hardships they had to cope with.

Each day, Doug recalled, the dummy aircraft and vehicles would be moved around the site to create the illusion they were operational. Sometimes the men would be formed into a guard party and marched around the 'station' with shouldered rifles. At night, a Glim electric 'Flare Path' would be illuminated along the false runway – and immediately dimmed if any raiders were reported in the vicinity, just as would occur at any real airfield. Occasionally, too, during an actual raid, special fire baskets would be lit to make the enemy pilots think they had hit a target.

By early November, incendiaries had been dropped on the area on several occasions, lighting up the sky with great flashes, and bombs had exploded with mighty roars on nearby Cox Hill, Hadleigh Road and Stone Street. On what in peacetime would have been Guy Fawkes Night, it was the turn of the 'K' site. Doug Patrick again:

> I remember Bill Peake's wife, who was in the farmhouse, saying the explosion was terrifying. The noise of the bomb must have woken up everyone for miles around. Fortunately, no one was injured.

The following morning, as the men on the site went about their usual duties tidying up what damage had been caused, further information was received about the raid. The aircraft involved had evidently been one of a force of thirteen bombers that had targeted the Ipswich area. The planes had dropped their bombs across a wide swathe of land, but caused little real damage.

In most respects, the incident was no different from countless others that had been reported all over the eastern counties during the year – except that on this occasion, the raiders had *not* been German. Indeed, a story was already circulating among local people – later described in the *East Anglian Daily Times* – that the engines of these aircraft had not sounded like the 'usual' kind at all, but made a strange noise 'like rattling tin cans'.

The nation's aerial watchdogs, Fighter Command, were of course on the alert and did not need the curious audio information to confirm the identity of the attacking force. They were, in fact, Italians, who had recently arrived at bases in Belgium on the specific orders of Mussolini to fly in partnership with the *Luftwaffe*. Soon, they would earn the nickname 'The Chianti Raiders' – and it is the extraordinary story of their intervention in the Battle of Britain that is told in these pages.

INCIDENT IN
RENDLESHAM FOREST

1

The sound of a tearing alloy skin, cracking metal struts and two screaming engines could be heard across Rendlesham Forest as a large aircraft belly-flopped into the scrubland, its propellers mangling up the turf as it juddered and careered erratically to a standstill. It was a November afternoon in 1940, and inside the shuddering bomber a group of men clung desperately to the super-structure and prayed for their lives... and probably wished they had never left the sunny climes of their homeland.

Rendlesham Forest is an unspoiled area of 1,500 hectares on Suffolk's coastal belt of heath land known as the Sandlings. Consisting of large areas of coniferous trees, as well as broad-leaved belts, heath land and wetland areas, it has long been a favourite spot for recreation and is easily reached from the nearby market town of Woodbridge, five miles from the coast.

The area is haunted by remarkable historical events. Here, for example, just before the Second World War broke out, a fabulous Anglo-Saxon ship dating from about AD 650 was found buried at the village of Sutton Hoo. It was piled high with an incredible treasure trove of jewellery, armour and ancient weapons. Some forty years after this astonishing find, in 1980, a report began circulating that an unidentified flying object had been observed smashing through trees in the forest on the night after Christmas. American airmen from the twin NATO bases of Bentwaters and Woodbridge were apparently quickly sent out to investigate, but it was not until some time later that a security police sergeant was encouraged by the media to tell his story:

> The object was lit up like a Christmas tree with white and a blue bank of lights. It moved slowly at first, but then it could move so fast and it turned at right angles in an impossible way. I do not know any technology, certainly not in 1980, probably not even now, that could do the things this did. It was just like magic.

The UFO was said to have damaged a number of the trees and left holes in the ground. The incident particularly excited the interest of those local people steeped in the supernatural traditions of the area. Yet, despite claims by several men and women to have seen weird lights and even an ominous-looking shape moving through the forest on the night in question, the defence agencies of both Britain and America remained silent on what exactly *had* happened – thereby generating a mystery that has remained to this day. Even when forced into making a public statement, a decade later in January 1990, a Ministry of Defence spokesman responded with typical evasion: 'The Ministry is content that the Rendlesham incident was of no defence significance, because whatever was witnessed was not apparently hostile.'

There is, however, rather more evidence and certainly no doubt about the intentions of the bomber that crashed in the forest in November 1940. It is a story that has intrigued many researchers and historians, all of whom are agreed that this incident was definitely the result of an intrusion into British airspace – and hostile in intent. Indeed, it was part of a determined effort by another enemy air force to influence the Battle of Britain in favour of the Axis powers.

The battered and crumpled fuselage of the bomber finally came to rest at Bromeswell, near a rifle range at the village of Eyke. This, too, was an ancient settlement with a name derived from the Scandinavian word *eik*, meaning 'place at an oak tree'. The site had been dug regularly by archaeologists, who had found Roman and Ancient British remains in the vicinity. On this occasion, the noise of the crash brought several labourers, who had been working in the fields nearby, stumbling through the undergrowth to the scene. A glance at the white crosses on the wings and twin tail fins, which were now draped with pine branches broken off as the aircraft had ploughed through the trees, made it immediately obvious to all of them that this was not a British machine.

For a few moments silence reigned and nothing stirred inside the aircraft. Then, wondering if the crew might all be dead after such an impact, one of the labourers moved towards the ruined fuselage. He peered in and immediately saw the body of one dead man, and four other crew who appeared to be still breathing. Amid the tangle of wires and smashed equipment, the labourer was surprised to see that all the airmen were wearing tin hats. One slumped figure even had a camera hanging from his shoulder.

The farm worker continued to peer around the carnage until he became aware of a handful of other men coming towards the aircraft. They were in army uniforms and immediately began looking around the wreck. One of the newcomers, evidently a sergeant, shouted for anyone inside to come out. Nothing stirred for what seemed like an eternity. Then a figure stumbled through the hatch helping a second man with one arm dangling at his side. A voice suddenly broke the silence.

'They're bloody Eyeties [Italians].' It was one of the soldiers, pointing towards the white crosses on the tail fins, as if to emphasise his words. 'They're fucking lucky our boys didn't kill them all.'

After two more dishevelled figures had struggled from the wreck into the clearing, the sergeant put his head inside the fuselage. The stench of burning fuel and bloodshed almost made him vomit. Then his features creased into a grin, as something else caught his eye.

'Look what the buggers have got here!' he said, to no one in particular, reaching inside and picking up two objects from behind

3

the floor. One appeared to be a large piece of cheese and the other a bottle of red wine. The man held up the trophies for those outside to see.

'What do you make of them! Planning a celebration after they'd bombed us, were they? Well, they bloody well haven't got anything to be happy about now!' he laughed.

The wine was unmistakably Chianti – and at that moment no one could have guessed what a far-reaching impact the simple discovery would have. It would, in fact, become synonymous with the Italian air force crews now attacking England – the *Corpo Aereo Italiano* (CAI), to give them their correct title – and result in a nickname that would be applied to them all throughout their raids during the autumn of 1940 and spring of 1941: 'The Chianti Raiders'.

* * * * *

The decision of the Italian dictator Benito Mussolini to join the Western world's other great despot, Adolf Hitler, in June 1940 in the war against Britain, amounted to Italy's first attack on England since the days when the great legions of the Roman Empire had crossed the Channel and enslaved the country. This 'second coming' two thousand years later was, however, greeted with differing opinions in a Britain already hardened to the Nazis.

David Garnett, a member of the famous English literary family, took an almost amused attitude to events in his contemporary account, *War in the Air: September 1939 to May 1941*, published in 1941. Having joined the RAF on the outbreak of war, Garnett was in a privileged position to describe the aerial battles that ensued:

> The Italian bomber and fighter squadrons were sent by Mussolini so that the Italian Air Force might share in the destruction of London before it was too late and there was nothing for them to bomb. Whatever their armament and aircraft, the Italians did not fare well. They were greeted with almost incredulous enthusiasm by the pilots of the British fighter squadrons when they intercepted them. We are rather bad haters, and while we are at war with the Nazis we have

no hate to spare for the Italians. The Chianti flask and the parmesan in that wrecked aeroplane went to our hearts.

Indeed, seen with the benefit of hindsight, it is not difficult to appreciate why a mixture of amusement and prejudice coloured the British view of their new enemy at this time, as James Hayward has pointed out in his *Myths and Legends of the Second World War* (2003):

> There was a strong perception that Mussolini's troops were a cowardly rabble, reluctant to fight, yet all too keen to surrender en masse, often while carrying neatly packed suitcases. The other stereotype was of 'a lot of opera singers' (according to Roosevelt), and vainglorious dandies 'pomaded and scented, accompanied by framed pictures, birdcages and similar domestic amenities, their elegant spare uniforms neatly folded in extra suitcases and trunks.' In North Africa, the Italian Army retreated so often that their trucks were said to be fitted with five reverse gears, while in London a popular dance-step called *The Tuscana* was 'supposedly based on the Italian's way of fighting, i.e. one step forward, two steps back.' Although there is a great deal of truth in these many anecdotes about Italian military ineffectiveness, the charge of inherent cowardice is a myth, for the Italian soldier was more often the victim of inadequate training, poor equipment and incompetent leadership.

This confusion of ideas certainly provided a rich source of inspiration for Britain's leading cartoonists at the time. Take Illingworth in *Punch*, who evidently shared David Garnett's levity when he drew 'The Roman Invasion, 1940 AD' for the issue of 20 November (reprinted here). Shortly afterwards, Wren of the *Air Force Times* – who, for once, had a chance to shift the focus of his weekly series of aircraft caricatures, 'Oddentification', from Nazi aeroplanes to those of their new allies – produced a picture of a very glum-looking Italian aircraft complete with the lines:

5

'The Roman Invasion, 1940 AD' (*Punch*, 20 November 1940)

Avanti! Avanti! Mid fumes of Chianti,
The vaunted Armada took off in the breeze.
Each bulging Caproni packed tight with Polony,
Ripe Macaroni and Parmesan Cheese.[*]

The great humorist A P Herbert was similarly unable to resist the opportunity and wrote seven verses for *Punch* on 13 November entitled, 'Oh, What a Flop'. In these he referred to Mussolini as 'that big, brown, bald adventurer and friend of every thug' and compared him to several other famous Italian villains including Nero, Caligula and Lucrezia Borgia. The dictator had 'come out like those old Roman geese,' Herbert wrote, and concluded:

What shall we do with Hitler, say we all, when war is done?
What shall we do to Musso when we've biffed his brother Hun?
Let's put the two together in a cell four feet by three,
And let them talk and talk and talk. And *what* a flop they'll be!

Such views were not, however, shared by everyone at the time. J M Spaight, the principal assistant secretary at the Air Ministry, who also wrote his memoirs – entitled *The Battle of Britain* – that same year, was at pains to provide information about the capabilities of the two principal aircraft the Italian air force had at its disposal – the BR.20M heavy bombers and the speedy little CR.42 biplane fighters, both of which were already veterans of the Spanish Civil War and the fall of France:

The Fascist airmen have shown that they are as foul fighters as their Nazi brethren. No doubt it is a satisfaction to the Italian fighter pilot to feel that sometimes at least he has the British pilot at his mercy; he cannot have that feeling very often.

---

[*] There were, in fact, only nine Caproni Ca164 aircraft sent to Belgium as part of the *Corpo Aereo Italiano*. The triplane, with its shorter upper wing and squat fuselage, carried a crew of two, had a range of 530 km (330 miles) at a top speed of 217 km/h (135 mph), and was only ever used during the operation for training and communication purposes.

RAF Intelligence was also not prepared to dismiss the new enemy quite so off-handedly as the humorists and cartoonists. A report in late October 1940 circulated to all pilots and their squadrons, with copies to the Prime Minister, Winston Churchill, and the War Cabinet, declared: 'The manoeuvrability of the CR.42s, in particular their capacity to execute an extremely tight half roll, has caused considerable surprise to other pilots and undoubtedly saved many Italian fighters from destruction.'

There are, as will become evident, elements of truth in all of the statements – as is so often the case in war. Mussolini was certainly arrogantly confident that his men would mop up the last of the British resistance and a number of his pilots did believe they were superior to the RAF. What neither Mussolini or Hitler had counted on was the extraordinary resilience and courage of the RAF fighter pilots and the British people during the summer and autumn of 1940.

The facts of the 'Battle of Britain' – as it was memorably first described by Winston Churchill during his 'Finest Hour' speech to the House of Commons on 18 June of that year – are so familiar as to need no more than a brief summary.

The first German bombs had fallen on mainland Britain on 10 May and five days later the RAF responded with a raid on the Ruhr. Following the French armistice with Hitler, the *Luftwaffe* launched *Luftschlacht um England* – the 'English Air Battle' – on 23 June, sending fighter sweeps to attack coastal convoys and hoping to lure the RAF into a war of attrition. The escalation of this strategy throughout July was followed on 13 August by the start of the *Alder Angriffen* – 'Eagle Attacks' – when the German air force commenced all-out raids, but suffered heavy losses of its Stuka dive-bombers.

On 24 August, the first bombs hit central London – despite the latter having been declared a forbidden target under a personal directive by the *Luftwaffe* chief, Hermann Goering. A day later, Bomber Command retaliated with a strike on Berlin. Before the end of the month Hitler issued instructions for finalising the ill-fated *Operation Seelow* – 'Operation Sealion' – for the invasion of England. Then, as the RAF continued its courageous efforts in the skies above the country, the Führer announced he would raze

British cities to the ground and inaugurated the *Blitzkrieg* – 'Lightning War' – on 7 September, 'Black Saturday'.

As German fighter attacks by day gave way to bombing raids by night throughout September and October, the country's new ally, Italy, moved into position in Belgium to aid the *Luftwaffe*'s efforts. A combat force of two bomber *Stormi* (each equivalent to an RAF wing), one fighter wing and a *Squadriglia* (Flight) of strategic recon-naissance planes had made their way from sunny Italy across the heart of triumphant Germany to the windswept, chilly coast of occupied Belgium. Just over the English Channel, so the pilots of the *Corpo Aereo Italiano* were told, lay a weakened enemy. They could take off with optimism in their hearts, as Alfred Price has written in *Blitz on Britain* (1976):

> In the opening phase of the Blitz, which lasted until mid-November, an average of 200 raiders, including Italian aircraft based in Belgium, bombed London each night except one, and to these attacks were added daylight raids by fighter-bombers, and by single bombers attacking targets of opportunity on cloudy days.

The first to see these Italian raiders were the people of East Anglia, whose stretch of coastline, between the Thames Estuary and Great Yarmouth, had been agreed with the *Luftwaffe* as the CAI's prime target. However, not all of those who were eyewit-nesses to what followed were immediately sure of what they were seeing – having endured a summer in which the only enemy had been German. Take the example of John E Wrathall of Ipswich, who wrote to the *East Anglian Daily Times* in May 2004 after a request for information about air raids on the port of Harwich in November 1940:

> I was then a 12-year-old living in Ipswich at Crane Hill Farm. I had gone down to Shotley [Peninsula] on the bus with my great-uncle for a pleasant Sunday outing. As I was only young it was exciting when we first saw the aeroplanes, but when anti-aircraft guns opened up we

realised they were not ours. We hastily retreated up the hill and joined other people under some trees and after a while we were taken into some shelters by sailors who were presumably from HMS *Ganges*.

It was not until later that John Wrathall learned the planes had been Italian – as did Peggy Emerson of Wood Farm House, Denington, who also contributed to the same appeal for details:

I was 10 years old and at Hollesley School at this time. We were being taken out to an air raid shelter at the farm across the road and we had a very clear view of the sea, which was only two miles away. There was a fight going on between enemy and British aircraft over the sea and, as it was not overhead, we were allowed to stay outside and watch it, for a little while at least. I remember seeing at least one plane shot down and going into the sea. I was later told the planes were Italian and, much later after the war, that this was the only time that Italian planes were engaged in battle during the Battle of Britain, but I do not know if this was true.

As both of these letters illustrate, the participation of the Italian air force in the war has long been the subject of much speculation, rumour and myth. In fact, the newspapers of the time and the transcripts of radio broadcasts are little help with information about the 'Chianti Raiders'. It is to the logbooks and debriefing accounts by pilots of the RAF and the CAI, along with records kept by the East Anglian police, the army and the County Archives of Essex, Suffolk and Norfolk, that the researcher has to turn for information about what the *RAF War Diaries* for November 1940 say became known among local airmen as 'The Spaghetti Party'. Truly, it was to be no party for the men from the southern climes – although many of them fought with skill and bravery against daunting odds.

* * * * *

The area of East Anglia over which this forgotten episode of the Battle of Britain was fought is very familiar to me. I have flown over it numerous times in a light aircraft little bigger than the Italian fighters – though I had the comfort of a closed cockpit and a radio, two features that were singularly denied to many of the raiders in the chilly autumn of 1940. It is not hard to imagine when flying across those big skies with the patchwork of fields and small communities spread out below that stretch towards the rugged coastline battered by the spume-covered waves of the North Sea, just how alien it must have seemed to the CAI pilots, the majority of whom had never flown in such conditions before.

My flights from Harwich going northwards over the sandy beaches of Hollesley Bay to Aldeburgh and Southwold and then on to Lowestoft and Great Yarmouth, have helped me to see through the eyes of the Italian pilots and turn their often matter-of-fact statements into something approaching the dangerous and emotional dramas they must have experienced. The search for information has taken me from Belgium to Italy, America to New Zealand – so far-flung are the elements of this extraordinary story. I have also found clues on the doorstep of the Suffolk village of Boxford, where I have lived for almost a quarter of a century. For not only was it the base for the dummy airfield bombed by the CAI, but later, from 1943, it was the location of a Prisoner of War Camp for the 129th Italian Labour Battalion who worked on local farms until finally vacated in 1948. This area, like Rendlesham, is haunted by memories of the war.

Mussolini's intervention in the Second World War cost the Italian air force dearly in terms of men and machines. Starting out as the 'pride of Fascism' – according to *Il Duce* – with a total of 1,753 frontline aircraft, the number had fallen to only a few hundred by the time the country surrendered. According to Derek E Johnson in *East Anglia at War 1939–1945*, between 25 October 1940 and 5 January 1941, 'The Italians dispatched some 87 bombers and 40 fighters against east coast targets, claiming to have dropped 50 tons of bombs.' The author added, 'There were no fatalities.'

In fact, the totals are inaccurate and it is wrong to say there were no casualties. The CAI combat force consisted of 170 aircraft – 87 fighters, 78 bombers and 5 strategic reconnaissance planes – and a total of 6,600 personnel of all ranks. The aircraft were to record a total of 1,076 operations in just over 1,800 hours of flight, for the loss of two dozen aircraft and twenty men. The cost to Britain amounted to much the same in terms of civilians and military personnel, including the particularly tragic loss of five Royal Marines at Deal in Kent.

The general consensus of opinion among historians who have studied this period of the war is that the Italian operations were a complete failure. The fighters and bombers were so badly mauled, says one account, that they were quickly retired to defensive duties. Michael J F Bowyer in his otherwise excellent *Air Raid! The Enemy Air Offensive Against East Anglia 1939–1945* is just as unequivocal in his verdict:

> There's no point in hiding it, wartime Britain was unimpressed with its Italian adversaries. Their uniforms converted them into operatic-like figures, martial gondo-liers who once produced splendid ice cream, who must dream of the grand days of Rome which still keeps many a teacher in business. Their leader, Benito Mussolini – fat, unpleasant and with a comic name – had hijacked an excitable, appealing nation.

The history that follows in these pages offers a rather different picture: less comic, arguably more impressive, but certainly much more packed with drama and incident than has heretofore been appreciated.

THE FLIGHT OF
THE FALCON

2

Sergeant Antonio Lazzari was flying for his life.

The air raid on England by his 85 *Squadriglia* and the other fighters and bombers of 18 and 99 *Gruppo* [Group] was going horribly wrong. Just minutes before, RAF fighters had appeared as if from nowhere as the CAI force was beginning its descent towards a large estuary. The Spitfires and Hurricanes had dived into their midst with guns blazing and all hell had been let loose, scattering the invaders right across the sky.

The wind howled around the open cockpit of Lazzari's biplane as the 23-year-old pilot from Milan turned desperately northwards and saw a stretch of wild-looking coastline. It was his first mission to England and he had set out across the North Sea from Belgium with high expectations. At last, he had thought, he would have a chance to prove himself as an airman and perhaps achieve his first 'kill'. Instead, it was now simply a race for life… or death.

Behind the goggles strapped around his metal helmet, Lazzari's eyes flicked anxiously between the nine whirling instruments of the two control panels on either side of his stick and from there up to the sky, fearful of an attacker 'bouncing' him from the piling grey clouds.

Already the sergeant had seen enough to convince himself just how superior in speed and firepower the British aircraft were to his little CR.42, no matter how hard-won its reputation might be.

In the short period of time since the two groups of almost one hundred aircraft had approached the east coast of England on the afternoon of 11 November 1940, Lazzari had already been an eyewitness to death and destruction in the sky. One of the BR.20M bombers had plunged towards the dark, heaving waves in a hail of bullets, while a CR.42 like his own had begun a fluttering descent that indicated things were not right with the aircraft or its pilot. In fact, wherever he glanced across the sky there were signs of high-speed dogfights taking place with the defenders falling upon the raiders with merciless efficiency.

The rattle of gunfire that reached him over the howling of the wind and the noise of his machine as he pushed the fighter's engine to maximum revs indicated starkly that the pride of Mussolini's specially formed corps of fighters and bombers were taking a pounding. So much, he thought, for the Nazis' claims that the English were broken and on the verge of defeat.

Despite the obvious differences in the capability of his aircraft and that of the RAF fighters, Lazzari was proud of his CR.42, number MM6976, with his unit numerals, 85/16, painted on the side of the fuselage. Indeed, he knew with a thudding heart that it now represented his only hope of survival in this damnable war.

The CR.42, known familiarly as the *Falco* [Falcon], had been acknowledged for some years as one of the finest biplane fighters – certainly the best in service in 1940, and that included its British equivalent, the Gloster Gladiator – and a worthy successor to the CR.32, which had achieved considerable success in the Spanish Civil War. In time, too, after its day had passed, experts would agree that it was the most agile biplane of the Second World War and a hard target to hit – a fact that had particularly inspired Lazzari when he was checked out for combat flying. The *Falco*'s top speed of 438 km/h (272 mph) also made it the fastest biplane in the present conflict.

Powered by the tried-and-tested Fiat fourteen-cylinder A74 RC 38 radial engine that could generate 840 hsp, the plane had a wing area of 22.4 m (73 ft 6 in), a height of 3.58 m (11 ft 8 in) and length of 8.26 m (27 ft). It had a service ceiling of almost 10,060 m (33,000 ft) and a range of 775 km (480 miles). If there was a down side, it was the *Falco*'s armaments – just two Breda Safat 12.7 mm machine guns, no more than a First World War fighter would have boasted – which, pilots like Lazzari all too soon discovered, were inadequate against the British Spitfire and Hurricane. The fact it could carry an additional 200 kg (440 lb) of bombs was no more comforting.

Yet, as every pilot who had flown a CR.42 knew, the plane was immensely strong – it had been a little sarcastically nicknamed by some 'The Flying Mule' – and was very manoeuvrable, like all aircraft with a fabric covering. It was also extremely light on the controls. The machine had been meticulously developed by Fiat from the biplanes of the First World War into a thoroughbred combat fighter that would remain in service until the war ended for Italy – with a number even then being made operational by the Allies for attacking the *Luftwaffe*.

Records of the Italian air force, the *Regia Aeronautica*, indicate that even before Mussolini took the country into war the service had more than three hundred of the little fighters operational, amounting to an incredible forty per cent of its strength. Other countries who had come to admire the CR.42 also purchased it in large numbers for their own air forces – including the Hungarians, the Swedish, the Finns and Belgians – and by a strange twist of fate, the very first *Falcos* to fire their guns in this war had been a squadron belonging to the Belgium *Aéronautique Militaire*, who vainly attempted to stem the *Luftwaffe*'s attacks on the Low Countries in May 1940. The Belgian CR.42s did, however, achieve five commendable victories against the loss of just two of their own planes before the nation surrendered the following month.

Like the other pilots in his squadron, Lazzari also knew that the CR.42 had already taken part in combat in Italy's fourteen-day war against southern France. There the planes had been pitted against two excellent, recently developed modern fighters, the Dewoitine D.520 and Bloch MB.152, without any serious losses. It was, indeed, all these comparative successes that had filled the Italians with a sense of optimism that their versatile biplane and their knowledge of aerial tactics would be a match for the British monoplanes.

As Antonio Lazzari sped along a wild and ever-changing coastline that November afternoon, he began to wonder whether this optimism was truly grounded in fact, after what he had just gone through. There was no time for reflection on the past glories of the *Regia Aeronautica* as he flew on, however, hoping the passing miles would put distance between him and the RAF fighters. With any luck, he had escaped them and might now be able to find his way back home to base in Ursel. Or anywhere in Belgium, for that matter.

As he looked down from the open cockpit between the struts of his lower wing, Lazzari saw a wide spit of shingle that must have been all of 10 miles long. At the southern end of this stood a red-and-white lighthouse and beyond that a river winding away into the hinterland. What really caught the pilot's eye, though, were the unmistakable signs on the island of a runway and two old buildings that looked just like hangars. Was it an airfield?

If the Italian pilot thought for even a second of landing on Orford Ness, the idea was instantly dispelled when he suddenly caught sight of another plane plummeting into the sea away to his right. He was still in danger, obviously, and his anxiety would certainly not have been any the less had he known that the very first bombs to have been dropped by an enemy on the east coast of England had fallen here from a German raider on 22 May 1940 – an event still fresh in the minds of the local inhabitants. Nor was he aware that it was from here that rumours of a 'Death Ray' had originated and become part of the gossip of local people as well as some of the Axis air force personnel stationed across the Channel. Apart from those to whom the whole idea seemed absurd, there was still a feeling among others that there might be an element of truth that some kind of secret work was going on in the vicinity. However, Lazzari at this moment in time had rather more immediate dangers to worry about.

No sooner had the mysterious strip of island passed behind him, than the sergeant saw an ancient building rising above a sandy beach: it was actually a Martello tower dating from the early nineteenth century, a defence measure against the possibility of invasion from Napoleonic forces. Behind this was what seemed like a deserted town – its shops and hotels boarded up – yet still defiantly facing the sea with an array of defences where dozens of fishing boats had once been at anchor. Aldeburgh had centuries of experience of the dangers of invasion: as long ago as the time of the Spanish Armada in 1588, cannons had been mounted on platforms close to the sea. It was now a 'prohibited area', most of its men, women and children having been moved inland.

The eerie desolation allowed the pilot of the CR.42 his first moments of calm in some time. He paused to check all his instruments and realised that his fuel was starting to run low. Lazzari was still at a loss, though, about which way to head and the little biplane's direction indicator, altimeter and compass wavered under his increasing uncertainty.

When he looked up again, his sense of confusion was further increased by what was hovering into view. In the midst of a stretch of heath land fringing the coast was a curious lake circled by several dwellings and a solitary house perched on top of a tower. The whole place was like something from the lakeland area of southern Italy where he had spent summer holidays with his parents back in the twenties, long before the clouds of war had gathered over his country. Indeed, the whole tower seemed almost Italianate in design.

In fact, Sergeant Lazzari was now flying over a famous landmark, 'The House in the Clouds' at Thorpeness. It served the dual role of unique residence and water tower for the community of half-timbered, mock-Tudor houses situated around the lake that had been constructed as a holiday village by an eccentric Scottish novelist and poet, G Stuart Ogilvie.

The airman was still puzzling over these curiosities as his plane roared on over a break in the miles of heath land and sand dunes. This was Sizewell Gap, once notorious as the base of ruthless and highly organised smugglers who had run contraband from France. The lawbreakers had also taken advantage of the notorious Sizewell Bank just offshore on which hundreds of trading vessels had been wrecked in the last two centuries, providing rich pickings of goods and casks of spirits for the local people, too.

However, all that Lazzari saw as his plane lost a little more height were huge rolls of barbed wire strung along the seashore. He also caught his first glimpse of human beings – a small group of soldiers manning an anti-aircraft (AA, or 'ack-ack') gun. The men looked up, startled, as he passed overhead but were, it seemed, too slow to identify him before he had gone.

There was now nothing, in fact, in front of his propeller besides sand and sea and several miles of railway tracks – until another curious ruin came into view. It was the last remnants of what appeared to be a church clinging to the edge of the cliffs. Coastal erosion had obviously been at work, though Lazzari had no way of knowing that a famous medieval port town, Dunwich, packed with houses, commercial buildings and eighteen churches, had once stood here until a great storm in 1286 followed by years of pounding seas had all but wiped it off the map. The particularly dark sea that the pilot glimpsed from his cockpit was now the repository of countless secrets and along with the formidable scaffolding defences that had been erected below the cliffs to prevent an enemy invasion, made it seem a place to avoid.

A panoramic heath land of bracken, heather and silver birch trees that unfurled beneath the CR.42's wings soon presented Lazzari with an even stranger sight – an aerial on top of a 180-ft steel tower planted to the ground on four huge concrete feet. A huddle of small buildings and a few piles of construction materials beneath the mast bore all the signs that the complex – whatever it was – had only recently been erected.

Lazzari was never quite able to explain to himself later *why* the idea had come into his mind – but he wondered if this tower might have anything to do with the secret weapon that the British were supposed to be using against enemy aircraft. When he got back to Ursel, he would be sure to mention it in his debriefing. That fate would deny him this chance, may well have proved significant in preventing the enemy an earlier knowledge of radar.

Another town – the largest Lazzari had encountered – was now coming into view ahead of his aircraft's buffeting nose. Marshland gave way to mudflats and then a river in which boats of varying kinds, including small fishing vessels, yachts and any number of dinghies, were moored alongside wooden stakes and hard standing. A small ferry boat with a group of passengers was crossing from one side of the river to the other, the occupants suddenly looking up as the CR.42 roared overhead, its height now down to just a few hundred feet.

Beyond the river over a rising stretch of grass, the Italian pilot saw rows of houses and shops that delineated a sizeable community. There was evidence that it must have some importance, as a number of the buildings bore the scars of recent bombing. The gaunt rafters of several burnt-out homes could be seen not far from other larger premises surrounded by scaffolding or covered in tarpaulin blankets.

As he gazed down, Lazzari allowed himself the first smile for some time. Right on the edge of a cliff overlooking the seashore were ranged six ancient cannons. They had to be centuries old, he thought, and would be useless against the weaponry of a modern invader. He had no way of knowing that for centuries the town had been under threat of invasion – particularly from the Dutch in the seventeenth century – and that one famous encounter, the Battle of Sole Bay in 1672, when the seamen of the English fleet had almost been caught unawares after a night of carousing in the Southwold taverns, had left the inhabitants wary of attack.

The presence of the six cannons on Gun Hill had resulted in the town being declared a 'fortified area' in the First World War and there were several of the older residents could still remember being shelled by a U-boat that had surfaced in the bay. That feeling of vulnerability remained, if anything more strongly, when the Second World War was declared.

There were a few people in the streets of Southwold staring upwards as Lazzari passed overhead, looking for any sign of an AA battery. When he caught sight of a large gun near a long pier that had evidently been blown in half as a defence measure, he summoned the last few ounces of speed from his engine and veered out to sea.

A new hazard now confronted Sergeant Antonio Lazzari. Although it was only still early afternoon, a mist was beginning to gather over the water, shrouding everything in greyness. He began to suspect the bearings he was reading on his direction indicator and tried adjusting the synchroniser. The hands on his altimeter were spinning rather more than he would like, too, and he suspected his fuel was now getting dangerously low. He was not sure whether he was flying straight and level or going round in circles.

The coastline that at last came in to view was pitted and scarred by erosion and, if anything, more bleak and desolate. There also seemed to be quite a lot of debris on the sea and even traces of it along the beaches. Lazzari wondered if this might be the result of bomb damage – and when he caught sight of several ruined houses on the edge of a cliff, decided he must be right. Of course, he told himself, he had seen ruined buildings like these before – on the coasts of France and Belgium during training exercises. Could he *possibly* be back in Europe?

Before he had another moment to think, the little CR.42 was flying over a large port, its waterfront covered by defences, barricades and barbed wire. The harbour itself was packed with vessels of every type, from motorboats to merchant ships, all ranged along the quays. Many were showing signs of damage – their superstructures bent and warped, their paintwork scorched, some even with gaping holes in their sides. Alongside these ships of war lay trawlers and drifters, quite a few of which had suffered the same fate. One of the shipyards and a timber yard nearby also bore the marks of heavy bomb damage.

An AA gun was pointed skywards, but this, too, did not break into fire as Lazzari passed by and found himself flying directly over a wide street of shops and offices. People in a mixture of overalls and uniforms hesitated as the sound of his engine broke the afternoon stillness. It was obviously a sound they had heard before and the sight of a shattered store, several ruined buildings and a row of demolished cottages was enough to convince the Italian pilot of the fact. However, with only one wing of the store still standing and its sign missing, he had no way of knowing that he was passing over Lowestoft – one of the prime targets of the *Luftwaffe* and his own CAI.

The greatest surprise of all awaited Lazzari as he crossed an open area of parkland known as Crown Meadow. For there in the middle of the park, surrounded by a group of people, stood an aircraft he recognised immediately. The black-and-white crosses on the wing were unmistakably German and the twin-engine pods and 'glasshouse' cockpit and nose cone marked it down at a glance as a Dornier Do.17.*

* This Dornier had actually been brought down virtually undamaged by AA fire and was being exhibited on Crown Meadow to raise money for the 'Spitfire Funds' to provide more fighters for the RAF.

The sergeant's head jerked back in surprise. 'O *mio Dio,*' he breathed, and then cursed through his teeth: '*Maledetto!*' That was one of the *Luftwaffe's* finest bombers – and it seemed as if it was being prepared for take-off. If that was the case, where in Christ's name was he?

Lazzari felt a new rush of sweat run down inside his flying jacket. The pounding of his heart was almost matching that of his engine when, suddenly, just as he was crossing a wide, open stretch of river flowing into the sea, the engine spluttered. The cylinders misfired once, twice and then – *mio Dio!* – picked up again. Lazzari knew he needed to land. And quickly.

In fact, his appointment with destiny as the first Italian pilot to be taken prisoner in Britain awaited just a mile away, in the little village of Corton...

* * * * *

Farmer Bob Wright and his gang of labourers had not long been back from their lunch break and were just starting to work again when they became the centre of a drama that is still remembered by the older inhabitants of Corton to this day. The day the Italian fighter plane crashed into their midst.

Corton lies just beyond the sprawl of Lowestoft, close to the Broads and the border between Suffolk and Norfolk. Its long, sandy beach and heath land behind cliffs that have been steadily eroded by the sea for centuries has made it a popular holiday resort for caravanners and campers. Despite the tranquil impression the village gives to visitors, with its pretty flint cottages, it has an exciting history. In the very earliest times, mammoths roamed the area – as bones found by several geological searches have revealed – and the Romans established a base here as one of the links in a chain of shore forts built around the East Anglian coast to guard against invasion by the Saxon marauders.

Corton's most imposing landmark is the fifteenth-century church of St Bartholomew on the northern outskirts of the village. With a 90-ft-high tower rising from flat pastureland, it can be seen from way outside the village and even by ships passing along the coast. The church is partly ruined, though, and half of it stands hollow and ghostly. This damage resulted from Cromwell's time – it was desecrated in 1642, its rich furnishings removed and the vicar thrown out on a trumped-up charge of drunkenness. It was to be over a century before St Bartholomew's gained a new clergyman, by which time much of the building had decayed beyond restoration. Despite being in use once again, the remote situation of the church has caused more than one visitor to declare that it feels as if it is somehow at the end of the world. Certainly, Corton is close to being the most easterly point in Britain.

Being located so close to Lowestoft had caused the village to suffer repeatedly during periods of war, from the Dutch, the French and, in the twentieth century, the Germans. A local tradition records its baptism of fire during the First World War, when the German navy bombarded the shore on 23 April 1916. Many of the villagers, so the story goes, had been up all night because of an expected raid by Zeppelins. However, at 4.30 a.m. word went around that everyone could safely go to bed as the British fleet had appeared offshore. In reality, this 'fleet' was a German battle-cruiser squadron, which soon began to fire on Lowestoft and the vicinity. Curiosity got the better of many of the people of Corton, who set off for the cliffs to see the ships, although on the way they were intercepted by an army officer and told to go inland. Stopping only long enough to gather as many possessions as they could carry – not forgetting any children or pets – the villagers made off along Cockles Path and Stirrups Lane.

As this stream of humanity passed the vicarage they were somewhat surprised to see their clergyman, the Reverend Sheppard Ward, sitting in a tree in his garden with a telescope pressed to his eye. The ships, he shouted to his flock, were 'ours' and they need not worry. The shells that flew overhead and exploded with the familiar loud, 'crump, crump' proved a rather more convincing argument than the Reverend Ward's words, however, and the entire population stayed clear of the village until the squadron departed later in the day. When the people of Corton returned home, so the story goes, one family arrived to find that the soldiers who had been billeted on them had stayed behind and breakfasted on six eggs each, declaring 'they might as well enjoy their last hour'.

Michael Soanes, the local historian who told me this story, added:

> I understand it was an attempt by the Germans to entice
> elements of the Grand Fleet from Scapa Flow to protect the
> east coast. In this they were successful, as some ships were
> sent down here and were consequently late getting to the
> crucial Battle of Jutland.

The Second World War found Corton under fire once again. On 22 June 1940, a German aircraft dropped two high explosives on arable land at Woburn Farm. In August there were raids on the 25th and 27th, with a high explosive landing in a field near a searchlight at Long Lane; this was followed two days later by an incendiary bomb that fell on Station Road. Another farm, Woodlands, was also the target of an incendiary bomb on 5 September.

These raids may well have been intended for Lowestoft and the other port to the north, Great Yarmouth, as both were subjected to repeated attacks throughout the early months of the war. An Italian plane crashing in the middle of the community was something quite different, however.

Bob Wright and his men were hard at work on Long Farm lifting sugar beet in a field east of Box Iron Wood, when the sound of an aircraft engine split the afternoon silence. To the south of them stood Corton station; the afternoon train from North Lowestoft would soon be along on its way to Hopton, Gorleston Halt and Yarmouth South Town. So far the line had escaped the attentions of the Germans, but the noise of the approaching aircraft made one of the men, Geoffrey Bullen, look up. It was immediately obvious to him that the plane was in trouble.

Moments later – as Bullen recalled afterwards – a small biplane with a distinctive yellow cowling and the emblem of three axe heads on each of its mottled brown-green wings appeared over the awning of the station's platform. It was descending rapidly and almost at once plunged on to an embankment and into the far end of the field. On impact with the sodden, rutted ground where the sugar beets had recently been removed, the aircraft's undercarriage collapsed and the fuselage skidded and swerved for almost 400 yards before coming to a halt, its pale blue propeller bent and twisted back around the cowling. Steam poured from the engine as it clattered vainly under the shock of the impact and then fell silent. The time, it was later established, was 2.17 p.m.

The group of workers stood transfixed. A final hiss and a small explosion in the engine was followed by the creaking of the wing struts as they collapsed. As silence once again fell over the field, the workers heard the sound of a groan from the open cockpit. A head could just be seen slumped to one side.

Bob Wright was the first to react. Apart from being a farmer, he was also the captain of the local Home Guard and had been trained for just such a moment – though he had never imagined that he might have to deal with an incident like this on his own land. He clumped across the muddy, rutted earth and peered into the crashed aircraft. The pilot was still alive, as he would later recall:

> The man was shaking with fear, rather than cold. He was obviously terrified of what would be done to him. He had a revolver by his side but made no resistance when I took this away and told him to get out of the plane. The stench of petrol made me worry that the aircraft might catch alight at any moment.

Local legend records several versions of the crash and arrest of Sergeant Antonio Lazzari of the *Corpo Aereo Italiano* on that November afternoon. One story claims that his plane had been hit by ack-ack fire from a battery in Lowestoft as he flew down the High Street. However, no evidence was found on the fabric of the plane or its engine to suggest it had been hit by bullets fired from the port or anywhere else.

There is also a dispute about the first words the dazed pilot spoke after crash-landing. The most popular version claims they were a mixture of bewilderment, even of vain hope. *'Questa è la Germania?'* he is said to have enquired falteringly – 'Is this Germany?'

Although there is no doubt from Lazzari's own detailed statement to the authorities that he was thoroughly confused about his whereabouts, other accounts differ from this version. The first of these is a brief report of the incident that appeared in the *Lowestoft Journal*, dated 16 November 1940. It states:

> When the men working in the sugar beat field in which he crashed told the pilot how far out he was in his reckoning, he raised his hands and the farm labourers mounted guard on him until the arrival of a military escort. The pilot told his captors that he had been over the Thames Estuary, where the formation of which he was a part was split up and driven out to sea. Afterwards he had lost his bearings and, when he sighted land and descended to come down, thought he was over Germany.

Among the local residents who saw the plane crash and went across the muddy field to examine it, were a schoolboy, Peter Smith, and a housewife, Edith Pepper. The youngster did not reach the field until the end of school, by which time Lazzari was under guard.

'He didn't speak any English,' the boy said later. 'I heard that he had told the men he had no idea where he was.' Mrs Pepper, on the other hand, was on the scene within minutes of the incident occurring, as her daughter, Valerie French, was to describe in her account of the events later provided for the Corton Historical Society:

> When she arrived the young pilot was in a very distressed state, hanging his head and shaking violently. He asked my mother, 'Is this London?' and was promptly sick – at which point my mother wondered if he might like a cup of tea. Just as she was asking him, several soldiers arrived on the scene, having run from the Corton Beach Holiday Camp, where they were stationed. Some of them, my mother said, were still clutching knives and forks – they had been having a meal!

Valerie herself was an eyewitness to the sequel to this encounter at the family home in Station Road that same evening.

> Just after we had finished our meal, there was a knock at the door. An army captain stood there and asked to speak to my

mother. He then reprimanded her for putting herself at risk. 'Mrs Pepper, that pilot had a gun and ammunition. He might well have killed you!' The captain presented my mother with a deactivated bullet from the Falcon and said it was to remind her of what could have happened. The bullet stood on our mantelpiece for many years.

If there was one thing that the people of Corton were soon in no doubt about, it was the identity of their unexpected visitor – the crashed plane and its pilot were Italian. Who, though, of the two parties, was the more shocked?

Of course, no one in the area was surprised any more when Nazi aircraft flew overhead bent on their missions of destruction. Indeed, quite a number of them had already been shot down or crashed and their crews taken prisoner. But few people in that part of Suffolk – or across much of the eastern counties, for that matter – were aware of the role the Italian air force was taking in the Battle of Britain.

So just how had events conspired to land the bewildered and unhappy Sergeant Lazzari in a field behind Corton station? Or, for that matter, a number of his other equally unfortunate fellow countrymen and their aircraft, who also ended up scattered along the East Anglian coast on that chilly winter afternoon.

The answer to the question lies in the life story of the megalomaniac dictator Benito Mussolini, his life-long obsession with flying, and a burning ambition he nursed that his *Regia Aeronautica* should be regarded as the equal of his ally's hugely effective and then all-conquering *Luftwaffe*.

IL DUCE – FANATIC FOR FLIGHT

3

Standing in unlikely isolation in Burnham Park, just to the east of the famous Soldier Field in Chicago, is an ancient column that is probably the last surviving relic of the passion for flying of two men whose names are inextricably linked with Italian Fascism – Benito Mussolini and Italo Balbo. The monument commemorates a great aeronautical feat and is another step on the path towards the formation of the *Corpo Aereo Italiano*, whose mission was to help in the destruction of the RAF in the Battle of Britain.

The Balbo Monument, as the artefact is known, is actually an Ancient Roman column dating from the second century AD and was once part of a portico near the earliest port city of Rome. It had stood there for two thousand years until it was unceremoniously removed in 1933 by Mussolini and shipped to Chicago to be erected there as a commemoration of Balbo's pioneer flight across the Atlantic with a squadron of seaplanes. Fixed on a travertine marble base, it bears an inscription, now fading with the passage of time, in both Italian and English, which reads:

> This column, twenty centuries old, was erected on the beach at Ostia, the port of Imperial Rome, to watch over the fortunes and victories of the Roman triremes. Fascist Italy, with the sponsorship of Benito Mussolini, presents to Chicago a symbol and memorial in honour of the Atlantic

> Squadron led by Balbo, which with Roman daring, flew
> across the ocean in the 11th year of the Fascist era.

The flight from Italy and the erection of the column had been deliberately planned to coincide with the city's 'Century of Progress' World's Fair. The event marked the one hundredth anniversary of Chicago's incorporation as a city and featured the scientific and technical achievements of the previous one hundred years. For Mussolini, the publicity-conscious and aviation-obsessed Italian dictator, it was a perfect opportunity to trumpet his own achievements in a US city with one of the largest populations of Italian immigrants.

The fair opened on 27 May 1933 on a site stretching from 12th Street to 38th Street alongside Lake Michigan. However, the homegrown successes were overshadowed almost at a stroke by the spectacular arrival of Italo Balbo and the 24 twin-hulled Savoia-Marchetti SM.55X flying boats of his 'Italian Formation Flight, 1933'. The flight had been planned and executed as a display of Italian air strength to impress the world and proved a triumph of airmanship and public relations.

The project had taken a year of planning and training the pilots and mechanics before the aircraft had left Italy on 30 June. En route, Balbo's close-formation flight made several stops in Europe and Canada – receiving the kind of welcome usually reserved for dignitaries and turning the pilots into heroes with the public – before arriving in Chicago at an optimum moment on Saturday afternoon, 15 July. The flying boats touched down in groups of three with barely a splash on the calm lake waters and taxied to the waterfront. It was an unforgettable moment for the thousands of visitors and a publicity triumph for Mussolini that found its way on to the front pages of the world's newspapers the following day. However, although many aviation specialists were impressed by the feat, others thought the whole mission had been a childish attempt at showing off.

The Fascist triumph did not end there, either. Balbo, one of the original group of Fascists who had helped bring Mussolini to power, was made Air Marshal of the *Regia Aeronautica* and determined to turn the air force into a global power. His transatlantic flight was also honoured by the Chicago authorities with the renaming of 7th Street in the city as Balbo Drive. It, too, survives to this day as a reminder of the flight. Curiously, though, the forgotten column is said to be the only structure remaining in the city from the 'Century of Progress'.

The two dozen huge flying boats on the waterfront attracted over a million visitors before Italo Balbo and his pilots returned to Rome on 12 August to be greeted by an ecstatic *Il Duce.* For Balbo, it was to prove the crowning achievement of his career – for within months, Mussolini, perhaps jealous of the accolades showered on his air minister, decided to oust Balbo and take personal charge of the *Regia Aeronautica.*

* * * * *

It has been claimed by more than one of Benito Mussolini's biographers that his fascination with flight began when he was a child, watching the effortless soaring of birds and wishing that he could emulate them. Margherita Sarffatti, who knew the future dictator intimately, said that during his youth he sometimes trapped birds and kept them as pets, being particularly fond of owls. Indeed, there can be little doubt that he developed an interest in flying early in his life and became a pilot when his rise to absolute power was still in its formative years.

Mussolini was born on 29 July 1883 at Dovia di Predappio in Forli province, the son of a blacksmith and an elementary school teacher. His father, a member of Italy's impoverished middle class, was an ardent Socialist, and the young Mussolini shared these political inclinations for some years. As the boy grew towards manhood, he revealed a sharp and lively intelligence, a powerful ego and a voracious appetite for sex. In his voluminous memoirs *Opera Omnia* (1928), he wrote of these formative years: 'I was a restless urchin, free with my fists. I was the head of a small band of urchins who roamed the riverbeds and fields. I pinched the girls and I brawled with the boys... I was a bold rural thief.'

Despite this unruly behaviour, Mussolini learned well at school and in 1901, at the age of eighteen, he took a *diploma di maestro* and went to work as a teacher in an elementary school. Soon tiring of this, however, he crossed the border into Switzerland and idled his time away until he was expelled back to Italy in 1904 for 'vagrancy'. After a period of soul searching and intensive study, the young rebel began to develop his own brand of Socialism that advocated force, will and the superego. He attacked clericalism, militarism and reformism and urged revolution at any cost.

The outlet for his 'concocted' form of Socialism were a number of small periodicals for whom he wrote rousing articles that first attracted attention, then acclaim and soon widespread admiration. In 1912 he became editor of the Socialist Party's daily newspaper, *Avanti*, where he began urging the people to 'unite in one formidable *fascio* [bundle] preparatory to seizing power'. In this expression some historians have seen the beginnings of the Fascist movement.

When the First World War broke out, the fascination that Mussolini had developed for aviation was revealed in a number of articles that predicted the coming power of the aeroplane. In November 1913, he founded a new paper of his own, *Il Popolo d'Italia*, and began recruiting a pro-war group, the *Fasci d'Arzione Rivoluzionaria*. It was his wish that the war would lead to a collapse of society and bring him to power. Instead, he found himself called up for military service – although after being wounded in 1917 while at grenade practice, he was allowed to return to journalism.

Two years later, Mussolini realised two powerful ambitions. He turned Fascism into an organised political movement, the *Fasci de Combattimento*, and with it decided to fulfil his long-held dream of learning to fly by taking lessons at an airfield at Arcore, just to the north of Milan. According to his instructor, C Redaelli, in *Iniziando Mussolini alle vie del cielo*:

> Mussolini arrived the first time in July wearing his editor's clothes, a dark suit, bowler hat and grey spats. On subsequent occasions he would bring family members or friends on an afternoon outing. On one occasion he was in a special hurry because he had a duel scheduled shortly after his flying lesson!

During the next year, Mussolini completed eighteen flights and logged up almost seven and a half hours in the air. Although this was below average for a keen pilot, it was no mean achievement for a busy man and certainly helped him in projecting an image of himself as the 'man of the future'. He would continue to promote his passion for flying in the years that followed, as Denis Mack Smith has noted in his biography, *Mussolini* (1981): 'Every year he liked the public to know exactly how many hours he had flown as an aircraft pilot, and some biographers have accepted a total figure of 17,000 flying hours – as many as a full-time pilot in a lifetime.'

Nevertheless, flying in an open cockpit, daring the elements and those who clung to material interests, seemed to Mussolini to exemplify reactionary modernism, as another biographer, R J B Bosworth has pointed out in his recent biography, *Mussolini* (2002):

> In the summer and autumn of Italian discontent, Mussolini was not just busy as an editor and polemicist. Rather, his life was enlivened by his hobby and one that could readily be adapted into a new politics – flying. The young socialist, who had hailed the French aviator Louis Blériot's conquest of the Channel in July 1909 as 'a triumph of Latin genius and courage', now had his own chance to soar into the skies. An infatuation with the cult of the air had lingered in his mind until, in August 1919, he imagined an empyrean future in which the tyranny of distance had been overcome along with the differences with people. Then, he mused romantically, 'all souls will be fused into a single soul.'

In 1935, an Italian aviation expert, Guido Mattioli, having observed the association between Mussolini's Fascism and aviation, wrote an absorbing if controversial book, *Mussolini Aviatore*, in which he explained:

> No machine requires so much human concentration of soul and will power as a flying machine to make it work properly. The pilot understands the fullest meaning of the word 'control'. Thus it seems that there is an intimate

31

spiritual link between Fascism and Flying. Every airman is a born Fascist.

Mattioli revealed that even then the tyro pilot was busy telling associates that he was contemplating departing on a 'raid' to Tokyo:

> Preparing for the prospect of such a world-girdling exploit was taking a lot of his time. When, six months later, the flight did go ahead without him, Mussolini still waxed lyrical about it. He said grandiloquently, 'A flash of green, white and red Italian light will stay in the skies signalling to the infinite what Italy stands for. Flight constitutes the greatest poem of modern times.

Mussolini campaigned vigorously in the press for Italy to achieve a 'primacy in the air' and referred to those who objected to such an idea as idiots and penny-pinchers who should be swept aside. Bosworth adds:

> From August 1919, *Il Popolo d'Italia* featured a *pagina aeronautica* which was meant both to favour the cause of the aeroplane and to underline the modernity and technological optimism of the *Fasci*. Mussolini took to defining himself as 'a fanatic for flight' and on at least one occasion aimed to stun a meeting of the *Fasci* by appearing dressed as an airman.

After two years of relentless campaigning and writing – during which he attempted unsuccessfully to gain a seat in the Italian parliament – Mussolini finally succeeded in 1921. These elections sent him victoriously to parliament at the head of 35 Fascist Deputies. A special assembly of his fledgling movement gave birth to a new party, the National Fascist Party (PNF), which could boast more than 250,000 followers, with Mussolini as their uncontested leader – *Il Duce*.

The year was not without its drama as far as the new leader's flying skills were concerned, however. In March, while he was doing take-off and landing practice at Arcore, his engine stalled and his small plane crashed. Mussolini escaped with only scratches to his face and a twisted knee, though he was compelled to use crutches for weeks thereafter. Any damage to his pride was swiftly alleviated two months later when the *Gazzetta dell'Aviazone* applauded him and a Fascist friend, Aldo Finzi, as 'the first flying members of parliament'.

Two other biographers, G Pini and D Susmel, note in *Mussolini* that *Il Duce* retained happy memories of this time all his life:

> Flying had something viscerally Fascist or Mussolinian about it as men flew heavenwards to challenge the very gods. There were times when the working dictator would take control of a plane in which he was travelling. Contemporaries noted how, even during the dark days of the Salo Republic, he sloughed off his usual gloom when again given the chance to be an aviator... Whatever else troubled Benito Mussolini, before and after 1922, it was not a fear of flying.

At this moment in time, both the sky and earth of Italy lay within Mussolini's grasp. By his side, too, was another young firebrand named Italo Balbo who shared his dream of aerial domination.

* * * * *

Italo Balbo has been described by a number of leading historians as Italy's most famous interwar pilot. A dashing and charismatic figure, he was also a pioneer aviator, Fascist leader, colonial governor and confidant and possible successor to Mussolini. To his admirers, Balbo seemed to embody a noble vision of Fascism and the New Italy; to others he was an ambitious, cynical and ruthless man who hitched his star to that of *Il Duce*.

Balbo was born in Quartesana in Ferrara on 6 June 1896, the son of middle-class parents, Camillo and Malvina Balbo. Like Mussolini, he became interested in aviation as a youngster and in 1911, at the age of fifteen, helped to tend fires to light the path of airmen competing in a race from Bologna to Venice and back sponsored by *Il Resto del Carlino*.

Called up in the First World War, Balbo served with Alpine troops and his bravery in action earned him a bronze and two silver medals as he rose to the rank of captain. After the war, he studied at Florence University and obtained a degree in Social Science and Politics. Returning to Quartesana, he worked for a while as a bank clerk, but like a lot of young men disillusioned with the way the country was being run found himself increasingly drawn to Fascism. According to Claudio G Segre, author of *Italo Balbo: Aviatore e Ministro dell'Aeronautica, 1926–1933* (1979), he joined the embryonic Fascist Party, becoming secretary of the section in Emilia Romagna, near Bologna:

> He began to organise fascist gangs and formed his own group nicknamed the *Celibano,* after their favourite drink. They broke strikes for local landowners and crushed trade union disputes, attacked communists and socialists. By 1921, Balbo was one of the most active and significant of fascist *squadristas.* Dreams of flight and of beating up socialists went together because, in the aftermath of the First World War, propagandists were sure that the individual courage needed to conquer the air, as the expression went, was fundamentally 'Anti-Marxist'. Darwinism, too, slipped easily into an aerial vocabulary.

Not surprisingly, then, Balbo was happy to throw in his lot with Mussolini and together the two men and their followers 'marched' on Rome, where the power of the Fascists broke the liberal governments of Giovanni Giolitti, Ivanoe Bonomi and Luigi Facta. In October 1922, the King of Italy, Victor Emmanuel III, had no option but to invite Mussolini to form a government. Naturally enough, the new leader saw the running of a government in terms of aviation, as he later recorded in *Opera Omnia:* 'For the first time I found myself squarely challenged by the gigantic problem of public finance. For me it was a new aeroplane. But there was no competent instructor anywhere on the field.'

Lack of instructor or not, Mussolini knew what he wanted and in the next few years he rid the cabinet of its liberal elements and appointed himself to all the major positions, including Prime

Minister, Minister of Foreign Affairs, Minister of War, Minister of the Navy and Minister of Aviation. He acted through undersecretaries who were usually also chiefs of staff of their respective branches enjoying a large measure of autonomy in exchange for public servility to *Il Duce*. Italo Balbo was rewarded for his support by being appointed Undersecretary for National Economy, but was a man with his own strong opinions and seemed to have his mind set on other duties, as he hinted in his *Diaro 1922*:

> Our movement has the good fortune to be both idealistic and realistic. Aviation is the synthesis of these elements. Aviation and heroic aviators offer a glimpse of tomorrow. Powered flight represents the synthesis of rational achievement and sublime achievement.

A number of other prominent Fascists had also become pilots, including the party secretaries, Pavolini and Muti, and Giuseppe Bottai, one of Mussolini's close friends had formed the 'Roman Club of Fascist Flyers'. Soon a modernist aeronautical town, Guidonia, was under construction to serve as a base for all of these enthusiastic airmen.

In November 1926, Italo Balbo was finally given the job he hankered after, Undersecretary for Air, and immediately set about turning the *Regia Aeronautica* into a world-leading force. He also took flying lessons and qualified for his pilot's licence after an intensive six-week course. Balbo knew he was inheriting a tradition of aeronautical excellence and was determined to use it for the greater glory of Fascism.

The new Undersecretary was aware that as far back as October 1911, the Italians had been the first to use the aircraft as a weapon of war during the conflict with Turkey. Two years later, the Italian military theoretician Giulio Douhet had published his *Rules for the Use of Airplanes in War*, the first doctrinal manual for airpower. And after the end of the war, Italian aircraft had won innumerable air races and aerial competitions. In 1920, for example, the Savoia S.12 won the Schneider Cup, to be followed the next year by the triumph of the Macchi M.7. A Macchi MC.39 won the cup again in 1926 and the final development of these great race-planes, the Macchi MC.72, achieved the world record for seaplanes of 709 km/h (440 mph) on 23 October 1934 at Lake Garda.

The significance of these achievements was immediately apparent to Balbo. He was particularly intrigued by Douhet's theories that in future conflicts, the nation that controlled the skies would win the war and long-range aircraft bombing cities would cause panic among the people and force their governments to surrender. In Balbo's view, later expressed in his book, *Stormi in Volo Sull 'Oceano* (1933), 'Closely formed units of bombers could operate over large distances and successfully fight their way through defences and saturate targets.' As to the weapons that might be used, the author revealed a little of the darker side to his character when prescribing 'the natural marriage between chemical weapons and the sky'.

With the enthusiastic support of Mussolini – along with rapid promotion to Minister of the Air Force on 12 September 1929 – Balbo directed all his energy and vaulting ambition to the task that lay ahead. It was with seaplanes that he saw the quickest and best opportunity to put his ideas to the test. The result was a fleet of Savoia-Marchetti flying boats that he and his officers were soon flying all over Europe.

But it was more than just Europe that Balbo and Mussolini wanted to impress. On 17 December 1930, the minister led a flight of twelve of the flying boats across the Atlantic from Orbetello to Rio de Janeiro, where the formation was greeted with open-mouthed aston-ishment. The airmen were fêted by the Brazilians over the Christmas period and then made for home, arriving back in Italy on 15 January. As we have already read, two years later, with twice as many seaplanes, the 37-year-old Balbo flew from Rome to America and upstaged the World's Fair in Chicago. During his time in the States he visited New York, where a ticker-tape procession was staged in his honour and he was invited to lunch with President Roosevelt. The American aviator Charles Lindbergh, who had been the first man to fly across the Atlantic in 1924, described Balbo's flight as 'the greatest aeronautical achievement ever'.

The flight was indeed a landmark in aviation: the first by a formation across the Atlantic, when previously no more than two planes had made the crossing in a single passage. It also proved beyond any shadow of doubt the potential of Giulio Douhet's theory, that Balbo had turned into reality. Thereafter the minister's name would be immortalised in the term a 'balbo', to describe any large formation of aircraft.

Sadly, this triumph would mark his undoing. Mussolini was not a man to have anyone else share the limelight and in mid-October Italo Balbo was sacked from his job and effectively 'banished' to be Governor General of Italian-occupied Libya, much to his disgust. There, in June 1940, the man who had done so much for Italian aviation would become the nation's first significant casualty of the Second World War.

On the morning of 28 June, he took off from Dernia in a three-engined Marchetti S.79 for Sidi Azeis to review Italian troops. As the aircraft flew over the port of Tobruk, anti-aircraft batteries and an Italian cruiser in the harbour opened fire. One of the shells struck Balbo's plane, which crashed, killing him and the crew. Because the British had been recently bombing Tobruk, it was claimed that the defenders had opened fire thinking the aircraft belonged to the enemy.*

Although this was the official line on the tragedy, there were other people – notably Balbo's widow, Emanuela Florio – who believed he had been assassinated. English historian Nicholas Farrell has examined the conspiracy theories that broke out in Italy and writes in *Mussolini: A New Life* (2003):

> There are still Italians today who believe that Balbo was the victim not, as is the case without doubt, of a friendly-fire accident, but of a friendly-fire plot to kill him. Mussolini was apparently unmoved by the death of the man who had been with him since the start of Fascism and who had given Fascism such a good name abroad, especially in America, but who had been one of the very few to stand up to him. This fuelled the conspiracy

---

* The respect in which Balbo was held, even by his adversaries, can be judged by the action of Air Commodore R Collishaw, Group Commander of No. 202 Group of the RAF units in the Western Deserts of Egypt, after hearing of the Italian's tragic death. According to Denis Richards in his *The Royal Air Force 1939–1945*, 'His [Balbo's] funeral was graced by a wreath from Collishaw, dropped by air.'

theories. The manner of the death of the most dashing Fascist was an ill-omen of things to come.

Farrell is absolutely correct. If the remarkable Italo Balbo had lived to promote the *Regia Aeronautica*'s role in the Second World War – in particular that of the *Corpo Aero Italiano* in its attacks on Britain – things might indeed have been very different.

* * * * *

If the departure of Italo Balbo in 1934 deprived the Italian air force of its driving force, the 'pride of Fascism' still seemed to be set fair. Certainly there was much in the tradition of the force to make believe anything was possible.

Formed in the aftermath of the First World War on 24 January 1923, the *Regia Aeronautica* had been created as an independent military force separate from the army and navy. In 1925 an air ministry had been set up to put it on a secure footing and this fact, along with the technical advances being made in aircraft manufacture and the progressive and imaginative ideas of the commanders, produced a force held in high regard. What no one had expected was the scale and size of *Il Duce*'s grandiose plans for the future.

Balbo had only been removed from his job as titular head of the *Regia Aeronautica* for a matter of months when Mussolini decided it was time the air force proved its mettle. Like many other nations, Italy had been suffering from the worldwide economic depression and by 1935 the middle classes were discontented with their leader's actions to counter this situation, while the working classes were suffering abject misery. Though *Il Duce* cynically initiated a public works programme, he knew a diversionary exercise was also necessary. What better than a foreign adventure against an unprepared and ill-equipped nation? The poverty-stricken North African country of Ethiopia fitted the bill perfectly.

On 2 October, Mussolini announced that Italy had been the victim of 'barbarous and unprovoked aggression' by Ethiopia and used this wholly fictitious story to carry out Douhet's long-prepared strategy of mass-bombing a civilian population into surrender. A fleet of

Caproni Ca 133 bombers were dispatched from Libya, flew unopposed across the barren terrain of Sudan to its neighbouring state and bombed the helpless town of Adowa. So confident of success was Mussolini, that two of his eldest sons, Vittorio and Bruno, were sent to fly in the planes – Bruno, the younger, having been taken out of school to share in this 'glorious' moment. Aged just seventeen, the boy had been given a pilot's licence after less than the required period of training in order to participate.

Vittorio Mussolini later published an account of his mission, *Voli Sulle Ambe* (1936), in which he expressed disappointment about the raid. He said he had hoped to generate explosions of the kind he had seen in American films and was unimpressed by the way in which the fragile Ethiopian huts had tumbled to the ground and the people had fled without attempting a single retaliatory shot. Both he and his brother received telegrams of congratulation from their father, he said – along with a suggestion that they write to their mother.

Il Duce, of course, reeled off all the superlatives to describe the success in Ethiopia – 'inexorable force' being a favourite description of his airmen – carefully avoiding the fact that the 'enemy' had only been armed with eleven slow aircraft, three of which could not even take off. A unanimous condemnation of Italy by the fifty members of the League of Nations did nothing to stop the dictator claiming a triumph and another piece to add to his 'Italian Empire' – which he hoped would ultimately control the Adriatic and Mediterranean seas.

Eager to raise his profile further, in December 1936 Mussolini offered assistance to the Spanish nationalist, Francisco Franco, who for some time had been expressing a desire to establish a government of 'the Fascist type' and was embroiled in a bloody civil war. Now the *Duce*'s pilots could experience real conflict and plans were made to send a strong contingent to Cadiz to form the *Aviazione Legionaria*. The force consisted primarily of Breda Ba.65s, a low-wing monoplane, armed with four machine guns and able to carry a 200-kg (440-lb) bomb load internally, plus an external ordnance that would make a grand total of 998 kg (2,200 lb). Later these planes would be augmented by the arrival of new Fiat CR.32 fighters and the Savoia-Marchetti SM.79 bomber, nicknamed 'Gobbo Maledetto' ('Damned Hunchback') because of its distinctive hump on the upper forward fuselage.

After a number of teething troubles, the *Legionaria* saw extensive action over northern Spain during the next two years. They attacked Republican artillery batteries and landing strips as well as railway lines and road junctions and by April 1938 had helped to cut the Spanish Republic in two. Indeed, when the war finally came to an end in March 1939, the Italian pilots were able to claim quite a bit of credit for their role – having logged 1,921 sorties, including 368 ground-strafing and 59 dive-bombing attacks, at the cost of just a dozen aircraft.

Unfortunately, however, Mussolini's 'intervention' in Spain did not yield any of the gains he had anticipated, and historians such as Ivone Kirkpatrick in his *Mussolini: A Study in Power* (1964) have suggested that this was a major factor in causing the opportunist *Duce* to seek a pact with the other great European dictator, Adolf Hitler. Mussolini had first visited Germany in September 1937 and culminated the trip with a speech to a vast audience in Berlin where he had spoken of the similarities between the Fascist and Nazi systems that were, he said, 'the greatest and most authentic democracies existing in the present-day world'.

Il Duce returned to Italy certain that 'the future of Europe will be Fascist', and in 1939 underlined his conviction by signing a 'Pact of Steel' with Hitler. But events were already moving more quickly than he had anticipated, as Michael Orleans has explained in *Benito Mussolini* (1998):

> World War II's surprise outbreak in 1939 left Mussolini standing on the margins of world politics and he saw Hitler redrawing the map of Europe without him. Impelled by the prospect of easy victory, Mussolini determined 'to make war at any cost'. The cost was clear: modern industry, modern armies, and popular support. Mussolini unfortunately lacked all of these. Nonetheless, in 1940 he pushed a reluctant Italy into war on Hitler's side.

If the aeronautically mad *Duce* harboured any reservations about the Italian war machine, his faith in the *Regia Aeronautica* remained undiminished after their 'triumphs' in Ethiopia and Spain. Indeed, during one of his subsequent meetings with Hitler he even took the opportunity to show off his own prowess as a pilot, as Alan Bullock has described in *Hitler: A Study in Tyranny* (1952):

> At the end of their meal, Hitler walked about among a crowd of soldiers talking informally, while Mussolini, to his annoyance, was left with Rundstedt. The *Duce* took this as a deliberate slight and remarked to his ambassador that Hitler in the middle of his troops looked anything but a soldier. Mussolini had his revenge, however, on the return flight when he insisted on piloting the plane in which he and Hitler were flying. Hitler's own pilot, Bauer, remained at the controls all the time, but Hitler never took his eyes off Mussolini and sat rigid in his seat until Mussolini left Bauer to his job. The Führer's congratulations were mingled with undisguised relief. Mussolini was childishly delighted and insisted his performance being recorded in the communiqué.

When it came to making the decision about joining Hitler in the war, the *Duce* ignored the typically outspoken advice of Italo Balbo when the Governor General was home on a visit from Libya and protested at the proposal. Balbo argued Italy would be better to join Britain. Several ministers also aired their misgivings that Mussolini was in danger of becoming Hitler's *secondo poco brillante* ('less-than-smart second') and reminded him that the nation was ill prepared for war.

There is no question, though, that Mussolini *wanted* war. He convinced King Victor to give his assent on the grounds that it was the wish of the people and that any conflict would be short and profitable. It did not matter to Mussolini how strong or weak Italy's armed forces might be, or that the country possessed no coal, oil or iron ore of her own – this was *his* moment. On the afternoon of 10 June, Mussolini made the fateful proclamation from the balcony of the Palazzo Venezia to a crowd hurriedly assembled by his staff:

> Destiny has decreed war. We go into the field against the plutocratic and reactionary democracies of the West who have repeatedly blocked the march, and even threatened the existence of the Italian people. Our conscience is absolutely clear. We want to snap the territorial and military chains, which suffocate us in our sea. A people of 45 million souls cannot be free if it does not have free access to the ocean.

It is equally clear that right from the start Hitler had strong doubts about the capability of his new partner to wage war. Historians Richard Overy and Andrew Wheatcroft make this point in discussing Mussolini's intervention in the Second World War in their excellent survey *The Road to War* (1989). *Il Duce* did not want to wait until France was beaten, the authors argue, for fear of having his offer rejected. Mussolini was also sure that Britain would not fight on alone.

> He made the best of Italy's military situation. The army was 'not ideal but satisfactory'. There were now 24 divisions fully prepared and 1,753 combat-ready aircraft. He privately believed that Italy might get its own phoney war on the French border, a belligerent at Hitler's side but without the risk of a disastrous offensive. On 10 June he declared Italy's belligerence. Hitler, unknown to his ally, considered Mussolini's commitment merely a 'foray for booty'.

The German army and air-force commanders were equally dismissive of Italian assistance and no more impressed when Mussolini launched his troops against France's last-ditch offensive in the south of the country. Five French divisions held at bay three times that number of Italian soldiers and the pilots of the *Regia Aeronautica* found the remaining French aircraft a tougher enemy in combat than any they had encountered in Ethiopia or Spain.

Nothing, though, would discourage Mussolini from seeking his 'destiny'. He was particularly anxious to send a special contingent of his aircraft to help the *Luftwaffe* complete the job of beating the beleaguered RAF, he informed Hitler while listing some of the grudges he held against the common enemy. In particular, the *Duce* knew from reading the foreign press and from intercepts that he was being increasingly mocked and ridiculed in London – a clear insult to his overweening vanity. To counter this, he had instituted a propaganda campaign to deride the British as a decadent and impoverished society that had not changed since the time of Charles Dickens. According to *Vita Italiana*, the average Englishman was 'stupid and took a week to puzzle out what an Italian understood in no time at all'. The *Azione Coloniale* went even further: 'The spread of Communism is a very real threat in Britain. Her fleet is no longer effective, which means that London is indefensible. Moreover, the Italian Air Force is so strong that war against Britain holds no terrors.'

Whether the Mussolini journalist who wrote these words believed in what he said no one will ever know. What *is* certain is that terror was precisely what the squadrons of Italian pilots who were on their way to the occupied coast of the English Channel would find themselves facing in the darkening autumn days that lay ahead.

MISSION TO THE UNEXPECTED

4

The omens for the *Corpo Aereo Italiano* – as Mussolini had ordered the force to be named – taking part in the Battle of Britain were not good from early September when the three *Stormi* began gathering in Italy before setting out for the Axis frontline on the English Channel. The CAI consisted of two bomber groups and a fighter wing amounting to 170 aircraft, and the logistics of moving them and almost seven thousand air-force personnel from Italy into position alongside the *Luftwaffe* squadrons already operational in Belgium was to prove an extraordinary episode combining elements of drama and farce, none of which was helped by the encroaching winter weather.

The force was scheduled to make the transition to its Belgian bases in two stages. The fighter aircraft, which would require several stopovers for refuelling in order to reach their destination, set off first. They were to be followed by the two *Stormi* of bombers that only needed a single stop en route in Germany.

Although September in Italy is normally a month of clear skies and pleasant temperatures, September 1940 was mainly wet and windy, the heavens full of louring clouds that seemed to cling for days along the spine of the country from Rome all the way up to Milan and the foothills of the Alps. The weather had certainly not helped the condition of the airfields where the CAI aircraft had been assembling ever since the decision had been made to send them to new bases in Belgium. Indeed, some of the pilots were in for a wait of days, even weeks, before their orders came through to fly north and join their German allies.

The man charged with coordinating the operation with the *Luftwaffe* was *Generale* [Air Marshal] Rino Corso Fougier. Archive documents reveal that his force was made operational on 10 September 1940, under the aegis of 1 *Squadra* based in Milan. This squadron was the equivalent of a British 'Group' and had been charged with protecting the northern half of the country – where the majority of Italy's industries were located – as well as training pilots from other units on the country's 'frontline'. The proximity to France had, of course, made it ideal for the early attacks on that country's southern coast and the duties also included escorting the Italian navy and patrolling neighbouring coastlines.

Air Marshal Fougier brought a wealth of experience as a pilot and as a leader of men to his posting as Air Officer commanding the *Corpo Aereo Italiano*. Born in Bastia, on the island of Corsica, in November 1894, he had initially been attracted to a career in the Italian army and in December 1912 enlisted as a reserve officer. In 1914, aged just nineteen, Fougier had become a second lieutenant in the Bersagliere Regiment and the following year won a medal for bravery when leading a reconnaissance mission that narrowly escaped death from an exploding land mine.

During this period of his life, Fougier was drawn to flying and in June 1916 signed up as a student pilot. By the end of the year he had achieved his pilot's licence and in February 1917 was a fully qualified military pilot, earning a posting to 113 *Squadriglia*. The remaining months of the First World War saw Fougier prove himself a daring and skilful pilot, scoring several 'kills' in combat, rising to the rank of captain and being awarded three *Medaglia d'Argento al Valore* for bravery. Surviving the war, he became a flying instructor and his potential was spotted by Italo Balbo, who saw him as one of the leading lights of his new *Regia Aeronautica*.

By 1931, Fougier – now a *Colonnello* [Group Captain] – was in charge of Number 1 *Stormo*, rated the best in the Italian air force

In 1933, when Balbo was relegated to Libya, he managed to secure the posting of Fougier, who took an important role in the subsequent operations in Libya and the raid on Ethiopia. Mussolini's decision to send the *Regia Aeronautica* to take part in the Spanish Civil War saw Fougier reassigned again, this time to the Iberian peninsula, where his skill and daring further enhanced his reputation. He was promoted again in September 1939 and on Italy's entry into the Second World War was made Air Marshal and charged with organising the mobilisation of the air force. When the fateful decision was made to join the *Luftwaffe* in the Battle of Britain, Fougier – always a man to lead from the front – decided to accompany the force to Belgium.

Despite the success that the Air Marshal had enjoyed, there is no doubt that although he was keen for more glory, he was not so carried away with his mission as to believe success was a foregone conclusion. He sensed from all that he had read and heard about the RAF that he would be up against an enemy much harder to crack than any he had so far encountered.

Because of the high priority put on the mission by Mussolini, Fougier was able to gather his three wings with the minimum of fuss and red tape. The two bomber units, equipped with Fiat BR.20Ms, were designated as 13 *Stormo*, consisting of 11 and 43 *Gruppo*, and 43 *Stormo* made up of 98 and 99 *Gruppo*. Both were largely already in situ on bases at Novara and Piacenza close to Milan. The fighters of 56 *Stormo* – divided into 18 *Gruppo* made up of 83, 85 and 95 *Squadriglia*, and 20 *Gruppo* of 351, 352 and 353 *Squadriglia* – were, however, more scattered and had to be rendezvoused at Rome. From these two units, the Air Marshal was hoping to reap the benefit of experience recently gained by some of the 18 *Gruppo* pilots who had seen combat duties in southern France, plus the added firepower from the 20 *Gruppo* men now re-equipped with the new Fiat G.50s.

Fougier also had a further *Squadriglia*, the 179, equipped with Cant Z.1007bis to carry out tactical reconnaissance, and a clutch of auxiliary planes including nine Caproni Ca164s for communications and a single, all-purpose, Savoia-Marchetti S.75. In all, he would have a force of slightly less than two hundred aircraft at his command.

The first of the CAI aircraft to leave for Belgium were those of 20 *Gruppo*, who gathered at the airfield of Ciampino Sud, some 15 km (9 miles) south-east of Rome. The airfield was an auspicious place for such a mission to begin. Inaugurated in 1916, it had served as a military base for airships, and it was from here that the small airship, the *Norge*, commanded by General Umberto Nobile, had taken off in May 1926 for its famous flight across the North Pole. Significant an event as this may have been regarded by some people, there were others familiar with history who knew that two years later Nobile had returned to the Pole in another airship, the *Italia*, which had been overcome by the forces of nature and crashed on the pack ice.

For days before departure, the pilots had been getting to know one another while the weather conspired to keep them on the ground. Lounging around the airfield's barracks and mess rooms, smoking, drinking, telling jokes and endlessly discussing their mission, it had become obvious to them all that there was something important about what lay ahead. Not least among the evidence bringing them to this conclusion were the modifications that had been made to their equipment and the new uniforms that had been handed out on arrival.

The traditional air-force uniform was virtually the same as that worn by the army – from which the air force had originally evolved – but this had been replaced by a version made of grey-blue cloth. The previously straight pocket flaps were now cut three-pointed, and the side cap had a pleat in the crown. The awful knickerbockers and puttees that dated from the First World War and made the men the butt of endless jokes had thankfully given way to trousers. Those other frills of the past, the shoulder straps and full-dress belt, had also gone, creating a more modern and fashionable-looking uniform. Certainly, those men who got leave from the airfield and were able to venture into Rome found themselves being given more appreciative looks by young women.

The new flying suits were, if anything, even more impressive. They came in two types: one, for winter use, made of brownish olive-green material with a full lining, while a summer version was cut from white linen. Both were available in one- or two-piece styles according to the pilots' preference. There were also flying jackets and helmets made of leather – the jackets decorated with the badges of rank on the cuffs, with the gilt metal wings of pilots and observers on the left breast. Italian style had now replaced the earlier rather functional uniform of the *Regia Aeronautica* to the benefit of the men in what was regarded as an exciting new arm of the service.

An interested and occasionally amused observer of this change of fashion was a well-known Italian pilot who had an advantage over many of the men in that he had already seen extensive combat action in Spain and France. He, too, was passing through Ciampino with 56 *Stormo* on his way to Belgium. The man was Gianni Caracciolo and during the course of a short but incandescent career as a fighter pilot he would become famous as 'The Fighting Prince'.

A tall, robust man who was sometimes referred to as having the look of a *scugnizzo* (a Neapolitan term for a quick and cunning rascal), Caracciolo actually had blue blood in his veins. His full name was Prince Gianni Battista Caracciolo Carafa and he was said to be descended from the famous Bourbon naval commander Francesco Caracciolo, who distinguished himself first by supporting the British fleet against the French and then, disgusted by the flight of King Ferdinand to Sicily, by supporting the Republic of Naples. When the French left and the Republic fell, however, and Bourbon troops and the British fleet reoccupied Naples, Francesco Caracciolo was arrested on the orders of Admiral Horatio Nelson. Refusing to accept the Treaty of Capitulation, Caracciolo was ordered to be hanged on the frigate he had commanded, the *Minerva*.

Gianni himself was born in Naples on 9 August 1910 and, true to his military background, entered the Naval Academy at Livorno when he was just eighteen. Following the sudden death of his father, though, the young man resigned from the school and instead channelled his sense of adventure into qualifying for a civilian pilot's licence. By the age of 24 he was thoroughly obsessed with the world of flying and joined the *Regia Aeronautica*, where he quickly became a *Sottotenente* [Pilot Officer].

Caracciolo's first posting was to the 4th *Stormo Caccia Terrestre* (a land-based fighter wing), where his quick brain and natural ability were honed to enable him to fly operational aircraft. When the Spanish Civil War broke out in 1936 and Mussolini offered support to General Franco's troops, the young prince – who had always been attracted to Spain – volunteered his services.

For the next year and a half he flew all over the Iberian peninsula, his skill and daring ensuring he claimed a number of 'kills' and earn decorations for gallantry from both the Spanish and Italians. Gianni's unconventional methods, his adventurous nature and his engaging manner set him apart as a leader, blue blood or not.

With the ending of the Civil War in March 1938, Caracciolo returned to Italy. Here, apart from his duties of administering the family estates, he took an instrument-rating course on his own light aircraft. When Mussolini joined the world war in June 1940 Caracciolo was immediately recalled to the *Regia Aeronautica* and assigned to 51 *Stormo* at Ciampino. After a brief period on combat service in southern France, he once again found himself in September in the midst of another group of raw young pilots anxious to get into the action.

Gianni Caracciolo was later to recall the days before the fighters of 56 *Stormo* set out for Belgium. His experience, though, did not allow him to share the rosy view of the future that these young men possessed. He sensed – correctly – that the new uniforms and equipment had been ordered to create a good impression on the German airmen already on the front. He also suspected that the *Luftwaffe* pilots might not be as impressed by the Italian planes as their own pilots were.

'The Fighting Prince' was not sure that the men had been trained thoroughly enough. They could handle their planes quite skilfully, certainly, and many of them were adept at aerobatics. But combat was something very different to practice missions – and the Italian tendency to become overexcited and a little too adventurous might well count against them in dogfights. Though he did not for one moment doubt the bravery of the men bound for Belgium, he wondered if they possessed the true killer instinct of the best fighter pilots in the *Luftwaffe*... or their opponents, the RAF. Caracciolo afterwards told his friend and biographer, Francesco Cavalera, author of *Fighting Prince* (1989):

The CAI had many good pilots and their aircraft were very manoeuvrable. But the RAF had faster aircraft and their tactics enabled them to attack with greater firepower and escape from retaliation with greater ease. The best of our aces had a good chance in combat, but those in the older and slower biplanes were up against long odds from the very start of the campaign. Also, the fine conditions that our fighter pilots had been used to in the Mediterranean and Spain proved a stark contrast to the bad weather that hung over the English Channel and the countryside of eastern England that winter.

The subject of the weather was very much on the minds of the CAI pilots gathered on the airfield at Ciampino Sud, and the men and their officers spent many hours poring over the daily forecasts before the first group was able to leave on the morning of 22 September. The first to go was 20 *Gruppo*, equipped with the G.50 single-wing fighters, commanded by *Maggiore* [Major] Mario Bonzano. Both the aircraft and their leader were reckoned among the best in the Italian air force.

It was somehow appropriate that Bonzano should be the first man to take off for Belgium. A career officer in the *Regia Aeronautica*, he had developed his passion for flying in his home town of Oneglia, which Mussolini had joined with Porto Maurizo on the opposite site of the River Imperio in 1923 to create the provincial capital of Imperia. The young Bonzano had also spent hours on the beach watching the hydroplanes being flown around the coast of the Ligurian Sea and vowing that one day he, too, would be a pilot.

Such was the skill that Bonzano demonstrated during his years of training and qualification as a military pilot, that he was selected in the initial group of Italian airmen sent to fight in the Spanish Civil War and led the first flight of twelve G.50s in the conflict. In July 1939, he was made the first commander of 20 *Gruppo* and in a career that would last until May 1942, he would see action in Belgium, France, Tripolitania and Cirenaica, claiming a total of fifteen 'kills' that would place him among the foremost of the *Regia Aeronautica's* Second World War aces.

After the declaration of war, 20 *Gruppo* was assigned to Ciampino Sud to form part of the defence of Rome. There the unit made use of four old CR.32s for the occasional night mission and 25 of the new G.50s for day sorties in order to gain experience for what lay ahead. When the time came to leave for Belgium, the CR.32s were detached to Guidonia, leaving the G.50s to head north.

Major Bonzano took off in his brown-and-yellow camouflaged single-seat fighter with all the élan of a man at ease in his aircraft and well prepared for action. Over a year of flying in the G.50 *Freccia* [Arrow] as it was known, had made him familiar with the capabilities of the Fiat A74 RC 38 engine that propelled the 7.8-m-long (25-ft 6-in) plane with its 18.25-m (60-ft) wingspan at speeds up to 470 km/h (292 mph). The 'Arrow' could operate to a ceiling of 10,750 m (35,000 ft), had a range of 580 km (360 miles), and was armed with two Breda-SAFAT 12.7 mm guns. The plane had already proved its efficiency and deadliness in Spain and Bonzano was optimistic that the 45 G.50s that made up 351, 352 and 353 Squadrons who followed in his wake off the runway and into the leaden skies over Rome would prove the same.

The first leg of 20 *Gruppo*'s flight took them 520 km (325 miles) – almost the limit of the fighter's range – to Treviso, skirting the Adriatic as they travelled north. Fog that the pilots saw gathering around the coast of the Golfo di Venezia did not bode well for the next stage of the journey, which would take them towards the Austrian border.

In fact, the next day ground fog had reduced visibility at the San Giuseppe airport to only a few yards and a delay was inevitable. This was no hardship for the naturally fun-loving pilots who knew all about the town's reputation as 'Little Venice' – a name acknowledging its similarities with its more famous neighbour some 40 km (25 miles) away.

Apart from the many areas of Provencal culture in the town, there was always the Calmaggiore, the bustling main street with any number of *divertissements* even in time of war, and the Piazza dei Signori – referred to as the place's 'sitting room', where the wine flowed freely and the girls were easily attracted by the glamour of airmen. If a stroll by one of the innumerable small waterways was not romantic enough, there was the seductive power of such favourite local dishes as *sopa coada* (pigeon soup) and the famous red chicory.

The fog stubbornly refused to lift and it was not until 6 October that the skies cleared and Major Bonzano was able to order his group to take off on the next leg of their journey to Bolzano, a city situated in a valley of the Tyrol Mountains, and the chief town of the Alto Adige region. Fought over in the past by Austria and Italy, the location of its airport near the junction of the rivers Talvera and Isarco did not make for the easiest landing for the pilots of 20 *Gruppo*.

Here, again, the late autumn weather held up the party for eleven days enabling the men to get a taste of this latest way station. Bolzano had long had the appearance of being part of the German-speaking world, but the influence of Mussolini since 1922 had gone a long way to 'Italianising' the district. Immigrants had been encouraged to move from all over Italy, an industrial area had been created and Italian was declared the official language. However, when Hitler annexed Austria, the alliance between the Führer and *Il Duce* allowed the *status quo* to continue, though the resentment of some of the old German speakers in the city was evident even to the carousing CAI pilots.

At last, on 17 October, the weather over the mountains cleared and the Italians flew over the Alps into Germany, landing at Munich. For all of the men this was to be their first taste of life in the Third Reich. Even on the final approach to the airport at Reim it was possible to see huge swastikas decorating many of the buildings and a host of other trappings of Hitler's regime.

Aware that German eyes would be watching them appraisingly, the pilots of 20 *Gruppo* were under instructions from their squadron leader to take especial care in landing. All the G.50s touched down perfectly. It was just the arrival Bonzano had hoped to put on for his new allies – whose national pride and competitive instinct, he knew, was every bit as keen as his own.

Blue skies over Munich allowed the *Gruppo* to fly on after refuelling for another 300 km (185 miles) to Frankfurt, which was scheduled to be their last stop before Belgium. Here again the Italian airmen found a new airport gleaming in the sunlight and splashed with swastikas and huge portraits of the Führer. The Rhein-Main Airport, as it was known after the confluence of the two rivers just to the west of the city, had been in use since 1909 when Count von Zeppelin had used the area as a landing site for his lighter-than-air dirigible, the Z-11.

In 1936, the base was refurbished and became one of the largest airports in Germany – second only to Tempelhof Airport in Berlin – with the intention that it should be one of the most important European air terminals. Aside from commercial use, the southern part of the Rhein-Main known as Zeppelinheim became the port for the *Graf Zeppelin;* its sister ship, the LZ-30; and the ill-fated *Hindenberg.* After the tragedy of 6 May 1937, the airships were dismantled and their huge hangars demolished. A year later the base had been given over completely to the military.

It was along the much-extended single runway and into a special hardstand zone between the new hangars and airport facilities that the crews of 20 *Gruppo* taxied after landing on 18 October. All but one, that is, for the mission suffered its first taste of the unexpected that afternoon. One of the CR.50s had developed a carburettor problem on the downwind leg of its final approach and the unfortunate pilot had no alternative but to make a forced landing that carried the plane skidding off the runway and on to its nose in long grass. The man was able to climb from his cockpit unhurt, but the damage to his machine was such that it would take no further part in any operations against the British.

The final leg of Bonzano's mission took him 400 km (250 miles) north-west over the German border and into occupied Belgium. Their destination was Ursel airbase just beyond Ghent and only 30 km (19 miles) from the coast. Here, for better or worse, they were to be stationed throughout the winter months ahead. A new concrete airstrip was visible from some distance as the aircraft flew in over the rural Flemish countryside – but it was evident, too, from the number of potholes around the runway and in the surrounding fields, that Ursel had been bombed not long before.

The aerodrome had, in fact, only been constructed in the summer of 1939 when, with the threat of war growing across Europe, the

14th Company Aviation-Auxiliary had laid out a grass landing strip 900 m (2,950 ft) long. On 11 May 1940 – with war now a fact – Belgian air-force pilots with Fairey Foxes and Renard R16s had moved in and begun operations in conjunction with the Belgian army against the Germans. Four days later, Ursel was the target of three Heinkels, which inflicted widespread damage. On 23 May a second attack by German bombers made the airstrip unusable and forced the entire personnel to evacuate the area.

The swiftness of the German advance into Belgium resulted in German troops taking possession of the badly damaged airfield on 27 May. Just a little over a month later, in July, the runway was re-laid in concrete and the hangars and operational buildings were restored. By the time Major Mario Bonzano and his three squadrons touched down on 19 October, there were only the scars left to bear witness to the bombings.

The pilots of 20 *Gruppo* settled into their new quarters, mustering as much enthusiasm as they could manage. Most of them were looking forward to meeting their new colleagues. However, their optimism about what the future held might not have been so high if they had heard some of the ribald conversations going on among the German pilots when news reached them that the first units of Italians were about to join the fray.

By good fortune, the second unit of fifty CAI aircraft – 18 *Gruppo* – had a much easier flight to Belgium after they left Italy on 6 October. The 83, 85 and 95 Squadrons were all equipped with new CR.42 biplane fighters and a number of the pilots had already been in action carrying out strafing attacks on bases in France as well as escorting bomber raids. In June the men had scored their first 'kills' – three French Bloch 151s – although at the cost of two of their own aircraft.

During the month of August, the *Gruppo* was largely occupied with ferrying CR.42s to strategic bases across Italy – including a brief stay for rest and relaxation in Monaco – before heading north and an appointment in Belgium. They were led by the experienced Squadron Leader Feruccio Vosilla, another veteran of the Spanish campaign. Born in Trieste in 1905, he had taken up flying in 1928 and joined the *Regia Aeronautica* the following year. By the time he was making his way to Belgium, he was already the possessor of three decorations for bravery.

The weather was much kinder to Vosilla and his men – which was something that the pilots in their open cockpits had every reason to be grateful for. In fact, the only delay for bad weather occurred at Darmstadt, the bustling German city just over 370 km (230 miles) from their destination. While approaching the airport at Griesheim, the men had a bird's-eye view of the first *Reichsautobahn* built in 1935 that stretched for 25 km (16 miles) to Frankfurt.

The *Autobahn* was busy with military and civilian traffic when 18 *Gruppo* took off on 19 October and headed for Ursel. The Italians touched down that same afternoon – just a few hours behind the earlier group and without a mishap to their name. In the following month, though, the word mishap would become one this particular group of pilots would come to dread hearing.

* * * * *

The area around the town of Novara in the far north of Italy is probably as unlike a Mediterranean landscape as it is possible to find. A vast, flat plain that stretches between Turin and Milan, it consists of huge paddy fields that for generations have produced more rice than anywhere else in Europe. For half of the year these fields are flooded, but in the autumn they are frequently shrouded in swathes of mist that allow rays of the sun to filter through and cast weird, dancing shapes on the water. Not without good reason, is it known as *un posto sinistro*, or a 'spooky place'.

It was from the airfield of Cameri in the midst of this ominous area that the first bombers of the CAI set out for the Belgian front on 25 September. It was a local saying that most people who came to the region were soon ready to move on, and the commander and pilots of 13 *Stormo* were no different. The men had sampled what was left of the historic old town, drunk in the bars in Corso Cavour and stared at the odd, syringe-like spire of the church of San Gaudenzio. The spire dominated Novara and acted as a useful landmark for any pilots flying in or out of Cameri airport, carefully avoiding the treacherous rice paddies that lay all around. More than one of the

13 *Stormo* crews had reason to be grateful to the spire when a fog suddenly descended and hid the town under a grey blanket.

The autumnal feel of the place was not lost on Group Captain Carlo di Capoa, the commander of 13 *Stormo*, who was responsible for getting the 38 bombers in his unit to Belgium. Born in Naples, he was a direct descendant of Leonardo di Capoa (1617–95), the Italian doctor of medicine and author of the controversial book, *Lezioni Intorno Alla Natura Della Moefete* (1683). His forebear had made a lot of enemies by his 'extreme scepticism' – an attitude that his descendant Carlo shared about the mission that faced him two and a half centuries later.

Not that Group Captain di Capoa lacked experience or courage. He had joined the air force in 1935 and the following year was assigned to bombers, in particular the Fiat BR.20 *Cicogna* (Stork). Well designed, its fuselage partly skinned with light alloys and fabric, it was in operation within seven months of its first flight. Carlo di Capoa trained on one of the first of the bombers in service and saw action in the Spanish Civil War, where he thought it performed well against the older biplanes, which it could outrun. The Group Captain sensed, though, that the 'Stork' might not be so lucky when it came up against the hawks of the RAF. He and his men just had to trust that the CAI fighters did their job.

What *did* please the Group Captain was that both his wing and the 43 *Stormo* under the command of Group Captain Ludo Questra had been supplied with the new version of the bomber, the BR.20M. His unit was divided into 11 *Gruppo*, led by Major Gino Mini and consisting of 1 and 4 *Squadriglia*; and 43 *Gruppo* with two squadrons, 3 and 5, under the leadership of Major Giovanni Monteleone. Questra's *Stormo* was also divided into two groups: 98 commanded by Major Giuseppe Tenti split into 240 and 241 *Squadriglia* and 99 *Gruppo* consisting of 242 and 243 *Squadriglia* led by Major Bernardo Ciccu.

Group Captain di Capoa had made full use of the 100 km (60 miles) that separated Cameri from the other CAI bomber airfield at Piacenza for training his five-men crews made up of a pilot, co-pilot, navigator/bombardier, gunner/radio-operator and gunner. Some of the crews had already operated over southern France in the BR.20 with its two Fiat A80 RC 41 radials that could generate a cruising speed of 343 km/h (213 mph) at 4, 600m (15,000 ft) and a maximum speed of 430 km/h (267 mph) at 4,000 m (13,125 ft). The plane had a range of 1,240 km (770 miles) and ceiling of 7,199 m (23,620 feet). With a wingspan of 21.5 m (70 ft) and a length of 16 m (53 ft), the *Cicogna* could carry a bomb load of 1,600 kg (3,527 lb) – usually consisting of two 1,764-lb (800-kg) bombs, two 1,102-lb (500-kg) bombs, four 551-lb (250-kg) bombs, or twelve 441-lb (200-kg) bombs. It was armed with one 7.7 mm machine gun in the nose turret capable of firing 500 rounds and two identical guns for rearward firing in the dorsal turret along with one 12.7 mm gun with the capacity to fire 350 rounds. The BR.20 also carried a 7.7 mm machine gun in the ventral hatch, which could fire 500 rounds at any pursuer.

The BR.20Ms (*Modificato,* or 'modified version'), which arrived at Cameri in June, boasted several new features that it was hoped would increase the bombing efficiency of Group Captain di Capoa and his crews. Foremost among these were a number of aerodynamic improvements, protective armour for the crew and strengthening for the centre of the fuselage. The nose had also been extended, another dorsal turret introduced and a revised tail wheel introduced for landing and take-off. Although the BR.20M was heavier than its predecessor, the performance soon proved to be superior.

The pilots who flew the aircraft, with its shiny brown, green and red camouflage, on training missions across the rice fields of northern Italy reported that it handled well and that the structural improvements gave an increased sense of protection. If there was a criticism, it was the *Modificato*'s noisy, vibrating engines, which it was felt might cause damage to the airframe on long missions.

The crews who formed part of Group Captain Questra's 43 *Stormo* based at the San Damanio airfield at Piacenza found off-duty hours a little more varied than their colleagues surrounded by the fog-laden paddy fields. Situated on the River Po and close to the border with Lombardy, the town had become used to being bypassed by travellers journeying to Parma and Modena in the south, but still offered attractions for airmen about to go to war. Especially those who enjoyed good food and wine, for Piacenza was reckoned to be the gateway to Emilian cooking and no Italian could consider going to battle on an empty stomach.

The long runway at San Damanio – just short of 2,990 m (10,000 ft) – was the longest to the south of Milan. Indeed, many a pilot in the CAI had cause to whisper a silent prayer of thanks for every extra metre as he took off with a bomb bay loaded to capacity on training flights. Landing again with the carefully defused payload could be an equal test of skill… and nerves.

A third independent combat unit – known as an *Autonomo* – was added to the mission before 13 and 43 *Stormo* left Italy for Belgium. This was 179 *Squadriglia*, commanded by *Capitano* Carlo Pirelli-Cippo, who were flying the versatile Cant Z.1007bis Torpedo bomber, known as the *Alcione* or 'Kingfisher'. The unit had been formed in June 1940 operating BR.20Ms in which they saw action over France before being re-equipped with the all-wood Cant that would subsequently earn the reputation of being Italy's finest three-engine medium bomber of the war. The purpose of the *Alcione*s – Captain Pirelli-Cippo was told – was to act as reconnaissance planes for the attacks on England. It would be the aircraft's first operational mission.

The plane's apt name had come about because it had originally been designed by a shipbuilding company keen to expand their manufacturing into aircraft production. It started life as the Z.506 Airone floatplane just prior to the Spanish Civil War. In 1938, however, the initial test aircraft for the *Alcione* threw up problems with the Isotta-Fraschini Asso liquid-cooled engine and these required a complete re-think. A switch of engine, the widening of the aircraft and an enlargement of the bomb load resulted in the effective three-engine, single-wing aircraft that would ultimately serve on all the Italian fronts of the war.

Powered by three 1,000-hp Piaggio XI RC 40 radial air-cooled engines, the 'Kingfisher' was capable of speeds up to 456 km/h (283 mph), had a ceiling of 8,080 m (26,500 ft) and a range of 2,000 km (1,243 miles). It was equipped to carry a crew of five – pilot, co-pilot, front gunner, radio operator/bomb aimer and a tail gunner – and its weaponry consisted of three machine guns: one 12.7 mm gun in the dorsal turret firing front and back and two similar guns in the belly, one able to fire backwards or forwards and the other obliquely. The *Alcione* could also carry up to 1,100 kg (2,430 lb) of bombs or two 450 mm (17.7 in) torpedoes.

Although – as is suggested by their very name, *Autonomo* – these units of the *Regia Aeronautica* usually flew by their own schedules, for the move to Belgium, Pirelli-Cippo and his men had been ordered to follow in the wake of 13 and 43 *Stormo* – though not necessarily along the same route.

By the morning of 25 September, all the pilots and crew assigned to the mission were in position and fully operational at Cameri and Piacenza, ready for departure. A satisfactory weather report for the day resulted in the men being roused from their beds before dawn.

Group Captain di Capoa was the first to depart northwards with his four squadrons of BR.20Ms, followed by the quartet led by Group Captain Questra. The *Alciones* of 179 *Squadriglia* took off last, and almost immediately headed west.

A watery sunlight was trying to pierce the clouds over the plains of Lombardy and Piedmont as the armada of two *Gruppos* climbed towards the Alps. The sight of the large number of aircraft prompted many people bound for work to stare upwards and perhaps feel a sense of pride at the might of Italy. For those piloting the bombers, though, there was no chance to enjoy the patchwork beauty of their native land slipping beneath as they headed for the north-east coast, keeping watch all the time for any sign of a change in the weather as they neared the great mountain range.

Records of the flight to France indicate that as the bombers approached the Alps they were navigating in 7/10ths cloud. As they increased altitude prior to levelling out for the crossing, the weather deteriorated to 8/10ths stratocumulus. Flying almost blind, each pilot virtually dependent on the aircraft ahead, the men were barely aware of crossing the Austrian border and flying over Innsbruck.

According to the logbook of Group Captain di Capoa in the lead bomber, navigation was particularly difficult at this point, not helped by the malfunction of some of the instruments in his plane. Thanks, though, to a visual fix made by the navigator, who spotted the River Danube passing beneath, the commander was able to order a new course to be set for Frankfurt. Others on the mission were not so fortunate, as Chris Dunning has related in his excellent history, *Courage Alone: The Italian Air Force 1940–1943* (1988):

> They [were] transferred to Belgium for what was intended
> to be a triumphal assault against a weakened foe. But bad
> weather scattered them all over Germany on the way. Poor
> navigational training and inadequate instruments resulted
> in an indifferent performance.

In those first minutes over cloudy Germany, the sceptical Group Captain from Naples probably began to realise his misgivings had been well founded. On the rest of the journey, they were reinforced. While still some distance from the Rhein-Main Airport, one of the BR.20Ms suddenly fell out of the formation, the pilot clearly in trouble and needing to land. Later reports stated he managed to locate a private airfield at Gaglinghen not far from Mannheim and put the aircraft down without loss of life, but seriously damaging the engines. A second bomber in 99 *Gruppo* also had to make a forced landing at Frankfurt when the pilot discovered the aircraft was losing engine lubricant. It, too, was unable to continue on the mission.

The second leg of the journey, which saw the units separate to go to two different Belgian bases – 13 *Stormo* to Melsbroech and 43 *Stormo* and 179 *Squadriglia* to Chièvres – also incurred the loss of three more bombers. One of these was flown by a flying officer from Group Captain di Capoa's 5 *Squadriglia*, Lieutenant Dino Bossi, who crashed his BR.20M at Spa, still almost 100 km (60 miles) short of Melsbroech. A second bomber from 13 *Stormo* got into trouble closer still to the large airfield near Brussels and had to force-land on final approach.

Melsbroech had, in fact, seen the arrival of invaders before – but the Italians who landed on 25 September are remembered by the local people as being more unprepared than any previous force. The base, built originally during the First World War and used by both airships and planes, had been turned into a civilian airport in the Twenties and became famous for its terminals that were often jokingly referred to by local people as 'looking like railway stations'! The return of the Germans after their conquest of Belgium had once again thrust it into the role of a frontline bomber station for attacks on Britain.

Just one more BR.20M failed to make its destination on that autumn day in 1940. This was one of Group Captain Questra's 43 *Stormo*, which had to make a forced landing on its final approach to the CAI's other designated base at Chièvres, closer still to the English Channel. The station had already played a significant role in the air war between Britain and Germany and was about to be a focus of attention again with the arrival of Mussolini's flyers.

The remaining men of the four squadrons were simply relieved to be touching down. They were followed shortly afterwards by the Cant reconnaissance planes of 179 *Squadriglia*, who had enjoyed a rather more pleasant flight by utilising their greater range to detour the Alps via Monaco and Frankfurt. For both sets of men, though, it would not be long before the harsh realities of the task ahead of them started to become *really* apparent.

'ATTACCA L'INGHILTERRA!' 5

A low sea mist was clinging to the darkened hulls of the destroyers, cruisers and minesweepers lying alongside the heavily guarded quays of Harwich as the last hours of Thursday, 24 October ticked away. Another anxious day at the frontline East Anglian port was drawing to a close and those who lived and worked there were thankful for what they now hoped would be 24 precious hours without a German bombing raid. Living as they did closer than anyone else to the armed might of the Axis forces lined up along the French, Belgian and Dutch coasts, there were some among them who swore that on certain still nights they could actually hear the enemy making his preparations.

The apprehension of the people of Harwich about invasion was understandable for a number of reasons, military as well as geographical. Only the previous day, the Air Ministry had released the first details of alleged German invasion plans focused on their part of England, and the previous month the local paper, *The Harwich and Dovercourt Standard*, had reported that an enemy aircraft had flown over the coast 'dropping bundles of leaflets headed, HITLER'S LAST APPEAL TO REASON urging everyone to surrender'. The paper had informed its readers, 'The leaflets were found suspended on the Church Tower and also hanging on tree tops and grave stones.'

These strident sheets of misinformation and intimidation had quickly become souvenirs, not to mention a topic of much amusement and raucous discussion in the town's public houses, service clubs and restaurants. Indeed, they were still occasionally being mentioned that October night – along with the more immediately pressing news that the local rates were about to rise by 4d, with a promise of 'worse to come'. By all accounts, though, that Thursday was a pretty lively evening, with large numbers of naval men and petty officers from the Women's Royal Naval Service (WRNS) intermingling with the local people, turning the area – to quote the *Standard* again – 'literally blue'. The situation was not without its problems, however, as the paper commented in an editorial:

> This [participation with the civilian population] is not always with the happiest results, for a certain element among the naval ratings do little to enhance the popularity of their fellows. By and large, the long-suffering local public make allowances for these excesses, realising that the men are having an arduous and dangerous time at sea.

Arduous and dangerous were also apt words to describe how life had been in the port ever since the outbreak of the war. Situated at the tip of a peninsula in north-east Essex, commanding the entrance to a wide sweep of harbour and the River Orwell beyond, Harwich had been an important port virtually since the day in AD 885 when King Alfred had destroyed a Viking fleet in the estuary. Subsequent battles off the coast with the Dutch and French – in particular the privateers known as 'Dunkirkers' – resulted in it being turned into a naval station where ships could be built, repaired and provisioned, as well as an important trading and fishing port. In times of peace, the proximity of Harwich to Europe and the coming of the railway and the ferry earned it the label of the 'Gateway to the Continent'.

The First World War had seen the town designated a 'fortress' – its inhabitants required to carry passes with them at all times – along with the formation of the 'Harwich Force', a small fleet of destroyers and light cruisers. This group had been responsible for some of the first air operations mounted from ships at sea. These vessels, though, were not aircraft carriers in the accepted sense – i.e. with flight decks – but seaplane carriers converted from the cross-Channel steamers operating on the Harwich-to-Hook (Netherlands) route.

The encounters of certain of the 'Harwich Force' with the German navy and its U-boats became legendary. The story of Captain Charles Fryatt, commander of the SS *Brussels*, who twice eluded submarines trying to make him surrender, is particularly memorable. On a third occasion, in June 1916, the captain was not so lucky. He was captured, summarily tried and executed – an action that raised a storm of protest in his home port and the rest of the country. At the end of the war, the 'Harwich Force' had the satisfaction of escorting almost 150 surrendered German U-boats into the port where they were moored in a long line (prior to being sold for scrap) nicknamed, 'U-boat Avenue'.

During the First World War, Harwich also received its first taste of aerial bombardment when German planes and Zeppelins dropped bombs on both the town and the naval shipping in the harbour. Records indicate that the fire brigade had to turn out to incidents on no fewer than 108 occasions.

The declaration of the Second World War in 1939 saw the port once again thrust into the frontline as one of the country's most important bases and a prime enemy target. Soon, all those inhabitants who could do so were advised to leave – and there were few who stayed who forgot the day when a train had taken all the pupils and staff of local schools away to the safety of Herefordshire and Gloucestershire.

The harbour had once more filled up with destroyers – as many as 22 at one time – plus corvettes, cruisers, minesweepers and submarines. Rumour had it that not all the submarines were real, but were instead wooden dummies that had been specially built and moored in the estuary to fool enemy reconnaissance planes trying to discover whether the fleet was in port at any given moment.

Harwich also became the first port to feel the impact of 'Hitler's unbeatable secret weapon – the magnetic mine', as Harry G

Hitchman and Philip Driver described it in their book, *Harwich: Five Years on the Front Line* (1985). The horror of these weapons of mass destruction was soon being brought home to people, he wrote, in particular after a 'week of tragedies in November 1939 in which women and children were the principal victims':

> At Harwich beginning on Saturday 19 November, there were unforgettable scenes as the maimed and injured from a mined Dutch liner, *Simon Bolivar*, were landed. On Tuesday people on the seafront saw an explosion when a Japanese liner, *Terukini Maru*, was mined and later saw rescue vessels bringing the crew and passengers ashore. On Wednesday night, a destroyer, the HMS *Gypsy*, struck a mine in the harbour and was subsequently beached, its back broken, and remained there for the rest of the war. Add to this the disasters and the damage to properties and ships that was a result of the natural damage from gales, and it can be seen that Harwich had a week which it never wished to see again.

Fortune – and the war – was destined to deny this wish in the months of trial and danger that followed in 1940.

The railway steamers that had once ferried holidaymakers across the North Sea now began carrying troops and ammunition to the battlefronts in France. When disaster struck the British Expeditionary Force in the spring of 1940, it was thanks to an armada of fishing boats, barges and small ships from Harwich and its sister ports around the south-east coast that the evacuation of Dunkirk was carried out with such success. From that day on, too, Harwich saw a constant stream of refugees from the conquered nations of Europe.

Right from the beginning of the war, Harwich was a 'high- security zone' and a likely focus of enemy attacks. The Admiralty had taken over the Great Eastern Railway Hotel as its headquarters and soon more White Ensign vessels could be seen sailing in and out of Harwich than from any other port in the country. A former cruise vessel, the A/S [Auxiliary Ship] *Westward*, which had previously been employed carrying up to eighty passengers on luxury trips, was also requisitioned by the Royal Navy and moored in Parkston Quay to serve as an operations base known as HMS *Badger* – thereby giving the port the codename by which it would be known for the duration of hostilities.

Parkston was, in fact, just one of many closed areas in the harbour to which admission was strictly controlled. Those civilians who worked there were sworn to secrecy and early in 1940 plans had been drawn up for them to be fed and quartered on the quay in the event of a total civilian evacuation from the town. Carefully positioned British mines were already in place in the harbour alongside demolition charges and sunken block ships to thwart any invasion from the North Sea. Overhead, 24 bulbous grey barrage balloons hung suspended with trailing cables to deter low-flying aircraft.

Ringing the port were seventeen heavy anti-aircraft guns and batteries of searchlights to spot any raiders. These had frequently been in operation already and there were very few people in or around Harwich who had not witnessed a dogfight between the RAF and German invaders and cheered at the sight of a Hun raider crashing into the sea. All along the coast, too, miles of barriers made of scaffolding poles had been erected on the sands to bar the way against any landing force.

Yet despite all this protection, the wail of air-raid sirens and the blaze of searchlights sweeping across the harbour had become an ever-present element of life throughout the summer and autumn of 1940 as the desperate battle for beleaguered Britain was waged on the sea and in the air. One Harwich resident graphically described the situation to a reporter from the *Essex County Standard* in September 1940:

> Every night seems to be brilliant with searchlights, noisy with gunfire and torn with the rip of machine guns in the sky. Sometimes it is punctuated with the awful scream of a plane diving out of control, a grim crescendo culminating in a dull thud and a red glow of flames.

In between these attacks, though, the people of Harwich continued to go about their war business as best they could in the pitch-dark community. On many a street after nightfall, members of the civilian

Air Raid Precaution (ARP), Home Guard officers and the occasional policeman could be glimpsed on patrol, keeping a careful watch. Those civilians who did not want to run the risk of a fine ensured their windows were 'blacked out' with strips of gummed paper – and never went anywhere without their ubiquitous gas masks. In the event of an air raid it was always as well for people to know where the nearest public air-raid shelter was located – except, that is, for those who had their own: a corrugated-iron shelter known as an 'Anderson' dug into the garden or underneath a mound of sandbags.

Then, just as the evening of 24 October seemed to be drawing to a close without incident, a curious sound was heard high above the town. The time was just after 10.30 p.m. and there were more people out on the streets than usual, as the last restaurants and public houses were just closing. Some of these men and women could be seen leaving the British Restaurant on Bathside ('Best Food, Well Cooked in Ideal Conditions'), where they had enjoyed the Thursday set meal of lentil soup, minced beef, beans and potatoes rounded off by a jam slice and custard at a cost of one shilling (ten pence). Others had made do with pints of beer and a shot or two of whisky at popular pubs such as the Hanover in the old town and the Samuel Pepys in Church Street.

Whatever these people had been doing, the noise they heard was quite unlike any other that had disturbed their peace during the past year. The best description was that it sounded like 'rattling tin cans'.

Barely had anyone time to gaze upwards before the air-raid sirens began their familiar mournful wail across the town and harbour. Beams of searchlights lanced into the inky blackness, probing for whatever was passing overhead. The noise became unmistakably that of aircraft engines – but not like those of the usual *Luftwaffe* aircraft.

There was no appearance of panic as the men and women hurried back to their posts or, alternatively, the nearest air-raid shelter. They had experienced many air raids before and this seemed much the same. The comforting sound of the anti-aircraft gunners firing off several rounds broke the silence before the intruders disappeared. But *who* were they?

It was not until later that week that the people of Harwich could be sure the planes had not been German. There was no doubt the port had been the target of a small force of bombers, but it seemed that such was the confusion of the pilots that they had flown right over the town and dropped their bombs on a number of innocent places spread between the little village of Trimley, almost four miles to the north and the seaside resort of Walton-on-the-Naze, some five miles south.

The *Corpo Aereo Italiano* had, in fact, begun its campaign in the Battle of Britain. As some of the aircrews had feared right from the start, it had not been a success. The reasons for this were not hard to discover, either…

* * * * *

The archives of the *Regia Aeronautica* state that the *Corpo Aereo Italiano* finally had all its aircraft, airmen and ground crews on station in Belgium by 22 October. The bombers at Melsbroech and Chièvres; the fighters at Maldegem and Ursel. Air Marshal Fougier had set up his headquarters at Petite Espinette in Rhode-St Genesis, a picturesque little village between Brussels and Waterloo, and taken up the *Luftwaffe* offer to base his technical services on the nearby aerodrome of Evere.

Evere, which sprawled across 24 hectares (60 acres) of grassland, had originally been built in the second half of the First World War by the occupying German forces. Four hangars had served to maintain the enemy's force of aircraft and Zeppelins until all of them departed at the end of the conflict. From 1919 onwards, Evere was home to three Belgian fighter squadrons and one reconnaissance squadron, until the heavy thud of jackboots overran the country again in 1940.

The arrival of the Italians had not, however, gone unnoticed. As soon as the Belgian government in exile in London received the news, war was officially declared on Italy. British intelligence also stepped up its surveillance and America was not long in receiving details about this new development in the Battle of Britain. Surviving reports by a US correspondent and British intelligence differ somewhat about the purpose of the Italians – but share a similar scepticism about their potential effectiveness.

Lars Moen was a Swedish-American newspaperman turned scientific researcher whose work in the late Thirties had taken him all over Europe. When war broke out in 1939, he was engaged on a project in Antwerp. Ignoring advice from the American consulate to get out because he believed that the Germans would respect the neutrality of Belgium, Moen continued his work. Day by day, though, as Hitler's forces swept across France and Holland, he came to appreciate the true intentions of the Nazis – and very soon found himself in occupied territory.

Deciding that it might now be best to return home, Moen began the laborious process of applying for an exit visa. It was not, in fact, until numerous applications had been ignored and he had 'practically abandoned hope that the German military authorities would permit my departure before the end of the war', that Moen was finally granted permission to leave – coincidentally, to our story, on 22 October 1940. A fourteen-day journey to Lisbon followed by ten days on a boat to New York at last saw him safely back in America.

Settled again in New York, Lars Moen decided to write about his experiences in Belgium, describing in detail the harsh lives of the people and their 'swaggering and brutal' occupiers. *Under the Iron Heel* was published the following year and provides one of the earliest insights into life in Hitler's 'new' Europe. Thanks to his years as a journalist, Moen was an astute observer and in the most telling chapter of the book describes what he had learned of the Nazis' plans for invading England. Little escaped his attention and even as he was leaving Belgium some new uniforms had caught his interest:

> The arrival in Belgium of two thousand Italian fliers and mechanics seemed to me significant, coming as it did, at a moment when German pilots were being transferred elsewhere in considerable numbers. Such a move presumably meant one of two things: a shortage of German flying personnel, or a transfer of Nazi pilots to a theatre of war considered more vital than the Channel ports. Since there was nothing to support the view that Germany was running short of aviators, despite considerable losses over

England, it was far more plausible to suppose that the Italians were taking over to release German groups for service elsewhere. The Germans have no high opinion of Italian fighting ability, and it was highly improbable that they would have been brought to Belgium if really important operations were planned in that sector.

Although Lars Moen was not aware of the fact, the Air Ministry in London had also received information about the Italians. In its 'Weekly Intelligence Summary' dated 23 October and circulated to Winston Churchill and his officials, the Ministry set out the basic facts of the new enemy presence and added a spot of speculation: 'It is now known that a *Gruppo* of BR.20Ms attached to the *Luftwaffe* in Belgium is carrying out daily navigational flights. Their purpose appears to be solely reconnaissance.'

Accurate as both Lars Moen's statement and the Air Ministry communiqué are, neither is correct in its assessment of the plans then being put into place by Fougier. The CAI was busy familiarising its pilots with routes for attacking England and on 22 October, a flight of some two dozen bombers and fighters from Ursel and Chièvres flew a training exercise over the English Channel – though keeping well clear of the British coast. The Italians were determined to show their Axis colleagues that they were no mere substitutes, but capable of carrying out their own major operations – perhaps with more success than the *Luftwaffe* had enjoyed.

The *Luftwaffe* had, publicly, extended a welcome to the CAI. The German commander in France, Field Marshal Albert Kesselring, presented Fougier with one of the remarkable short-take-off-and-landing German aircraft, a Fiesler Storch FI-156, for his personal use. A single-engine Junkers Ju52 – the seventeen-seater cargo and passenger aircraft – was also offered on permanent loan to serve as a courier between the Air Marshal's headquarters in Rhode-St Genesis and the *Regia Aeronautica* in Rome.*

* Appropriately, it would be a Fiesler Storch with its capability to take off in less than 61 m (200 ft), flying at 40 km/h (25 mph) and landing within 15 m (50 ft) of touchdown, flown by the German pilot Walter Gerlach, which would snatch Mussolini after he had been deposed in the autumn of 1943 and was being held captive by the new nationalist Italian forces in a ski lodge 1,908 m (6,500 ft) up in the mountains of the Italian Alps.

Once the pleasantries were over, however, Kesselring wasted no time in issuing orders for integrating the Italians into the existing *Luftwaffe* structure. The CAI were to focus their initial operations on a 'vulnerable front' of the east coast bounded by the parallels 53 degrees north and 01 degrees east. This gave them a number of important targets including military installations, naval ports and major towns between the River Thames and Harwich and including the estuaries of the rivers Orwell and Stour.

Once fully operational, Kesselring told Fougier, the CAI operations could be extended farther north up the coasts of Suffolk and Norfolk to take in the other key ports of Lowestoft and Great Yarmouth. There was the possibility, too, of inland attacks over the Kent coast in the direction of London. *Luftwaffe* pilots who had already flown missions over this sector of eastern England would be made available to brief the Italian pilots before their missions. Among those who gave talks was the German ace Adolf Galland, who claimed that 'The only way to get a British fighter off your tail is to turn to starboard and swallow-dive away.' They would not follow, he assured his listeners. The logbook of Captain Gino Lodi of 56 *Stormo*, who attended one of these briefings, adds an interesting footnote:

> The Germans supplied armour plates for pilot seats. Very pistols, life jackets, aerodrome anti-aircraft defence and intelligence. However, they kept their secrets to themselves. The Germans planned an operation without giving many details to us and then told us to do a diversion.

The German 2nd *Fleigerkorps* were to control formations and facilitate communications. Each of the Italian units was given a German designation: the bombers in 13 *Stormo* became KG13 (for *Kampfgeschwader*) and those in 43 *Stormo* KG43. The fighter *Gruppo*s numbered 18 and 20 were designated 18/JG56 and 20/JG56 (*Jagdegeschwader*), while the independent 179 *Squadriglia* was referred to by the figures 1(F) 172. The three major airfields were also given codenames: Ursel was 'Saturn' and Melsbroech 'Dedalo', with Chièvres referred to as 'Icaro'.

The first meetings between the Italians and the battle-hardened *Luftwaffe* pilots were not easy. Language difficulties did not help and there is evidence that the Germans were not slow in using slang terms about their new colleagues.

Puppchen was apparently a favourite German term for the little CR.42s, while the bombers were laughed over as *Pantechnicon*. The word *Junk* was used to describe what were regarded as clapped-out Italian aircraft. A popular expression for a pilot was an *Emil*, though the less masculine aircrew found themselves being referred to as 'Blonde Arses'.

The Germans sometimes made fun of the Italian pilots' curious-looking cork-striped lifejackets, which they nicknamed *Wursts* (sausages). When Kesselring got to hear about these primitive lifesavers, however, he gave orders they were to be replaced by the new and more efficient model in use by the *Luftwaffe*, which was inflatable and fitted with a fluorescent bag to make it easier to spot a pilot who had crashed into the sea.

Despite the scepticism on the part of many of their hosts, the CAI pilots got on with familiarising themselves with their new surroundings. The word was that actual operations against England would begin within the month. A sense of urgency grew among the crews and the airfields were soon busy with fighters and bombers flying across the Belgian landscape and getting to know the terrain from base to coast.

The differences between northern Europe and the sunny climes of Italy were immediately apparent, especially with the murky weather, as it began to decline towards winter, making flying in aircraft with inadequate navigational aids all the harder. Nor was it easy for the Italians to integrate into the German style of operations for bombing England – an island country that few of the Italian airmen had seen and which now possessed a reputation for being ferociously defended. The men had heard stories of well-protected coasts, and accurate anti-aircraft fire, and rumours of secret weapons – one to spot aircraft approaching and another that could apparently set the sea on fire, shooting flames and smoke hundreds of feet into the sky!

It was not an inviting prospect for those preparing to take part in the very first raid – a night mission against the port of Harwich on the evening of 24 October. The man chosen to lead the operation was Captain Franco Bassi of 3 *Squadriglia* based at Melsbroech. Born in Trapani on Sicily, he had won a gold medal for bravery in the Spanish Civil War and had selected several other veterans of the campaigns on the Iberian peninsula and France for the raid.

Bassi led a dozen BR.20Ms from 1 and 3 *Squadriglia*, followed by six more bombers from 5 *Squadriglia* under the command of the experienced Captain Carlo Pagani. The force was scheduled to take off at 20.35 hours and fly directly to their target, where they would unleash their payloads of 680-kg (1,500-lb) bombs from a height of 5,000 m (16,400 ft).

The technicalities of the mission were something that Captain Bassi had performed many times in practice, both as a trainee pilot in Italy and recently in flights across the Belgian countryside. He was a superstitious man, though, and ever since he had been assigned to 13 *Stormo*, the unlucky number had always unsettled him. He took off from Melsbroech trying to put such thoughts aside, but with a sense of foreboding continuing to nag at his mind. Bassi just prayed that having his friend, Captain Luigi Gastaldi, flying in the bomber immediately behind would bring him good luck.

In fact, it was the leader of the second group, Captain Pagani, who had also flown in Spain and France, who needed the luck. Just fifteen minutes after Bassi had roared off into the night sky, Pagani and his crew in MM21928 also lumbered down the runway and took off. Within 'a few minutes' – a later report states – the bomber suddenly went into a dive and crashed beside a church in the village of Houtem.

There was no time, it seemed, for either the captain or the five members of his crew to take any action and all were killed instantly in the terrible impact amid the church's graves and ornate tombstones. Apart from Pagani, the others who died were his co-pilot, Giovanni Favia, who had served with him in the *Regia Aeronautica*'s two previous campaigns; *Tenente* [Lieutenant] Arrigo Vardabasso, likewise a very experienced aviator who had been flying in BR.20s since 1936; two flight engineers, Sergeant Paolo Biziocchi and Sergeant Aldo del Monte; and air gunner Sergeant Paride Astesati.

The mystery of what caused MM21928 to crash has never been solved. A sudden engine failure seems the most likely explanation, though Pagani's experience might still have enabled him to land a crippled plane. The stark fact remains that the CAI's war against England had claimed its first victims even before a single bomb had been dropped in anger.

Captain Bassi was, of course, unaware of this disaster as he and the other bombers flew over the darkened countryside and then across the misty North Sea to reach Harwich about an hour later. According to the only account of the raid that has survived by *Primo Aviere* [Corporal] Renzo Guglielmetti, a gunner on a bomber in 1 *Squadriglia*, ten of the aircraft dropped their bombs from an altitude of 5,000–5,500 m (16,400–18,050 ft). Their views were obscured by the mist and a blackout shrouding the town, however, so no one was sure if they had hit the port.

Corporal Guglielmetti reported that his plane had been struck a glancing blow by anti-aircraft fire, but he and the other crew members had escaped injury. The BR.20M had then turned for home and had been one of the first to land at Melsbroech at 23.50 hours. The gunner's report also reveals that others in the raiding party were not so lucky. A bomber flown by Captain U Machieraldo had to make a crash-landing at Lille, while another piloted by Lieutenant M Pesso suffered navigational difficulties and became lost, forcing the crew of six to bale out between Namur and Charleroi.

The misfortune he had feared also struck Captain Bassi on the return journey to Belgium. He, too, became lost in the bad weather, but still confident he was over occupied country, he ordered his crew to bale out. The captain followed and all the men landed in fields near the town of Cambrai, escaping with just minor bruising. Only the radio operator, Armando Paolini, suffered a more serious injury to his foot.

By one o'clock the following morning, the remaining bombers had arrived at Melsbroech and the loss of four aircraft was accounted for. It had not been an auspicious start to the campaign – and it was as well that the men were not aware of how wide of the mark their bombs had fallen, although the evidence is inconclusive. One report has claimed that only four bombs at all fell on land that night. Another eight were dropped on marshland and six more fell into the sea. A second account maintains that the bombs fell near three villages around Harwich – Trimley, Wrabness and Beaumont – with the remainder on Pye Sands at Walton-on-the-Naze and close to a drifter steaming off the coast near Clacton. A suggestion by Julian Foynes in his book, *The Battle of the East Coast* (1992) that other Italian planes 'seem to have gone to Yarmouth, near where bombs were reported at the appropriate time' would appear, on the lack of any specific evidence, to be a case of mistaken attribution, for there were also German raiders active that night. There was certainly no damage to property and no casualties anywhere in or around Harwich.

It was clear the Italians' first raid had been a failure. But such facts were not to be allowed to interfere with the possibilities of propaganda. The following morning, Mussolini's favourite radio stations and newspapers were reporting a triumph in the battle for Britain. An account in *Avanti* of 25 October – bearing all the hallmarks of having been written before the events took place – declared: 'A large force of Italian bombers raided London [sic] during the night. They have returned bearing the marks of combat, but with the glorious certainty of great victory.'

The only certainty was that, under prompting from *Il Duce*, the CAI would soon be setting out for England again with redoubled activity, 'marks of combat' or not.

* * * * *

In fact, Fougier waited only two days before agreeing on a new strategy with Kesselring – a daylight bombing raid with a strong contingent of fighter aircraft for protection. It was also decided to shift the target zone to the other side of the Thames and aim for the resort of Ramsgate on the exposed tip of the Isle of Thanet, which the *Luftwaffe* had already bombed on several occasions.

For centuries, Ramsgate had been in the forefront of any war fought by Britain, especially as a refuge for vessels and as an embarkation port for troops. Its main thoroughfare, Military Road, bore witness to this tradition and it was due to the hospitality offered by the residents to George IV in 1821 that the port now had the unique title of 'Royal Harbour'. Since 1939, Ramsgate had served as a base for Motor Torpedo Boats and provided one of the main disembarkation points for the thousands of soldiers rescued from the beaches of Dunkirk. Just three miles inland stood the RAF station of Manston, a frontline base in the Battle of Britain, with a long and very wide runway frequently used by damaged aircraft for emergency landings.

Details of what would prove to be the Italians' first foray against Ramsgate are scant. According to the logbook of one of the fighter pilots who acted as an escort – *Sergente Maggiore* [Flight Sergeant] Giuseppe Ruzzin of 85 Squadron, who flew a CR.42 from Ursel as protective cover – a total of 12 BR.20Ms were accompanied by a similar number of the biplane fighters. The group crossed the Straits of Dover at around 16.00 hours, but found much of the English coast shrouded by low cloud and the operation was abandoned without a bomb being dropped.

It is possible that this operation may have been no more than an exercise to familiarise the bombers and fighters in a dual operation. But when the same target was earmarked two days later, the force was considerably increased in size with the addition of *Luftwaffe* fighters for their experience. In all, fifteen bombers of 98 *Gruppo* from Chièvres commanded by Major Tenti, accompanied by 39 CR.42s and 34 G.50s and a dozen German planes were ordered to rendezvous near Ostend before crossing the Belgium coast for England.

The German fighters were the powerful Messerschmitt Bf 109s with their 1,175-hp Daimler Benz DB 601 engines capable of speeds of up to 560 km/h (348 mph), a ceiling height of 11,125 m (36,500 ft) and a range of just over 640 km (400 miles). Armed with two MG FF cannons firing sixty rounds per gun, the Bf 109 had proved its worth in the *Legion Condor* in Spain and at the commencement of the Battle of Britain was reckoned to be the best single-seat, single-engine fighter in the world. During the months that followed, of course, this claim was challenged and arguably overturned by the Spitfire.

Once again, the CAI hit problems even before the rendezvous over Belgium. Three of the bombers developed engine problems as they flew across the 160 km (100 miles) to the coast; two returned immediately to Chièvres, while the third had to make a forced landing at the Ostend-Stene airfield.

The rest of the still sizeable force flew on to England and reached the coast in clear weather. Contemporary accounts of the raid refer to the bombers and fighters flying in at a low level, almost wingtip to wingtip, in what seemed to some observers almost like an air-show display. The green-and-blue camouflage markings of the bombers also contrasted with the darker markings and yellow cowlings of the fighters. It is said, too, that the bright colours and unusual shapes of the planes took those on the coast who saw them somewhat by surprise. Certainly, the anti-aircraft guns did not open up until virtually all of the raiders had passed overhead and were beginning to swing north.

Almost immediately afterwards the bombers scattered a total of 75 bombs over the coast and then quickly headed east with the fighters buzzing around them like so many attentive worker bees. The first Italian bombs to hit English soil were recorded at 17.45 hours according to an entry in the Dover War Command Diary (PRO ADM 199/360). It is from this source, too, that it can be established that it was *not* Ramsgate that was hit as several reports have stated, but the town of Deal, midway between the resort and the famous port.

Indeed, this diary also reveals that the raid caused the first casualties inflicted by the Italians: the death of five Royal Marines at Deal. There is very little information about this tragedy beyond that stark fact and Major Mark Bentinck, the Royal Marines Historical Records Officer, admitted to me, 'This incident is not recorded in our history.' However, research in the Register of Royal Marine Deaths in the Second World War finally brought to light the names of these men as Marines Drake and Girling, who were in the port, Second Lieutenant Nelson of the Siege Regiment, Marine Lewis of HMS *Eaglet* and Bugler Clemson from HMS *Dolphin*. Despite the indiscriminate nature of the bombing, no civilians were killed.

The CAI did not escape without casualties, either. Five of the bombers were hit by anti-aircraft fire and a number of the aircrew suffered injuries. The plane to suffer worst was BR.20M of 243 *Squadriglia* piloted by Captain Romualdo Montobbio, which barely reached the welcoming shore of Belgium before rapidly losing height.

As the plane neared Courtrai, the gunner *Primo Aviere* [Leading Aircraftsman] Giuseppe Monti apparently jumped from the rear door of the aircraft, trying desperately to deploy his parachute. He struck the ground before it opened and died instantly. However, Captain Montobbio maintained control of the stricken plane and carried out a perfect belly-landing near the village of Kurne, saving the lives of the four other crew members, who only suffered minor injuries.

The safe return of the rest of the bombers and the fighters comparatively unscathed made even better copy for the media back in Italy the following day. The fact that the CAI had actually gone inland and bombed the English coast was 'spun' into another propaganda triumph that delighted Mussolini. This was just what he had been hoping for from his airmen.

Heartened by the success of this operation, Fougier pushed for his men to undertake an inland mission. On the afternoon of 1 November, 26 of the crack pilots from Squadron Leader Mario Bonzano's 20 *Gruppo* were dispatched from Ursel and after a rapid Channel crossing swept inland over Sandwich for 25 km (15.5 miles) as far as the ancient cathedral city of Canterbury. Those of the pilots with an eye for architecture were struck not only by the beauty of some of the old buildings, but also the damage that had clearly been inflicted by the *Luftwaffe*. On the return journey, the pilots had to avoid a barrage of anti-aircraft fire that greeted them as they passed over Folkestone.

The 20 *Gruppo* planes did not encounter any RAF opposition on either leg of their journey. The same good fortune also smiled on another fighter mission of 39 pilots in the slower CR.42s of 18 *Gruppo*. Their flight path took them over Ramsgate, via Canterbury and back home by Dover. The fact that both groups had flown to within 80 km (50 miles) of London without any interception from the RAF made a few of the men begin to wonder if perhaps the German claims about the British being on their knees might not have some truth in them.

On the evening of 5 November, another group of eight bombers from 13 *Stormo* were sent on a second night raid to Harwich. The significance of Guy Fawkes Night was, of course, lost on the Italians – although, obviously, no bonfires were alight on the mainland – but the planes were spotted at 5,000 m (16,400 ft) overhead and fired on by the port's anti-aircraft guns. According to a report by a soldier in an army detachment stationed in ancient Languard Fort across the harbour from Harwich, 'We counted several explosions in the sea and flares being dropped.' During the raid, a number of the Italian bombers were hit by ack-ack fire and one was damaged quite extensively, though it still reached base safely. Most of the bombers did manage to drop their bombs, though – one pilot, of course, being completely taken in by the 'dummy airfield' at Boxford!

CAI records state that a total of 44 bombs of 90 kg (220 lb) and 267 kg (500 lb) were dropped during the mission – along with the flares that were intended to help the aim of the pilots overhead. No serious damage was caused to Harwich, however.

This same archive indicates that on the afternoon of 8 November, 22 of the new G.50 fighters from 20 *Gruppo* flew an offensive patrol between Dungeness, Folkestone, Canterbury and Margate and 'reported a combat with four RAF fighters'. Neither side submitted any claims for this particular day, though. There were also a scheduled daylight bombing raid by 43 *Stormo* on 10 November, but this was apparently aborted because of bad weather, via a radio call to the commander after the planes were already airborne. Legend has it that one of the pilots was so delighted at being called back that he thought 'an armistice had been declared', according to a log record.

In fact, quite the reverse was true. Air Marshal Fougier and his staff were on the verge of launching the biggest operation yet undertaken by the Italians. It would bring the strength of the CAI into direct conflict with the RAF – and turn out to be one of the most extraordinary days of the Battle of Britain as well a crucial moment in the story of the Chianti Raiders.

THE HAWK AND THE FALCONS

6

The story of the first aerial battle in the skies between the *Corpo Aereo Italiano* and the RAF has its beginnings not in England, but on the other side of the world in New Zealand. It was a young man born and raised there who, as a result of an extraordinary sequence of events, became the first pilot to set his gun-sights on an Italian raider and notch up the first success against the new enemy. Such, though, was the surprise of Pilot Officer Edward 'Hawkeye' Wells over his lone encounter with a group of CAI fighters that he was convinced it must be an 'aberration' and had nothing to do with the Battle of Britain in which he had been fighting for much of the long, hot summer of 1940.

Pilot Officer Wells was a member of 41 Squadron based at Hornchurch near the coast of Essex. A tall, languid man with an engaging smile, he had travelled halfway round the world to join the RAF and become a Spitfire pilot in what was the toughest training ground in the world – with the shortest odds of survival. He is acknowledged today as one of New Zealand's ace wartime pilots as well as one of 'The Few' who lived to tell his story.

Edward Preston Wells was born on 26 July 1916 in the rural town of Canterbury, situated to the south-east of Hamilton on New

Zealand's North Island. Known as the 'Town of Trees and Champions', the picturesque little community is located in the heart of Waikato's affluent farming and horse-breeding district. Despite its thriving businesses, the town has remained small enough to retain a relaxed country atmosphere where the houses, shops and tree-lined streets demonstrate a pride in its old-world English heritage. Even before its settlement by the British, the area was well known as Horotiu Pa, a powerful Maori stronghold.

It was here that young Wells grew up on the family farm, learning about agriculture and breeding livestock. He was also taught how to handle firearms and his proficiency earned him the nickname 'Hawkeye', a handle that stuck with him into manhood and the services.

Wells fell in love with the idea of flying while studying at Cambridge High School, a top achievers' academy that implanted in every student the words of its motto, *Fortiter et Recte* – 'To have the Strength to do the Right Thing'. On leaving school, though, he went naturally enough into farming until the outbreak of the war. Then he joined the Royal New Zealand Air Force and in October 1939 began his training. Wells proved to be a natural pilot – skilled and proficient and as keen-eyed as his nickname – and with Britain staring defeat in the face, offered his services to the RAF.

'Hawkeye' Wells arrived in England in May 1940 after a tortuous journey by plane and boat via the USA. The proficiency he had shown with the RNZAF got him a posting to 266 Squadron based at Eastchurch, 'The Home of British Aviation' on the Isle of Sheppey, where he was converted to Spitfires. It proved to be a case of man and machine perfectly suited to one another. From the moment that he slid into the cockpit of a Mark I, Wells sensed both the power and efficiency in the single-seat fighter and why its brilliant design by R J Mitchell had made it such a favourite with pilots. The name, he was interested to learn, was a euphemistic translation of *Cacafuego*, after a Spanish treasure ship that had been captured by Sir Francis Drake in 1579.

Although the Spitfire had only first flown in 1936 and not entered service until August 1938, it had rapidly become the darling of the media and instantly recognisable by the public. This was largely due to the plane's elliptical wings, which gave it a very distinctive look while their thin cross-section gave it terrific speed. The wings spanned some 11.2 m (36 ft 10 in) and were beautifully balanced with the Spitfire's length of 9.1 m (29 ft 11 in).

The first time Wells ran the aircraft's Rolls-Royce Merlin II engine he felt the throbbing pull of 1,175 hp that generated a maximum speed of 570 km/h (355 mph) and would give him a ceiling of 10,360 m (34,000 ft) and a working range of 1,065 km (575 miles). There was comfort, too, in the aircraft's four 7.7 mm Browning machine guns. If necessary, the Spitfire could also be armed with a 500-lb (230-kg) bomb.

After several flights, Wells told some of his fellow pilots that he compared flying the Spitfire to 'driving a sports car'. Although it would not roll very fast, the plane climbed and descended easily. If there was a slight problem area, it was that the ailerons were rather stiff and it was said that some pilots had to jam an elbow against the side of the cockpit to get enough leverage to move them.

Wells soon experienced what other pilots had nicknamed the Spitfire's 'washout' feature. The incidence of the wings was such that a twist on the stick would cause the wingtips to stall before the wing roots, thereby giving a slight judder to warn the pilot. When the New Zealander first experienced this judder he knew he had sufficient aileron control to recover the plane before it went into a full stall – and in that instant joined the ranks of other pilots with cause to be grateful for the 'washout' when carrying out tight turns to the aircraft's limits during combat. Apart from the manoeuvrability of the Spitfire, the good visibility from the cockpit also gave the pilot a slight edge on the Messerschmitt Bf 109, which was virtually its equal in the Battle of Britain.

After just a few weeks of intensive training – and with enemy action over south-east England hotting up every day – Wells was posted to Hornchurch, a frontline base some 16 km (10 miles) from the Thames Estuary. It would become one of the country's most famous airfields during the Battle of Britain.

When Wells first set eyes on Hornchurch airfield he noticed a certain similarity to the rural district where he had grown up. The strip had once been part of agricultural land known as Sutton's Farm and a small and rather primitive airstrip had been built on it in 1915.

The base had been one of the initial Home Defence airfields constructed to counter the threat of the German airships that were then flying across the Channel to raid London and the south-east, bringing aerial terror to the civilian population for the first time. The success of the early Royal Flying Corps pilots from Sutton's Farm had earned them the soubriquet of the 'Knights of the Air'.

After the First World War, the small site was purchased by the Air Ministry and, along with some adjacent land, became RAF Hornchurch on 1 April 1928. Despite that slightly inauspicious date and its association with April Fool pranks, the station was soon the proving ground for much new aviation technology, notably ground-to-air wireless communications. The first squadron to use the all-grass airstrip was No. 111, equipped with Armstrong Whitworth III aircraft.

As the RAF expanded, many new pilots who would become aces began their careers at Hornchurch, including Brian Kingcombe, Paddy Finucane, AG 'Sailor' Malan, Eric Lock, Bob Stanford Tuck and Alan Deere, also a New Zealander. With the outbreak of the war, Hornchurch was designated as a Main Sector Station of No. 11 Group of Fighter Command, with the job of covering the important south-east approaches to London. The base also gained two satellite airfields under its control at Rochford near Southend and Manston on the Kent coast

Each day as the struggle with the *Luftwaffe* grew in intensity, massed ranks of Spitfires flew off from the strip that was divided into three runways of 759 m (2,490 ft), 777 m (2,550 ft) and 1,097 m (3,600 ft). After aiding in the evacuation of Dunkirk, the Hornchurch pilots played a crucial role in attacking the German fighters escorting the bombers intent on bringing Britain to its knees. In the early days of the war, these planes belonged to 54, 65 and 74 Squadrons, but from May onwards they were also joined by 19, 92, 222 Squadrons in company with Pilot Officer Edward 'Hawkeye' Wells and his colleagues of No. 41.

Like other sector airfields, Hornchurch had its own defence gun emplacements and pillboxes. Nonetheless, it was a regular target for the *Luftwaffe* – who first struck on 24 August – and by late 1940, the airfield had survived thirteen more bombing raids. In answer to this, by the end of September the various squadrons stationed at the base had claimed 411 'kills' with another 235 'probables'.

Wells flourished in the Hornchurch environment and was soon a prominent member of No. 41 Squadron, which claimed its own glories that summer. It, too, had a long and distinguished history, having been formed in July 1916 when its pilots served courageously on the Western Front. Although disbanded at the end of the hostilities, the squadron was reformed four years later and in January 1939 received some of the very first Spitfires brought into service. Throughout the entire conflict, in fact, 41 Squadron constantly received the latest versions of the plane as they came off the production line – testimony to the capabilities and achievements of its pilots.

These achievements had begun with air cover for the evacuation of the British Expeditionary Force from France and then redoubled with their major role in the summer-long conflict with the German air force. It was a period of his life that Wells never forgot, as he recorded in several combat reports that are now on file in the National Archives at Kew, in west London. Here is a typical extract from one:

> I was often asked if, during the Battle of Britain, I felt fear. My answer to this was that being fired at on a daily basis when flying was not a pleasant feeling, but I was so committed to the task of trying to repel the *Luftwaffe* that this overrode whatever personal feelings I might have felt.

'Hawkeye' Wells' first victory occurred on 17 October, when he shot down a Bf 109 into the sea just off the French coast near the port of Boulogne. On 29 October he had a 'probable' over the Channel and on 2 November made a definite 'kill' when he downed another Bf 109 while on convoy patrol off the east coast. By the time winter came, he and the others in 41 Squadron would be able to claim a total of 100 combat victories.

The pilots were also active in a number of other roles, of course, including bomber escorts and 'rhubarb' interdiction flights, as well as being 'scrambled' countless times to intercept inbound enemy aircraft that might or might not materialise in their sector. It was one such call that earned Wells his place in the story of the Chianti Raiders and which he recorded in graphic detail.

Shortly after the clock in the Hornchurch mess had chimed 11 a.m. on 11 November, the call to scramble echoed across the airfield. Wells and six other pilots were ordered to gain maximum height on a vector towards North Foreland. The location, on the southerly entrance to the River Thames, was the farthermost point of the coast of Kent and one of the closest spots to occupied France. All the pilots had flown over the spot numerous times and occasionally even taken a visual bearing on the ancient North Foreland lighthouse, which for centuries had warned seamen of the treacherous Margate Roads. The mission did not have a very auspicious start for the New Zealander, as he wrote later:

> Unfortunately my Spitfire was slow to start, so my squadron had to leave without me. Within a minute or so my engine fired and as I was keen to join the squadron and already knew the vector to follow I set off at full boost hoping to catch them. But the sky is a very big place and by the time I reached Southend there was still no sign of them. Shortly after this, and still climbing, I had to enter cloud. At about 10,000 feet I broke cloud to find myself surrounded – or so it seemed to me – by a very loose and open formation of biplanes flying just above the cloud sill. I could not recognise them, but I assumed them to be a friendly training flight that seemed to have lost its way and strayed into a highly operational area.

It is hard to imagine who was the more surprised: Wells in his lone Spitfire or the fleet of biplanes that the New Zealander thought might be old Gloster Gladiators, the single-engine aircraft with a Mercury radial engine that had been in service with the RAF since 1937. There is, though, no doubt as to who reacted first, as the pilot officer's surprise rapidly turned to annoyance:

> Almost at once, two or three of them opened fire on me at what seemed extreme range. I found this behaviour to be

unacceptable, irritating and even slightly dangerous. Then the nearest three dived straight down to attack me, firing tracer as they came. I evaded and climbed at full throttle; others from higher up came down in dive attacks in two's and three's [sic]. As I gained height I got clear of most of them.

Still unsure as to just *who* he was dealing with, but certain their intentions were hostile, Wells put into play all his training on the Spitfire, which had already stood him in good stead against German bombers and fighters. He returned to the fray without a moment's hesitation:

I then chose one [of the aircraft] slightly below me and dived to attack him. I gave him a good burst of 3 or 4 seconds. As I fired he half rolled very tightly and I was completely unable to hold him, so rapid were his manoeuvres. He immediately disappeared into the cloud sill and was not seen again. I attacked two or three more and fired short bursts, in each case the enemy aircraft half rolled very tightly and easily and completely out-turned me. In two cases as they came out of their rolls they were able to turn in almost on my tail and opened fire on me.

For a veteran of several encounters with the *Luftwaffe's* newest fighters whose manoeuvrability he had been able to match in every respect, the versatility of these little biplanes, as they twisted and turned with apparent ease, came as something of an unpleasant surprise. 'Hawkeye' was not a man to be easily outfought, though.

To one of the other planes I gave a longish burst and saw large black sheets, which I took to be engine cowlings, fly off the front part of the engine, also grey wisps of smoke (or petrol) came out of the root of his top wing where my ammunition was striking. He half rolled and went into cloud. I got into position on another and saw my de Wilde ammunition hitting the rear part of his fuselage. He half rolled and went down into cloud.

Wells repeated his attacks until he had exhausted his ammunition – Spitfires at that time had only about fifteen seconds of fire time – and decided to return to base at Hornchurch, having now given up any idea of trying to find the rest of his squadron. He was also anxious to give a report of his extraordinary, not say mystifying, encounter:

> There the intelligence officer, who saw my gun ports blasted open, was all agog to know what had happened to the rest of the squadron. When I told him I had never made contact with them, but that I had been attacked by a formation of biplanes, he was as astonished as I had been. I told him they seemed to be able to pull their noses up very high to enable them to get in a short burst, without stalling, at a Spitfire climbing at maximum range.

After puzzling for a moment to try and identify the hostile little planes, the two men decided to consult an identification chart of enemy aircraft that hung in the dispersal hut. After running through the variety of German fighters and bombers, 'Hawkeye' Wells spotted his assailants on a panel of pictures that had been added just a few months earlier. He concluded his report:

> There on the chart I was able to identify the aircraft as Italian Fiat CR.42 fighters. I claimed only one damaged, as I had seen some parts fly off one of the targets before he disappeared in the cloud. I now believe that four CR.42s must have fallen into the sea somewhere between Southend and the North Foreland. As far as I know, the Italian Air Force never came to England again.

Undoubtedly when he wrote these words, Wells believed this to be the case. The truth is that he could not have been more wrong. The Italian threat was only just gathering momentum and before the day was out, other people would come face to face with CAI raiders in the air and on the land. Among the first of these eyewitnesses was a young man working on the edge of the Suffolk coast. His name was

Harry Hawes and his story, like that of 'Hawkeye' Wells, has waited over sixty years to be told in full.

* * * * *

That November morning had been taken up with the usual variety of jobs for teenager Harry Hawes who worked as a farm labourer at Gedgrave Hall on Havergate Island. A strapping seventeen-year-old, he enjoyed his job, but was sometimes unable to prevent his mind from wandering to thoughts of the war. Certainly there were plenty of reminders all around him in Suffolk – the army, for example, had a number of depots and installations located around the countryside and along the seashore. There was also the gossip about 'secret work' being carried out on Orford Ness, the splinter of wild terrain separated from Havergate by a channel that could only be crossed by boat.

The island was a picturesque and interesting place to work, though. Apart from the miles of open pastureland on which the cattle that Harry tended would graze, Havergate was also a haven for avocets, the beautiful black-and-white wading birds with their distinctive long legs and upward-curved bills. Whenever he saw groups of them on the estuary or the shore, he hoped that the enemy bombers that were an almost daily sight flying overhead towards targets such as Harwich, Felixstowe and, further inland, Ipswich, would not scare them away.

These attacks by the Germans had already resulted in a routine for Harry Hawes and all the others who worked on the land along the vulnerable coast of East Anglia. Their first job each morning was to check for any unexploded incendiary devices or pieces of shrapnel that might have fallen in the night – especially in places such as old barns and haystacks – and make sure there was nothing that could harm man or beast. If any worker came across *something* that looked dangerous, his initial duty would be to set his horse free – it was reckoned the animals would always find their own way home – and then report the suspicious object to either the army, the police or the Home Guard.

That particular morning had been grey and overcast since dawn, and after stopping for his usual lunch break from midday to one o'clock, Harry set off in a horse and cart loaded with cattle feed. His destination was the grazing land near the eastern flank of the 28-hectare (70-acre) island and his route took him through the cutting known as Havergate Drift. Harry was jogging along, the horse's reins held lightly in his hands, when the calm of the day was suddenly shattered by an incident that would remain etched on his memory for the rest of life. Now a genial, bespectacled pensioner, Harry recalled the events at his home in nearby Wickham Market:

> All at once the sky was full of aircraft. They just seemed to appear from nowhere over the sea. There were Spitfires and Hurricanes and what were obviously enemy planes. A strange thought occurred to me as I watched. It seemed as if the RAF fighters were trying to round up the others into a group – like sheep dogs herding sheep – with the intention of attacking them and perhaps shooting them down before they could reach Harwich.

As Harry watched transfixed, his emotions an understandable mixture of fear and fascination, the scene above Orford turned into a melee of twisting, climbing and diving aircraft. Then, a few moments later, his view of the aerial battle changed from being a panorama played out at a distance to something much closer – and deadlier:

> One of the enemy planes dived down pursued by a Hurricane. The pair passed no more than a hundred feet above me where I was stood on Havergate Drift. There seemed to be bombs and bits of shrapnel flying around all over the place. Though nothing hit me, a piece of shrapnel struck the horse and grazed his side. It was pretty fright-ening, I can tell you.

Despite his proximity to the action, Harry gritted his teeth. He was, after all, the great-grandson of the intrepid John Green, one of the crew who had braved the elements with Admiral William Parry, the nineteenth-century Arctic explorer, and who now lay buried in Orford Churchyard. Harry steadied himself and remembered the instructions he had been given for such eventualities. Although almost deafened by the roar of the conflict and exploding bombs, he leapt down from the cart and struggled to free the terrified horse from its harness. When, finally, the animal galloped off up the Drift, Harry ducked down beside the cart and held his breath.

The youngster remembers the dogfight lasting for about fifteen minutes. He saw a number of enemy aircraft taking desperate avoiding action from the Hurricanes and Spitfires. Several appeared to be hit and plunged towards the sea, while at least a couple tried to dodge their tormentors by heading inland. He saw one aircraft quite distinctly begin to career downwards and disappear from view over Orford Ness. He would later learn this enemy plane had crash-landed on the shingle beach about half a mile from the famous Orford lighthouse.

When all fell silent again over Havergate Island, Harry Hawes took stock of the situation. Across the ground he could see small craters that had obviously been caused by bombs. The raiders trying to escape from their pursuers had, it seemed, jettisoned these in panic. The holes have remained there from that day to this as a reminder to Harry – and others who were in the vicinity at the time – of the events that afternoon in 1940.

As he stood gazing out towards the North Sea, Harry was conscious of another figure approaching across the battle-scarred earth. It was the familiar figure of Herbert Mann, the local 'road man', whose job was to keep the area tidy. The two shaken men swapped experiences for a while, before Harry headed back to Gedgrave Hall. There he was pleased to find his horse being tended by a group of farm workers who were equally relieved to see that he had not been hurt in the raid.

Another surprise awaited the young man when he went home that evening. He lived in a council house at 3, Nightingale Piece – named after the birds that had lived in Orford for many years and brought people from miles to hear them sing – where his parents and brother were also pleased to learn he had not come to harm in the affray over Havergate Island. There he learned that his father, William, a general labourer, had been working on Orford Ness only a short distance away from where the enemy plane had nose-dived on to the shingle.

Indeed, his dad had been one of the first to reach the aircraft and had his photograph taken by a local newspaper photographer standing beside the crashed plane while it was awaiting collection to be taken away for examination. The picture, with an RAF technician and a guard giving the thumbs-up sign, remained a family memento for years afterwards.

Both Hawes – father and son – realised they had probably had narrow escapes that winter afternoon. Sadly, though, fate was not finished with the family. On 22 October 1944, a German raider dropped four bombs on Nightingale Piece – one scoring a direct hit on number three and instantly killing Harry's mother, Alice, and his brother, Jack. Several cousins who lived in the same road were also among the thirteen victims. William Hawes, however, had been at work at the time and young Harry had joined the army and was already serving with the Gordon Highlanders at Felixstowe. The memory of that night, though, remains as painful for him as the sense of relief he felt at his escape on Havergate Island.

One fact that initially puzzled Harry and his father were the numbers 13/95 and the symbols on the crashed plane. They knew it could not be German – the swastika was already familiar to everyone – and the symbols, which looked like three axes, were in any case very different. Indeed, it would be a while before they learned they had been on the spot for the biggest Italian raid so far. A raid later referred to by locals as the 'Spaghetti Bombers', but officially codenamed by its instigators *L'Operazione Cinzano*.

L'OPERAZIONE CINZANO

7

In the hours immediately after dawn on 11 November, the atmosphere in the dispersal hall at Chièvres was a mixture of anticipation and apprehension. The Italian bomber pilots and their crews assembled in the large room on the Belgian base for a briefing were only too well aware that this was the day that had been earmarked for the first major air raid on England. The men and their aircraft had now been in the country for over a month and the weeks of intensive training on the ground and in the air – including practice bombing runs – were about to be put to the test for real. Some of their compatriots had, of course, already been on raids across the Channel with a conspicuous lack of success. Now it was time for *quello grande* – 'the big one' – *L'Operazione Cinzano.*

The sprawling airfield just 60 km (45 miles) to the south-west of Brussels was somehow an appropriate place for such a mission to begin, as it had a long, if tortuous, association with aerial warfare. Situated in the heart of expansive farmlands, it had become an airfield almost by chance during the First World War when Germany had invaded the country. A German biplane that had suddenly landed on the grassy fields of Chièvres one summer morning in 1917 was the first indication local inhabitants had that the enemy considered the location important strategically. Located halfway between Germany and the British coast, it seemed to the Kaiser's top airmen the ideal place for a major military airbase.

Time, however, ran out for the Germans before they could fulfil their grand design. A year later – on 11 November 1918, to be precise – during which time only a small number of flights had taken place to and from the levelled grass runway, the Armistice to end the war was signed and the Germans went home. Within a season, the 'airfield' had been allowed to return to peaceful grazing and agricultural land.

The Belgian government had learned a lesson from the German plan, though, and when the possibility of war again threatened the country, Chièvres was once more earmarked as a prime site for an airfield. During the autumn of 1939, plans were drawn up for a military airbase and work was actually in progress when, in May 1940, the country was invaded for the second time that century by its neighbour. On 19 May, Germans arrived at the fields of Chièvres again – this time an entire corps of soldiers from the 35th Infantry Division under the command of General Hans Reinhart.

On this occasion, though, there was to be no hold-up in turning the grassland into a Nazi airfield to be designated 'AirBase 404'. Over nine thousand men and women were 'recruited' from the local district to work on the construction of two concrete runways, 2 km (1.24 miles) long (camouflaged in brown and green paint) along with rows of hangars, sheds, barracks, control towers and eight fuel depots

To begin with, all fences, hedges and ditches on the grassland were torn down or filled in. Next, a number of houses were levelled to the ground while those close to the site of the runway had their roof peaks lowered in order to allow bombers time to gain altitude. Thirdly, a line of tall trees that had stood for years alongside the main road from the towns of Ath to Mons was ruthlessly chopped down. By the end of the month, the Germans had incorporated a further 405 hectares (1,000 acres) into the site – giving the airfield a total area of 500 hectares (1,235 acres), almost eight times larger than the Belgians had originally envisaged in 1939! (Towards the end of the war, when Chièvres fell into Allied hands, it had doubled again to more than 1,497 hectares [3,700 acres], making it possible for the site to become a NATO airbase in 1968.)

Because of the strategic importance of the airfield, the Germans also erected six anti-aircraft batteries around the perimeter of the base, each with its own shelter, ammunition bunker and communications system. Chièvres was even equipped with a sophisticated radio transmission service for outgoing and incoming flights. Within two years it would have its own radar system to detect enemy aircraft.

Such was the speed with which the base was constructed that it was soon being used operationally by one of the most famous *Luftwaffe* fighter wings – the *Jagdegeschwader* 26 flying Messerschmitt Bf 109 fighters. Their first missions were to attack the beaches of Dunkirk as the last remnants of the British army fled across the English Channel. After this, the fighters were dispatched to bomb and strafe airfields and aircraft factories around Paris until the French surrendered.

By the end of the summer the *Luftwaffe* had less need for Chièvres, however. So when the Italians entered the war, it was agreed that the airfield would be a convenient bomber base for the CAI to operate against the British. There was only one proviso to this agreement, of course: that the pilots operated under German command.

The numbers of German ground staff at Chièvres had varied considerably since the airfield became operational – from a few hundred in the early days to almost two thousand by the autumn of 1940. Many of these men were involved in the mechanical and engineering sections, servicing aircraft and repairing those that had been damaged in action. There were another six hundred in the technical section who operated air control, radio transmissions, weather forecasting and the general administration of the base.

The relationships between these *Luftwaffe* personnel and the Italian ground staff who began arriving at the base in October were often as fraught as those between the German pilots and the CAI aircrews. Quite a few of the Germans resented what they felt was 'baby-sitting' the ill-experienced newcomers and their inferior aircraft – and they made little effort to conceal their feelings.

By all accounts, the feelings between the two groups were no better when the day of the first big Italian raid on England dawned, on 11 November.

* * * * *

It is not clear why the *Corpo Aereo Italiano* chose the unusual codename 'Operation Cinzano' for their biggest mission to date. The name of the popular Italian drink had never been used on a military operation before, certainly, but it still seemed to have little relevance to the plan for mass destruction of ports, towns and military installations that Air Marshal Fougier and his staff had drawn up with the *Luftwaffe*. One historian researching the story of the Italian air force in Belgium has suggested – tongue-in-cheek – that maybe it was chosen by an officer with a sense of humour who thought that they would 'all end up in the drink'!

Whatever the reason for the name, there is no doubt that the CAI wanted to carry out something more spectacular than anything they had previously attempted. For a third time, Harwich and its harbour full of ships was to be the target – but this time in broad daylight. It was to be a maximum effort with bombers and fighters, as Fougier was anxious to demonstrate Italian prowess to the Germans in Belgium and – more especially – Hitler, Goering and the Nazi high command in Berlin. Not forgetting *Il Duce*, of course.

So, with an obvious nod to history, the date of 11 November was settled for the strike. This, in fact, was the day that Germany had signed the Armistice in the First World War and the Axis powers knew that it had become a day of remembrance in Britain with services of commemoration and the observance of a 'two-minute silence' still going on regardless of the war.*

As he was required to do, Fougier informed Field Marshal Kesselring of his plans and the *Luftwaffe* chief offered some of his own aircraft to bolster the chances of success. Deception was to play an important part in 'Operation Cinzano', as two British historians have explained while trying to unravel the facts of this landmark

---

* Since 1945, this day has been known as Remembrance Sunday and observed on the second Sunday of the month with a silence at the actual moments of the signing.

day. According to Michael J F Bowyer in *Air Raid! The Enemy Air Offensive Against East Anglia 1939–1945*, it was to be preceded by, 'Morning *Luftwaffe* fighter sweeps over Kent, two attacks on Channel shipping and an inland raid near Dungeness before the appearance of the Italians.' For his part, Julian Foynes goes into the details of the Italian preparations in his book *Coastal Blitz* (1992):

> Two Italian forces, one of five Cant Z 1007bs from 172 Squadron at Chièvres, the other 24 GR.50s from 20 *Gruppo* at Ursel, were to launch preliminary diversions off Foulness and Yarmouth, and to sustain these feints for the maximum time made use of the forward airfields at Coxyde and Raversyde on the Belgian coast. Still more diversionary cover was promised by German raids on London and a convoy in the Thames Estuary.

Italian accounts of the operation give a different version of events, however. To carry out the deception raid, it was decided to use the Cant trimotors, as the crews were undoubtedly better trained in navigation than their colleagues flying the BR.20s. However, as the men of 172 *Squadriglia* had no experience of bombing, this would have to be left to the pilots of the BR.20s who would follow behind to deliver the knockout blow when the RAF had been diverted away from Harwich. Both groups would, though, have their own fighter escorts.

The man chosen to lead the five *richiami* [decoy aircraft] was Captain Ernesto Vassallo, from Padua, another veteran of the Spanish Civil War, in which he had become very versatile at flying BR.20s. He made the transition to the new Z 1007 effortlessly and found it a superior bomber in every respect. His five-man crew for the mission had flown in from their base at Melsbroech the previous day and included co-pilot Lieutenant Ugo Pierotti, an observer, engineer, radio-operator/gunner and one additional gunner.

None of the five planes was armed and they had no armour plating or bulletproof tanks to protect them if British fighters ambushed them. What *did* encourage Captain Vassallo and the other crews as they were briefed that morning in Chièvres was the knowledge of the Cant's 'superior speed and its excellent high-altitude performance', to quote a memo by Air Marshal Fougier. Although the men were told that the weather forecast for the area was 'uncertain', it had been decided to go ahead notwithstanding.

The logbook of Lieutenant Pierotti indicates that the five planes took off from the airfield at 12.15 hours and, settling into a V formation, followed a direct flight path via Bruges and Ostend to Harwich. When they neared the coast they were due to be joined by twenty G.50 fighters from 20 *Gruppo* at Maldegem. They would then carry out two 'sweeps' over Harwich, while the accompanying fighters would tackle any defending aircraft. This, it was hoped, would leave the dock installations without any cover when the main strike force arrived.

But the bad luck that had hindered the CAI in the past month struck again. In poor visibility, the G.50 fighters were unable to find the Cants and turned back to their base. Captain Vassallo, though, was determined to press on with his mission and 45 minutes later the five aircraft were nearing the coast of south-east England. Aeronautical historian Thomas Potts takes up the story in his article, 'L'Operazione Cinzano' for *Aerospace Historian*, describing what he calls, 'the only operation against the British Isles in World War Two by three-engined aircraft':

> The crews had every confidence in their machines. Unprotected and in broad daylight, they flew to Harwich at an altitude of 5,000 metres [16,400 ft], reaching there at 13.15 hours. The five Italian bombers flew over the town in formation to simulate a bombing attack and then set off in a southeasterly direction over the North Sea. There was still no sign of the fighter escort. However, the bombers changed course and made a second sweep over the town at 13.20 hours. This time the crews could see RAF fighters taking off from Martlesham and, it seemed, climbing to meet them. The Italians wisely turned tail.

Whether or not they had been spotted, Captain Vassallo decided his crews had played their part and ordered them to head for home.

Lieutenant Pierotti recorded in his log that their plane, with its nose down, 'registered 500 km/hr [310 mph] on the ASI on the return leg'. Another aircraft actually lost its canopy due to excessive speed and was forced to land as soon as it had crossed the Channel at Ghent. The remaining four Cants finally touched down at Chièvres at 15.15 hours.

The captain considered his mission a success. He had fulfilled his instructions to the letter – even without the fighter protection. What he could not be sure of was whether the RAF fighters had been drawn away from Harwich – or, alternatively, whether the presence of his aircraft had warned the defenders that there might be more to come.

* * * * *

The ten BR.20M bombers that formed the heart of the attack force were airborne from Chièvres within fifteen minutes of the departure of Captain Vassallo's decoy group. These bombers, though, from 242 and 243 *Squadriglia* of 99 *Gruppo*, were fully armed, laden with three 250-kg (550-lb) bombs each. The crews flew due north towards England filled with the same optimism as their predecessors – though their spirits might have been a little dampened if they had known that at that very moment on the other side of Europe half of their famed battle fleet was being knocked out by a daring raid by 21 torpedo-carrying Fairy Swordfish on the port of Taranto in the heel of Italy. A port that, in terms of size and defences, was not unlike their target, Harwich.

The bomber crews, under the leadership of Commander Bernardo Ciccu, also a veteran of the action in Spain and southern France, had trained hard for this mission. They were a mixture of experienced airmen and recruits who had joined the *Regia Aeronautica* when Italy entered the war. Some were natural flyers; others were uncertain of what actual aerial combat would be like.

Typical of the five-man crews who flew across the gathering murky skies in two Vics of five aircraft each were the airmen in bomber 2/MM22621 of 243 *Squadriglia*. At the controls of the plane at the head of the formation was Flying Officer Pietro Affiani, who had been in the air force for five years and experienced tours of duty in

Spain and France. He had already encountered several enemy fighters, dodged anti-aircraft fire and knew that it was best to be a little nervous and always on the look-out for danger. His co-pilot, Sergeant Giuliano Ripolini, who had flown with him on numerous operations in the past year, admired Affiani. If ever a good-luck token was needed in these dangerous times – Ripolini had told the rest of the crew – it was to fly with a man like Lieutenant Affiani.

The other members of the crew were an *Aviere Motorista* [Flight Engineer] Emanuele Degasperi, an *Aviere* [Aircraftsman] Mario Pensa, who also doubled as the unit photographer, and Armando Paolini, the radio-operator. Of the five, Paolini was the most apprehensive as he had only just been reassigned to an aircraft after his brush with death on 24 October when he had had to bale out over Belgium. Though his injuries had been mercifully few, his anxiety was evident from the moment of take-off. Fate, in fact, was lying in wait for all of these men, as it was also for two of the other pilots in the formation, Pilot Officer Enzio Squazzini and Pilot Officer Ernesto Bianchi, though in a very different way.

The rendezvous for the bombers with their fighter escort had been set for 14.10 hours at a height of 4,000 m (13,120 ft) over Ostend. Little had been overlooked in planning the escort in order to boost the morale of the Italian crews – at the same time making it as intimidating as possible for the enemy in the air and on the ground. The line-up consisted of 46 G.50s, 42 CR.42s and a dozen Messerschmitt Bf 109s, all of which had been dispatched on schedule from their bases at Ursel and Maldegem.

Within a short time of this armada climbing into the skies over northern Belgium, however, the CAI plans were thrown into disarray. 'Again the bad weather became an important factor,' Thomas Potts recounts, 'causing the G.50s and Bf 109s to abort shortly after take-off and return to base, leaving the CR.42s as escort.'

Although the *Luftwaffe* archives state that the Messerschmitts went straight home, there is evidence that seven of the G.50s continued as far as the east coast, where they carried out a sweep of the area around Clacton and Frinton, flying at 3,500 m (11,483 ft). What *is* certain, is that they did not attack any targets and were not spotted by RAF fighters or anyone on the ground.

The remaining biplane fighters of 83, 85 and 95 *Squadriglia* pressed on with the mission. At their head was the tough and experienced Squadron Leader Feruccio Vosilla, who was determined to prove the courage of the men of the CAI. Because of their open cockpits, the pilots may have been more exposed to the elements than the other Italian aircrews, but they were undoubtedly in a better position to fly in poor visibility.

When, at last, they made contact, 95 *Squadriglia* rose above the bombers to provide top cover – flying at 7,000 m (22,965 ft) – while the other two groups dropped beneath, flying at 6,800 m (22,310 ft). Among the pilots in 85 *Squadriglia* was a man aptly named Giulio Cesare – 'Julius Caesar' – who later provided an eyewitness account of this moment when a massed force of Romans again approached the shores of England for the first time in two millennia:

> On the way to the English coast, the bombers flew most of the way in clear air with cloud above and cloud beneath. One bomber developed engine trouble and began to fall behind. Later during the flight there was trouble with cloud. Ultimately the bombers were divided into two groups, with the defective machine bravely bringing up the rear. The cloud beneath cleared as we approached the English coast. Flying at about 6,000 m (19,685 ft) – the same height as the bombers – we saw our squadron commander, Captain Anelli, signal with his hand from the open cockpit that we were to turn to starboard. Of course, most of the planes still had no radio – and to think, Marconi was an Italian!
>
> We all obeyed and kept our formation in Vics of three. Then just before we crossed the English coast, Hawker Hurricane fighters intercepted. By then there was a gap of about one kilometre [0.6 mile] between the two bomber formations and the Hurricanes fell on the rear group, coming up from astern before we could intervene. From then on, the action was fast and furious…

* * * * *

The origin of the initial RAF counter-attack on the Italian force had not been from the coastal airfield at Martlesham Heath as the crews of the decoy flight had supposed, but a small grass airstrip in the rural heartland of Essex known by the picturesque name of Stapleford Tawney. Located not far from the town of North Weald, which also had its own airfield that featured prominently in the Battle of Britain, it had originally been opened as a private airfield. During the war years, though, it became home to several of the top squadrons as well as playing a highly secret role in flying special agents into occupied France.

Stapleford had actually begun operating in 1933 with charter flights to and from Paris, which earned it the name of 'Essex Aerodrome'. Two years later, however, the operators were in financial difficulties and the airstrip fell silent until 1938 when the Air Ministry took it over and utilised the facilities for the No. 21 Elementary and Reserve Flying Training School. The most famous pupil to pass through Stapleford was J E 'Johnnie' Johnson, who trained on Tiger Moths and during the war became the RAF's top-scoring fighter ace. Johnson loved to tell the story of his instructor warning him to, 'Keep a good look-out for Hurricanes out of North Weald, they come at you at high speed and look no bigger than a razor blade.'

In March 1940, Stapleford Tawney became a satellite station for North Weald, under the control of No. 11 Group, Fighter Command. The first squadron to become operational was 151, followed a few months later by the renowned 46th with its badge of three rising arrowheads, signifying speed in getting into action, and the stirring motto, 'We Rise to Conquer'.

Formed originally in April 1916 as a reconnaissance unit, the squadron had performed invaluable missions over the Western Front. The following year it was re-equipped as a fighter squadron and saw action both in England defending against heavy German air raids and then taking the fight to France in 1918. Disbanded in December 1919, No. 46 remained in limbo until 1936 when it was re-formed at Kenley in Surrey. When the Second World War broke out, the squadron was converted to Hurricanes and relocated to Stapleford Tawney to help defend London during the Battle of

Britain, as Group Captain Dougie Barr has explained in his history, *No. 46 Squadron RFC & RAF* (2002):

> The *Luftwaffe*'s main effort at the time was against coastal objectives and shipping off the coast of Essex and Kent. The squadron was in action continuously and had many successful engagements against far superior numbers of enemy bombers and their escorting fighters. The enemy sustained such shattering losses amongst his long range bomber force that a change of tactics was necessary, and he tried to force a decision by using fighter bombers flying very high and making every possible use of cloud cover.

One of the vital elements in beating the Germans was the Hawker Hurricane 1 – or 'Fury Monoplane' as it had been called by its designer, Sydney Cam – which was brought into service in December 1937. Although often regarded as inferior to the more glamorous Spitfire, the single-seat, low-wing monoplane fighter with its new retractable undercarriage and enclosed cockpit actually saw more action in the war, and shot down more enemy aircraft, than any other fighter. Powered by a Rolls-Royce Merlin II liquid-cooled piston engine, which generated 1,030 bhp, it could fly at a maximum speed of 531 km/h (330 mph) at 5,335 m (17,500 feet), climbing to a service ceiling of 10,970 m (36,000 ft) and with a range of 684 km (425 miles). The 'Hurry', as it was known by its pilots, had a wingspan of 12.2 m (40 ft), a length of 9.73 m (31 ft 11 in) and was armed with four .303 Browning machine guns in each wing capable of firing 9,600 rounds per minute. The high-speed, controllable-pitch airscrew, wide-track undercarriage that folded inwards, and the medium-pressure tyres made it ideal for quick take-off and landing on indifferent landing strips… like that at Stapleford Tawney. The Hurricane's high rate of climb and wonderful manoeuvrability, combined with its firepower, made it a formidable fighter in the hands of crack pilots.

By the time the group of Hurricanes from 46 Squadron encountered the Italian raiders on 11 November, the pilots were combat-hardened veterans with a fine, if rather costly, record. The squadron's first kill had been on 2 September with the destruction of an ME 109; and the following day – when North Weald suffered its heaviest attack – two enemy bombers were accounted for. During the month, the pilots of No. 46 logged a further nineteen victories for the loss of twenty aircraft, with eight pilots killed.

Seven members of the squadron were already in the air on a routine patrol when the CAI bombers and fighter escort were first spotted approaching the English coast. This group, under the command of Flight Lieutenant Lionel Gaunce, had been 'nursing' a convoy of ships off the east coast near Foulness Island when they were contacted by an urgent voice from RAF Fighter Command Operations Room in Bentley Priory, Stanmore, on the outskirts of London. They were vectored to 'Intercept Bandits over the Thames Estuary.'

Flight Lieutenant Gaunce – known as 'Elmer' to his friends – needed no second invitation. A Canadian by birth, he had volunteered his services to the RAF in September 1939 and quickly proved himself a brilliant fighter pilot with No. 615 Squadron. In July 1940, with two other pilots, he had destroyed three Bf 109s attacking a convoy off the east coast. On 18 August, Gaunce was wounded while in a dogfight with another Messerschmitt and had to bale out of his stricken aircraft near Sevenoaks in Kent.

The indomitable flight lieutenant was back in the air again within a matter of days, but met a similar fate on 26 August when his Hurricane was shot down off Herne Bay. Fortunately, he was rescued from the sea and returned safely to his base in Essex. Gaunce was leading his umpteenth patrol with all his usual verve when the call from Stanmore crackled over his r/t (radio transmitter). He gave immediate orders to the five other planes to turn south-east. Almost at once, Gaunce was to recall in his debriefing afterwards, they spotted a small group of aircraft high above:

> It was difficult to tell at a distance if they were friend or foe. I gave the 'Hurry' a boost of power and climbed towards the group. They probably saw my identification at the same moment as I saw theirs. They were friendly. I told the others to make a wide circle before we went in to attack the Italians.[*]

_____

[*] The evidence suggests that this small group were also Hurricanes of 249 Squadron based at Church Fenton, part of No. 12 Group, who were known to have been patrolling the same convoy off Foulness Island.

For the first time, Gaunce and his men encountered the new enemy. There was no mistaking the insignia on the side of the bombers and the little biplanes, which immediately broke formation on sighting the seven fast-approaching RAF fighters. The men from 46 Squadron peeled off from their leader and dived into action.

The flight lieutenant immediately throttled in the direction of one of the fighters and moments later had to concede a grudging admiration for the little CR.42's manoeuvrability. As Gaunce twisted and turned the 'Hurry' into position to let off a burst of fire, his opponent matched each move and even tried to reverse their positions. When the little plane suddenly dipped out of view without a shot having being fired by either, 'Elmer' found himself angling in towards one of the bulbous-looking bombers.

The BR.20M tried to manoeuvre away – only managing a sluggish turn – and Gaunce fired off a burst that raked the fuselage. The bomber seemed to falter and begin smoking. Gaunce was just about to attack again, when he was conscious of an enemy fighter diving on to him from above. He pulled hard on the stick and sidestreamed away as the Italian flashed past.

The rest of the engagement went on at a similar hectic pace; the flight lieutenant was able to fire on two more of the biplanes, one of which disappeared into cloud, and a second that took the full impact of a twenty-second burst before plunging down into the sea. Gaunce would later claim a half-kill for the bomber and the disappearing fighter and a 'destroyed' for the CR.42 of Sergeant Enzo Panicchi of 83 *Squadriglia* that fell into the estuary. It was Gaunce's fifth kill of the war and is credited with being the RAF's second success against the CAI.

Another of the 46 Squadron pilots, Flight Lieutenant Norman Burnett, was also relishing the combat. Burnett, who learned to fly before the war and was a member of the RAF Volunteer Reserve in Sussex when it broke out, had flown on numerous occasions with 'Elmer' Gaunce. On 8 September he had been wounded in a dogfight with the *Luftwaffe* and crashed his Hurricane on the Isle of Sheppey. Not deterred, he had returned to action a month later. On this occasion, though, he had lost sight of Gaunce when the skirmish began and concentrated his attention on a CR.42, which had dived at him as he approached the rows of bombers.

Just like his friend, Burnett was initially surprised at the ease with which the old-fashioned-looking biplane climbed, turned and dipped. It was, though, he claimed afterwards, the technical superiority of his Hurricane that enabled him to get in several bursts on the Italian. On his return to Stapleford Tawney, Burnett claimed a 'probable destroyed'. (Tragically, on 11 June 1941 the Flight Lieutenant would be shot down and killed, while serving on Malta, by a Macchi MC 200 flown by Sergeant Domenico Facchini of 76 *Squadriglia*.)

Another of the group to enjoy a confirmed kill was Sergeant R J Parrott, a former university student who had joined the squadron early in the year. He, too, had flown before while a student and found himself perfectly at home in the Hurricane. Parrott had attacked one of the bombers that had become detached from the rest of the force and appeared to be heading back towards Belgium. He poured a long burst of machine-gun fire into the BR.20M and saw it burst into flames before spiralling down towards the spume-tipped waves of the North Sea.

It was the joint action of a trio of 46 Squadron pilots that achieved the most famous 'kill' of that winter morning, however. The men were pilot officers G Leggett and J Hedley and Sergeant Norman Walker who converged on the BR.20M bomber being flown by Lieutenant Pietro Affiani, and by so doing brought down the first Italian bomber to crash on British soil.

When the aerial battle had begun to rage, Affiani found himself caught between continuing the raid or turning for home – and fell victim to his own indecision. Bullets from all three Hurricanes struck the bomber as he sought to avoid the withering hail of fire and, losing direction, he turned northwards along the east coast of the country he had come to bomb.

Inside the doomed aircraft, all was pandemonium. The frightened radio-operator, Paolini, who had already had one narrow escape from death, now found his luck had run out. He was hit by the first bullets and died instantly. Alongside Lieutenant Affiani, his co-pilot, Ripolini, was almost in the same instant clutching at a wound in his arm and trying to stem a flow of blood. Behind them, the engineer Degasperi had slumped to the floor, obviously wounded, and was moaning softly to himself. Only Mario Pensa, who had busied himself as the bomber crossed the Channel taking photographs of what was supposed to be a CAI triumph, appeared unscathed.

Affiani continued to wrestle with the controls of the dying bomber as it started to lose height. Smoke was now pouring from one of the engines and the controls of the plane were only responding errati-cally to his touch. The lieutenant knew there was no hope of making it back to Belgium. His mission to bomb Harwich was over. His only job now was to try and land MM22621 and its crew without killing those who were still alive.

As the bomber sank slowly towards open countryside just behind the coast, Affiani looked from one side of the cockpit to the other, hoping for somewhere to ditch. Then, thankfully, after just a few minutes more, a large tract of forest hove into view. Nearby were some open fields and beyond that what looked like a small village. Almost before he was aware of it, the Lieutenant was hitting the ground, his propellers mangling the turf and the aircraft sliding to a halt. The silence that enveloped the inside of the fuselage when it was finally stationary was eerie, broken only by the cracking of the frame and the hissing of the dying engines.

Lieutenant Pietro Affiani did not know it yet, but he had landed on the outskirts of Rendlesham Forest near the village of Eyke in Suffolk. He and the others were about to become the first Italian crew to be made prisoners of war.

Another pilot who had witnessed the crash was Pilot Officer Karel Mrazek, who also belonged to 46 Squadron, but had arrived too late on the scene to join in the 'kill'. A formidable 28-year-old Czech airman, he had been a fighter pilot and regular officer in his national air force in the years before the war. Mrazek had been commander of No. 3 (Fighter) Squadron and flown in Poland and France before escaping to England after the fall of France. He had offered his services to the RAF and soon become a much-valued member of 'Elmer' Gaunce's group. He never forgot the events of 11 November, which began high up over Maidstone, as he recalled in an anthology of airmen's stories, *Winged Words*, published in 1941:

It was just my luck that on that, of all days, the Rolls-Royce engine in my Hurricane began to play up and lose power. Inevitably, I started to lag behind dangerously. All I could do was to hang about, keep my eyes open, and see if I could find any stragglers making for the Channel and home. Well, I found two – both CR.42s – which fell to my labouring aircraft. But I could not claim them. The squadron, together with 245 and 257 had had a field day and, all by myself, I had no witnesses as I made my way back almost out of fuel. In my excitement, you see, I had forgotten to switch on my camera gun!

Mrazek was, though, just in time to witness the crash of the Italian bomber as he headed back to Stapleford Tawney. This, though, would not be the end of the story for him or, more particularly, for the leader of his patrol, Flight Lieutenant Gaunce. Indeed, the skipper would soon discover that a close friend he had known from childhood had been up in the skies over East Anglia that morning… and involved in some even more remarkable action with the raiders from Belgium.

DAY OF THE GLORIOUS DEADBEATS 8

Flight Lieutenant Peter Blatchford was one of those brave, irrepressible characters to be found on the airfields of southern England during the Battle of Britain, their numbers being depleted every day, but still resolutely fighting on against the *Luftwaffe*. In the case of Peter, an easy-going, slow-speaking Canadian known to everyone by his nickname of 'Cowboy', he was to earn the dual distinction of fighting the Germans and the Italians and scoring 'kills' against both.

In November 1940, Blatchford was a member of 257 Squadron based at Martlesham Heath near Ipswich. He had been posted to the squadron in answer to a request by its commander, Squadron Leader Robert Stanford Tuck, who was in need of an experienced flight commander. Born in Edmonton, Alberta, Blatchford had joined the RAF two years before the outbreak of war and had already seen action in Hurricanes with No. 17 Squadron at Debden, Essex. His arrival at Martlesham, however, was remembered initially more for his physical attributes than his accomplishments, as Larry Forrester, a former wartime pilot himself, noted in his biography of Tuck, *Fly For Your Life* (1956):

He [Blatchford] was cheery-faced, chunky and chuckle-voiced with an extraordinarily large backside that made him waddle and roll like an overfed puppy. The slowness of his movements and mannerisms proved wholly deceptive – his mind was rapier-swift, his reflexes instantaneous. He was a brilliant shot, never got excited – all told, a 'natural'.

Tuck and Blatchford got on well from the moment they met – though they were both from very different backgrounds. The squadron leader was London born, had been educated at St Dunstan's College and had gone to sea at sixteen as an officer cadet in the Merchant Navy. There the young Tuck remained for two and a half years until he decided that flying offered bigger thrills and opportunities than being at sea. In 1935 he entered the RAF and won a reputation as an exceptional pilot and crack shot, quickly rising through the ranks. Along the way, Tuck also survived two air collisions, crash-landed several times and ditched in the Channel – his luck was regarded as so phenomenal that he became a legend as 'the immortal Tuck'.

Blatchford also grew to admire Tuck's leadership skills – but his natural sense of humour prevented him from always showing due respect for his superior's rank. In private, Blatchford referred to Tuck as 'Beaky' (after Tuck's aquiline nose), which would prompt the response, 'Fat Arse'. The Canadian's better-known nickname of 'Cowboy' had apparently been inspired by his passion for American Country and Western music. The pair also delighted in ribaldry and jokes – which undoubtedly helped relieve the strain of the grimness of war – and Blatchford was probably the only man who ever flew with Tuck to respond to an instruction in the middle of a dogfight with the words 'Get stuffed', or a long, loud raspberry. For all this, he became 'the boss's' best friend, closest confidant and an eyewitness to the career that would see Tuck become one of the war's greatest fighter pilots and air-leaders with an eventual score of 29 confirmed 'kills' and numerous 'probables'.

The affinity between the two men was also evident to the other members of the squadron at Martlesham. Indeed, the pair were often to be found in the mess sharing a drink and discussing the two things they *did* have in common – a love of beer and flying – whenever there was a break from 'ops'. Their inspiration would help to forge a unity and dedication among the men who would collectively become known by the self-deprecating tag of 'The Glorious Deadbeats'.

The squadron they all served was another that had been formed in the First World War, with a mission to fly anti-submarine patrols off the coast of Scotland that lasted until the end of the conflict. Reformed at Hendon in May 1940 as a fighter squadron, No. 257 had flown Spitfires for two months until exchanging them for Hurricanes in June. In the following months, it had endeavoured to live up to its resounding motto – 'Death or Glory' – while taking part in sweeps over France, escorting shipping and intercepting enemy fighter-bomber raids during the Battle of Britain. These had, though, extracted a heavy price in terms of men and machines in return for what Forrester describes as 'a negligible bag'. This would all change in one autumn day.

Martlesham, where Tuck and his men were based, was located on flat heath land to the east of Ipswich and had originally been opened in January 1917 as the base of the Aeroplane Experimental Unit operated by the Royal Flying Corps. For the next quarter of a century all manner of new aeroplanes and experimental projects were put to the test. In October 1922, a serious fire caused extensive damage to the hangars and airfield, but two years later the site was rebuilt and became home to the Aeroplane and Armament Experimental Establishment, which also tested military and civilian machines. Some of the earliest experimental tests with parachutes were also carried out at Martlesham.

The 1930s saw the trials of a number of prototype aircraft intended for the RAF, including the Wellesley, Battle, Lysander, Blenheim and those two 'star' fighters, the Spitfire and the Hurricane. In 1937, with tension mounting in Europe, it was felt that greater security was required at Martlesham and an operational fighter squadron, No. 64, flying Hawker Demons, was moved in. Under conditions of tight secrecy, tests were carried on into the performance of the Spitfire, Hurricane and several new bombers, as well as trials of such unconventional activities as the validity of cannon armament and the laying of aerial minefields.

When war was declared, however, it was decided that the position of Martlesham near the coast was particularly vulnerable to attack, and so the A&AEE was moved to a safer venue at Boscombe Down in Dorset. By contrast, the very situation of the base with its two runways, one 1,829 m long (6,000 ft) and the other 1.582 m (5,190 ft), made it ideal for the early interception of raiders and a haven for damaged fighters and bombers returning from missions. The RAF therefore decided that units from stations further inland should send detachments on a rotation basis and early 'residents' included 264, 17, 85 and 151 Squadrons, who all claimed successes against the raiders attacking convoys off the east coast. On 15 August, Martlesham itself was raided, causing considerable damage to the hangar complex, although no human casualties were suffered.

After surviving another smaller raid on 25 August, the base was soon back to normal and became home to 257 Squadron detached from North Weald, complete with its Hurricanes and pilots, Tuck, Blatchford and the rest of the 'Glorious Deadbeats'. Michael J F Bowyer in another of his excellent histories, *Action Stations: Military Airfields of East Anglia 1939–1945* (1990), refers to this period in Martlesham's history and notes what he calls, 'the pathetic attempt to attack Britain by the Italians'. Their target was Harwich harbour, he says, but 257 and the other eleven group squadrons, 'treated the visitors with the contempt they deserved'.

The facts of the engagement are, however, anything but prosaic.

* * * * *

The details of 257 Squadron's role in the aerial battle with the CAI on 11 November 1940 is probably the most fulsome and certainly the most colourful to have survived. This is thanks largely to Peter 'Cowboy' Blatchford writing down the details in an account that he subsequently broadcast on BBC Radio later in the month under the title 'The First Fight With the Italian Raiders'. Although the speaker was simply credited on air as 'a Canadian Flight Commander' – a great deal of anonymity surrounded the identity of many broadcasters throughout the war – his identity is easy to detect from the vibrant and racy style of the account. Although no copy of the transmission has survived in the BBC Sound Archives, Blatchford's words were transcribed on to three sheets of typescript paper, now faded and yellow with age, that provide a unique picture of the day that began as Larry Forrester has described it in his book as 'the only big opportunity missed by Tuck during his whole flying career'.

Squadron Leader Tuck had, it seemed, awakened that autumn morning with a painful eardrum – caused by flying with a cold – and was instructed by the medical officer to take the day off. By mid-morning he had become bored with nothing to do and went hunting with a gun in nearby woods. When he emerged from the trees a couple of hours later with thoughts of lunch in his mind, Tuck was just in time to see three arrowheads of his squadron taking off from the airfield and heading south-east. Anxious to know what was happening, he returned to Martlesham and was informed that 257 had been scrambled because 'a big force of bandits was approaching the mouth of the river Thames'. In his absence, Blatchford had assumed the role as leader. It was not something Tuck resented his old friend doing, of course – it was, after all, his number two's duty – he was just frustrated at the thought of missing some action and knew he would just have to kick his heels until the flight returned. Blatchford, who was by now high in the sky, takes up the story in his broadcast account:

> When we were about 12,000 feet [3,658 m] up, I saw nine planes of a type I had never seen before, coming along. Bombers – big and fat – like flying slugs. They were in a tight V formation. I didn't like to rush in bald-headed until I knew what they were, so the squadron went up above them to have a good look. Then I realised that at any rate they were *not* British and they were armed and that was good enough for me. I led the boys in from the back, line abreast. We went into attack starting with the rear starboard bomber and crossing over to attack the port wing of the formation. It was then, when we got in close, that I saw the Italian markings.

Blatchford, like other RAF pilots involved that day, soon appreciated that there were some among the Italian pilots who had been well trained and were practised in the art of aerial combat.

> They kept their tight formation and were making for the thick cloud cover at 20,000 feet [6,096 m], their gunners firing all the way. But our tactics were to break them up before they could reach the clouds and we succeeded at the second pass. Two of them were badly shot up and when they dropped out the others started turning in all directions. I singled out one of the enemy and gave him a burst. Immediately he went straight up into a loop. I thought he was foxing me – trying to make me break off – as I had never seen a bomber do anything nearly so violent before. He was right on his back. I thought to myself the crew must be rattling around inside there like peas – unless, of course, they were strapped into their seats. Anyhow, I followed him when he suddenly went in a vertical dive. I still followed, waiting for him to pull out. Then I saw a black dot move away from him and a puff like a white mushroom – someone baling out. The next second the bomber seemed to start crumpling like wet newspaper and it suddenly burst into hundreds of small pieces. They fell down to the sea like a snowstorm.

Later, the 'Canadian Flight Commander' told his radio listeners that when he had time to analyse his 'kill', he came to the conclusion that something quite extraordinary must have caused the sequence of events he had witnessed:

> I think my burst must have killed the pilot. I think he fell back, pulling the stick with him – that's what caused the loop. Then when the plane fell off the top of the loop, he probably slumped forward again, the weight of his body putting the plane into an uncontrollable vertical dive. She kept on building up speed. What usually happens then is that the wing or the tail falls off, and it was a surprising sight to see the plane just burst into small pieces.

Despite his amazement at these events, 'Cowboy' Blatchford had been in combat too long to relax his attention. He felt a momentary pang of sympathy for the pilot and his crew, but knew it could just as easily have been him on the receiving end. He started to climb again and almost at once saw two more bombers in the sky, apparently sticking together, covering for each other.

> Both seemed to have been badly shot up – streaming smoke and oil. I was just getting set to have another go when right out of nowhere a third bomber came straight at me in a dive, flaming like a torch. I was sure he was going to hit me and I whipped the stick over. I could *feel* the heat of the thing going by me and it plunged into the sea. When I stopped shaking, there was no sign of the couple I had been going after.

Blatchford admitted that at that moment he would have been very happy if the battle had finished and he could have gone home. But now something else was happening in the grey skies over the east coast.

> Just as I was about to turn, I saw a dogfight going on up above with another queer type of aeroplane I had never seen before milling round with the Hurricanes. They were *biplanes*. I was sure they must be Fiats – I had seen pictures somewhere, maybe in the recognition books. There must have been between twenty and thirty of them, camouflaged in brilliant colours. Really pretty, but full of fancy tricks. I went up to join in the party, but the fighter I singled out saw me coming and whipped round in a quick turn with me on his tail. His plane was very manoeuvrable, but so was the Hurricane and we stuck closely enough together and I got in one or two bursts.

What happened in the next few minutes amounted to one of the longest dogfights in which 'Cowboy' Blatchford had ever been

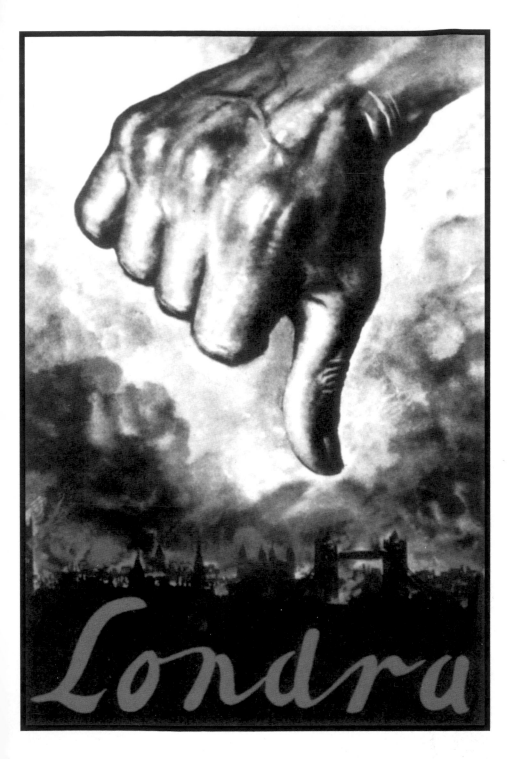

A 1940 Italian poster utilising the classic Roman 'thumbs down' killing sign to promote the belief that the *Corpo Aereo Italiano* would be invincible in the Battle of Britain.

BLACK-OUT 9.44 p.m. to 4.15 a.m.
Sun rises 4.45 a.m.
sets 9.14 p.m.
Moon rises 10.59 a.m.
sets 12.55 a.m.

DAILY SKETCH, TUESDAY, JUNE 11, 1940.

LONDON ITALIANS ROUND-UP PAGE FIVE

Daily Sketch

More Please!
BROWN & POLSON Custard

No. 9,702   (E')   TUESDAY, JUNE 11, 1940   ONE PENNY

ITALY TAKES THE PLUNGE INTO THE WAR AT MIDNIGHT

HOUR BY HOUR

4 p.m. ITALY DECLARES WAR ON FRANCE AND BRITAIN AS FROM MIDNIGHT.

5.50 Announced Paris placed in state of defence.

6.0 Mussolini to Rome crowd: "The hour of destiny has arrived."

7.0 Ribbentrop gloats: "Victory is guaranteed."

7.5 ANNOUNCED TODAY'S SECRET SESSION OF PARLIAMENT POSTPONED.

7.30 Official London statement: "Allies' preparations complete."

7.45 Officials say Turkey resolved to fulfil pact with Allies. M. REYNAUD TELLS FRANCE: "THE WORLD WILL JUDGE THIS ACT."

8.0 Telephones between Turkey and rest of Europe cut.

9.0 Duff Cooper broadcasts. He says: "Mussolini will leave nothing behind him but the curses of those he has betrayed."

10.0 French G.H.Q. announce Germans across the Seine west of Paris.

10.30 Bulgaria announced she looks to Russia for protection. Turkish and Greek frontiers guarded.

12.15 a.m. Roosevelt declares "Full speed ahead to aid Allies."

ITALY IS TO-DAY AT WAR WITH FRANCE AND BRITAIN, AFTER EIGHT HOURS' NOTICE OF HER DECISION.

At 4 p.m. yesterday Count Ciano informed the Allied Ambassadors in Rome that Italy would enter the war on the side of Germany at midnight.

At 6 o'clock Mussolini proclaimed to a war-fevered crowd that Italy had made her "irrevocable" decision.

IT WAS MET BY THE FIRMEST REPLIES BOTH FROM LONDON AND PARIS. IN LONDON IT WAS OFFICIALLY STATED THAT THE ALLIES KNEW HOW TO MEET SWORD WITH SWORD.

PRESIDENT ROOSEVELT, BROADCASTING EARLY TO-DAY, REVEALED THAT MUSSOLINI HAD TURNED DOWN HIS OFFER TO MEDIATE ON ITALY'S CLAIMS, AND SAID THAT HE HAD GIVEN THE ORDER "FULL SPEED AHEAD" FOR ARMAMENTS FOR THE ALLIES.

Violent fighting was continuing last night along the whole Weygand Line, and Paris was placed in a state of defence as the Germans were reported across the Lower Seine at certain points.

—See Pages Two and Three.

New theatres of war are opened up by Italy's entry into the conflict.

Left: An English newspaper announces Mussolini's entry into the Second World War on 10 June 1940.

A photograph of *Il Duce*, the aeronautical fanatic, which was actually banned from publication during his dictatorship.

Above: *Il Duce* inspecting some of
the Italian Air Force in 1927 with
Air Marshal Italo Balbo to his left.

Left: Mussolini meeting with his
ally-to-be, Adolf Hitler, in 1934.

Below, left: The isolated and rather
neglected Balbo monument in
Chicago today.

Below, right: The pioneering flights
of Italo Balbo lead to the use of his
surname to describe any large
formation of aircraft.

What do I do...

if I come across German or Italian broadcasts when tuning my wireless?

I say to myself: "Now this blighter wants me to listen to him. Am I going to do what he wants?" I remember that German lies over the air are like parachute troops dropping on Britain — they are all part of the plan to get us down — *which they won't*. I remember nobody can trust a word the Haw-Haws say. So, just to make them waste their time, I switch 'em off or tune 'em out!

Cut this out — and keep it!

Issued by the Ministry of Information

*Space presented to the Nation
by The Brewers' Society*

England prepares for attacks by Italian aircraft in the autumn of 1940. Great Yarmouth was one of the CAI's targets on the English coast.

Harwich ready for a night-time attack by Italian bombers in November 1940.

Italian CR.42 fighters gather
at Ursel in Belgium prior to
raiding England.

Left: Italian ace, Giani Caraccioli, 'The Fighting Prince'.

Below: Another Italian ace, Squadron Leader Feruccio Vosilla, checks out his CR.42 at Ursel.

Camouflaged hangers specially built for bombers at Melsbroeck, Belgium.

A pilot and ground crew at Ursel prepare a CR.42 fighter for a mission against England.

One of the new G.50 fighters taxiing at
Maldegem in November 1940.

Bombs being loaded into the bay of a
BR.20M at Chièvres.

A BR.20M bomber crossing Belgium towards the English Channel.

A unique shot of the Italian invasion force en route to England on 11 November 1940, taken by unit photographer Mario Pensa on board the BR.20M, which later crashed near Woodbridge.

Pilot Officer Edward 'Hawkeye' Wells, the first RAF fighter pilot to attack the CAI raiders.

Artist's impression of Flight Lieutenant Peter 'Cowboy' Blatchford's daring attack on a CR.42 fighter.

Two of the leading 'Glorious Deadbeats': Flight Lieutenant Blatchford (left) and Wing Commander Robert Stanford Tuck.

Sergeant Antonio Lazzari's CR.42 after he had crash-landed in a field at Corton on the Suffolk coast.

Another CR.42, piloted by Sergeant Pietro Salvadori, which also force landed on the shingle beach at Orfordness. On the extreme right is William Hawes, father of one of the eyewitnesses to the 11 November raid.

RAF technicians examine Sergeant Salvadori's CR.42 before removing it from Orfordness.

Army personnel and civilians looking over the wreckage of Flying Officer Pietro Affiani's bomber at Woodbridge.

An RAF technician examines the crashed bomber. Note the missing emblem from the tail 'removed' by Wing Commander Tuck's party.

The BR.20M pilot, Pietro Affiani, manages a smile for the *News Chronicle* photographer while on a railway journey to London.

Bawdsey Manor, the 'home' of Radar on the Suffolk coast, which the CAI pilots used as a marker for their raids. Did they know its real purpose?

Sergeant Pietro Salvadori's CR.42 fighter under test by the RAF in early 1941 with new markings.

Harry Hawes, who witnessed the aerial battle between the RAF and CAI, visits Salvadori's CR.42 fighter now on display at the RAF Museum in Hendon, London.

A reunion of surviving *Corpo Aereo Italiano* pilots in 1980, including Giuseppi Ruzzin (far right), Luigi Gorrini (to his right) and beside him, Giulio Giuntella.

involved. He had encountered some of the *Luftwaffe's* finest before, of course, but the pilot of the almost comic-looking little biplane, which had none of the sophisticated technology of the Germans, was giving him a runaround the like of which he had never had before. Quite unsuspectingly, he was heading for one of the most extraordinary combat finales of his life.

> We did tight turns, climbing turns and half-rolls till it seemed we would never stop. That Italian could certainly fly! Neither of us was getting anywhere until one of my bursts seemed to hit him amidships and for just a moment he looked to be waffling [completely out of control]. Suddenly he did something like an Immelmann turn and came in at me head on. I went into a diving turn and we started all the merry-go-round business over again. I got in two or three more bursts and this time knocked some fair-sized chunks out of his wings and fuselage. Then my ammunition ran out. That put me in a bit of a fix and I didn't know what to do next. I was afraid if I left his tail he would get on to mine the moment I broke off. So we kept on this turning and twisting routine until suddenly – more by luck than judgement – I found myself bang on his tail only about 30 yards [27 m] ahead and a few feet higher.

In that moment, Blatchford felt exhilaration turn to a deep sense of frustration. As he looked, he saw his adversary turn his head and stare back. He could not make out the pilot's features – just a white splodge under his goggles. Fate had dealt the man the worst kind of hand any fighter pilot could experience. But 'Cowboy' also had a problem:

> If I had had even a dozen bullets I could have finished him off easily. It was enough to make anyone swear. In a flash I decided that if I could not shoot him down, I would try and knock him out of the sky with my aeroplane. I went kind of haywire. It seemed to me that the biplane was only made of boxwood and string and could not possibly damage a Hurricane. But just as I started to close with him, I had

> second thoughts and decided I would just try scaring the living daylights out of him. I aimed for the centre of his top main plane, did a quick little dive and pulled out just before crashing into him. The idea was to pass very close over his head and maybe send him into a spin. I felt a very slight bump and a shudder and reckoned I must have misjudged. I climbed and circled, but I never saw him again. Somehow I don't think he got back.

So focused had Blatchford been on his prey, that he had hardly noticed that his aircraft was now vibrating and the engine revs would not stay steady. When he looked outside the cockpit, the vista around had changed. Another squadron of Hurricanes had joined the dogfight and were chasing the remaining Italians all over the sky. His day of surprises was not quite over yet.

> I heard their leader on the r/t and recognised his voice. It was 'Elmer' Gaunce with Number 46. 'Elmer' was an old friend of mine – I had known him back in Edmonton when we were both kids. I heard later that he had bagged a couple in the fight. Now I thought it's home for me, but it *still* wasn't over. As I was flying back, keeping a good look-out behind, I saw a Hurricane below me, having the same kind of affair with a Fiat as I had just had and run out of ammunition. I went down and did a dummy head-on attack on the Italian. At around 200 yards [180 m] he turned away and headed out to sea. Again I thought, 'Good, I really can go home this time', but just before I got to the coast, still keeping a good look-out behind, I saw another Hurricane with three Fiats close together worrying him. So I went down again, feinting another head-on attack, and again when I was about 200 yards away the Italians broke off and headed for home. That really was the end of the battle.

The Canadian headed back to Martlesham with a grin of satisfaction over his face. But this could not altogether disguise his anxiety about the state of his Hurricane, which was now vibrating quite badly. He was relieved when the heath land around Ipswich finally came into view and he prepared to land.

> Just as I was about to enter the circuit I saw this bomber being followed inland by two of our boys. It was obviously going to crash nearby, but I had no time to think about it. I had to get my own damaged aircraft down. I managed to land all right, but it was a close thing, so badly was everything shaking. I was very relieved to get out of the Hurricane and walk towards the mess where I could see the boss waiting, hands on hips. I didn't look back until I suddenly heard my rigger running after me shouting that it was a 'bloody miracle' I was still alive. There were six inches missing from one of my propeller blades, he exclaimed, and nine inches from another. The result, obviously, of my direct attack on that Fiat fighter!

* * * * *

Flight Lieutenant Peter Blatchford ended his broadcast by telling his listeners that it had been a 'grand day for the squadron'. What he did not tell them was the sequel, when he recounted his exploits to Squadron Leader Tuck and the pair decided to go and see the bomber that had crashed nearby.

Tuck was relieved when all of the members of his squadron touched down on the runway, their broken gun-ports whistling and their engines sounding rough and breathless after the bruising dogfight. He needed only one look at the grin on Blatchford's face, as his friend shook his curly hair free from his leather helmet, to know that he had missed something special. According to Larry Forrester, the Canadian blurted out: 'Hey, boss, guess what? A mob of bloody Eyeties – Mussolini's boys! Jesus, what a helluva day for you to be sick! One of them pancaked just a few miles away over by Woodbridge. Let's get in the car and take a look.'

Another pilot who had just landed and overheard this conversation was Pilot Officer Karol Pniak, a Polish veteran who had escaped from his native country when it was overrun by the

Germans, and had been reassigned to 257. A very independent-minded man, known to some of his colleagues as being 'bloody thirsty', Pniak had also seen the bomber shot down. He, too, was keen to see the downed bomber and Tuck and Blatchford welcomed him to go along with them.

No doubt the trio of airmen would have liked to be the first on the scene after Flying Officer Affiani's bomber crashed at Bromeswell, but others were there before them to investigate the strange, bullet-riddled machine and its injured and traumatised human cargo. The pilots were, though, the first to positively identify it as a BR.2OM of the *Corpo Aereo Italiano* from Belgium.

A small group of workmen and a policeman were gathered around and appeared to have got the crew out the wreck. PC Thurston Clarke, a young bobby in the East Suffolk Police, had been near to Martlesham Heath and had seen the Italian bomber plunge to earth after the battle in the sky. He later described how he came to be on the scene in a police report of the incident.

> I was on patrol in the Waldringfield area. I saw the bomber being chased inland from the south bank of the River Deben. As soon as I saw it go down, I decided I had to get to the scene and crossed the river in a boat with my bicycle and cycled to where the accident had occurred. I found the crashed aircraft partly buried in a forest of conifers. A gang of foresters had rounded up four airmen, who were sitting on the ground.

It was the first crashed aircraft that PC Clarke had seen and the combination of the twisted metal, the reek of fuel and oil and the dishevelled, bloody condition of the airmen made him feel decidedly unwell, he admitted later. All the men looked injured and one had an almost completely severed right forearm that was bleeding profusely. Clarke had expected the plane to be German – perhaps one of the Dorniers or Heinkels that were being shot down by fighter planes over East Anglia – and was as surprised as the workmen that it was obviously not. One of the workers had mumbled to the young bobby that he thought the airmen were 'Eyeties'. PC Clarke continued his report:

DAY OF THE GLORIOUS DEADBEATS

> All the airmen appeared to be very frightened. They were apparently under the impression that they would be shot, either immediately or after interrogation. The effect of British bullets on their plane, contrary to what they had been led to expect, had made a profound impression upon them. With the exception of the pilot, who was dressed in a flying suit, the other airmen were wearing thin dungarees made of poor quality material. They were each equipped with a shrapnel helmet and bayonet.

The policeman had no difficult in relieving the stunned and silent men of their weapons. But this was nothing to the surprise that he got when the three RAF officers from Martlesham arrived and virtually took over the crash scene. Squadron Leader Tuck absorbed what had happened at a glance. He could tell that the airman with the bleeding forearm needed medical attention quickly and barked out instructions to PC Clarke. The young copper nodded obediently and set to work applying a rough-and-ready tourniquet. While he was doing this, he saw a faint smile of recognition cross the man's face as he caught sight of the uniforms of the newcomers. His mouth moved slowly: '*Pilota*,' he said – and fell unconscious.

According to Larry Forrester, Blatchford was about to have an even more unnerving moment – although I suspect it is the first of several apocryphal stories associated with the crashed bomber. It is nonetheless worth repeating here, with that proviso clearly in mind:

> 'Cowboy' led the way to the wreck, not looking at the other men stretched out on the grass. The side door of the bomber was huge, but just as he approached it he trod on what looked like an old piece of Hessian lying on the ground. His foot sank into something soft and there was a loud, vulgar noise like a belch. 'Cowboy' sprang back like a cat. Now, on closer inspection, they could make out the vague hump of a body under the hessian. There was a man, still alive. But no, said Tuck, Blatchford had stood on the stomach and released some gasses. Then he gave a short, hard laugh, because it

seemed the only thing to do. 'Cowboy' shook himself, grinning sheepishly.

There is no doubt about the grisly sight that awaited them inside the aircraft. Just behind the door, there was a body in a harness surrounded by wrecked radio equipment. It was riddled with bullets and had clearly been dead for some time. Tuck paused for a moment and looked at the corpse he would later discover was that of the hapless radio-operator Armando Paolini. The squadron leader had been a collector of firearms for years and could not miss the holster hanging from the man's waist. Without a second thought, he pulled out a Brevetta automatic and stuck it in his pocket.

Spoils of war, Tuck told himself. Then something else caught his eye, according to Forrester's book – two large hampers at the front of the aircraft. In one he found loaves of bread, a selection of cheeses, salami, sausages, cake and several kinds of fruit. In the second were several straw-jacketed bottles that he recognised as bottles of Chianti.

In an instant Tuck had decided to add the hampers to his spoils – although to do so he was forced to pull rank on PC Clarke, who was reluctant to allow the airmen to remove anything from the scene of the accident. If anybody objected, Tuck told the young bobby, then he should refer them to him. It was an unwritten law in the RAF's books that successful pilots were entitled to 'souvenirs', he insisted.

The three officers were not quite done. From inside the shattered fuselage they also removed two steel helmets and a bayonet – and were mystified as to just why the Italians should have been carrying such equipment in the first place. As a final memento, Tuck, Blatchford and Pniak sliced off the squadron quests from the tails of the bomber to hang in their mess. Then they left the wreck and the Italians to the responsibility of the police and the army and drove back to Martlesham.

It was time for a tankard or two of good beer, washed down with Chianti and the best Italian cheese, courtesy of the latest of their country's enemies to be brought down to earth.

* * * * *

In the weeks and months that followed, versions of 257's dogfight with the CAI grew in number and improbabilities – fanned by word of mouth and several newspaper stories. The most far-fetched of these claimed that it was Tuck who had brought the bomber down single-handed. This story began with photographs of the crashed bomber and a portrait of Tuck, captioned 'The Man Who Smashed the Italians'. It was followed by an article in the *Daily Herald* by its columnist, Arthur Helliwell, their much-travelled 'War Reporter'. The article was headlined 'CHIANTI TUCK' – TERROR OF THE WOPS and read:

> For weeks, Squadron Leader Tuck and his men had been waiting for just such an opportunity. They descended upon the Macaroni airmen like avenging furies and played swift havoc among these ancient planes from ancient Rome. 'They were easy,' said Tuck, 'just dead meat of the skies.'

The angry and embarrassed commander – who was afterwards occasionally referred to, usually behind his back and by other squadrons, as 'Chianti Tuck' – tried his best to refute the story, pointing out that he had not even been flying that morning. There was no truth in the claims of the press that the Italians had run away at the first sight of a Hurricane, he said, adding that his men admired the Italians for their bravery and courage in inferior aircraft. But British wartime propaganda was not above stretching the truth from time to time and the legend continued for years, even after the conflict was over.

In August, 1950, for example, Christopher R Elliott a specialist on East Anglian history, demonstrated how deep-rooted this 'version' of events had become in an article, 'Italian Encounter' in the *East Anglian Magazine*:

> During this time [November 1940] what was probably the most thrilling battle of the day was fought out in the skies between Orford and Woodbridge. Wing Commander R Stanford Tuck, famous World War II pilot, was driving an Italian bomber inland. Tuck, a great individualist, so legend

has it, hoped to persuade the pilot to fly his disabled plane to Martlesham. Flying low over the countryside and banking to avoid trees and farmhouses, the lone Hurricane and the green and brown bomber battled grimly. The pilot did his best to ward off the attacker. Two members of the crew were seriously wounded and one gunner was dead. Over Moorfield Road, Woodbridge, the crippled bomber shed one of its propellers. At 2 p.m. it landed on the edge of Dangham Forest, Bromeswell.

Aside from the involvement of Tuck and other obvious inaccuracies, the article does contain a few tit-bits of detail not noted elsewhere. But it still took many more years before the squadron leader's ire was pacified and 'Cowboy' Blatchford's role in the drama fully recognised.

The Operational Record Book of 257 Squadron that is now held in the National Archives at Kew contains the irrefutable facts of the day and the achievements of its pilots in the dogfight with the Italians. Blatchford, of course, comes out on top with one BR.20M destroyed, a quarter share in another of the bombers and two CR.42s damaged. Cowboy's next opponent was probably also attacked by Pilot Officer Pniak. The Pole fired at a second bomber, which began to smoke and burn. It then turned on to its back and dived into the sea 10 miles off Harwich, one man baling out just before impact. The trio of Leggett, Hedley and Walker each shared in the shattered bomber that glided towards the coast and ultimately crashed at Bromeswell.

A bomber on the extreme right hand of the Italian formation was attacked by Pilot Officer J K Kay, and then broke away from the rest of the group and headed for the coast. Pilot Officer S E Andrews, who was passing, gave it another burst and it dived into the North Sea. Shortly afterwards, Kay was also able to claim a further half share in the destruction of a second bomber with one of his friends in the squadron, Pilot Officer Andrews. Another colleague, Pilot Officer B Davey, used up all his ammunition on a BR.20M, which began to belch black smoke from both its engines. The aircraft was finished off by a pilot from 46 Squadron with whom he had to share the prize.

Two more of 257 Squadron's airmen, pilot officers G North and P A Mortimer, shared the destruction of yet another bomber that extraordinary morning. North had first made an unsuccessful beam attack on one bomber and then tried a stern pass on another – which immediately fell away from him and dived towards the coast. Giving chase, he used up all his ammunition, but was suddenly startled to see the pilot release four bombs and drop his undercarriage. At that moment, Mortimer – who had also made an earlier head-on attack and hit one aircraft – arrived on the scene to lend assistance. He fired several bursts into the dropping machine, which caught fire and spiralled towards the sea. The two men watched from their cockpits as a single figure baled out. Tragically, the Italian pulled his rip cord too quickly and in seconds the canopy had become entangled with the bomber's tail and he was dragged to a watery grave.

A further pair of 257 pilots made claims that day. Sergeant L D Barnes, who reported sighting approximately ten groups of the biplanes in sections of four, attacked one group and used up all his ammunition. One of the little aircraft dived past him almost vertical and he claimed a 'probable' destroyed. Sergeant S E Lucas began his skirmish with a burst at a BR.20M that he believed was disabled. He then broke away from the disintegrating formation of bombers and attacked a fighter head-on. As he turned to find cloud cover, the plane crashed into the waters below.

In the final reckoning of five BR.20s and two CR.42s destroyed and one bomber and three fighters damaged, it had indeed been 'a grand day' for the 'Glorious Deadbeats'.

* * * * *

One other RAF squadron chalked up a definite 'kill' and a mysterious 'possible' that morning. The squadron was No. 249 and the pilot responsible for the destruction of an Italian fighter was Wing Commander Victor Beamish, another larger-than-life character whose achievements as a fighter ace entitle him to comparison with such other legendary figures as Douglas Bader, Johnnie Johnson and, of course, Stanford Tuck, although his fame would not be assured until long after the war was over.

Born in Dunmanway in Ireland at the turn of the century, Beamish gained entry to the RAF Training College at Cranwell as a flight cadet. There the stocky Irishman proved himself a star pupil and an excellent boxer and rugby player whose unmistakable dialect further distinguished him from the other cadets. For a time he was an aerobatic ace with the Royal Canadian Air Force, but at the peak of his powers in 1933, he was struck down by the 'killer' disease, tuberculosis, and had to be invalided out of the service. Showing great determination and courage – shades of the Bader legend – Beamish fought his way back to full fitness and gained entry to the RAF two years before the outbreak of the war.

During the Battle of Britain, although he was already aged 37, Beamish flew an incredible 126 fighter sorties, far more than most of his contemporaries, many of whom were almost half his age. A lot of these missions were on his own in his favourite Hurricane. As a result, Beamish gained a reputation for doing things his own way and steadfastly refused to stay on the ground whenever there was the possibility of some action. He was decorated three times for courage in combat and his bravery proved an inspiration to everyone who served with him.

It was in September 1940 that 249 Squadron moved to North Weald and two months later Beamish flew out for his solo confrontation with the CAI. The squadron was another that had been originally formed in Scotland in the First World War for coastal patrol duties. In May 1940, it was re-formed at Church Fenton, initially with Spitfires, but re-equipped with Hurricanes before the transfer to North Weald. Flung into the maelstrom of the battle with the *Luftwaffe*, Beamish the pugnacious, cauliflower-eared station commander and his men daily lived up to the squadron's apt motto, *Pugnis et calcibus* – 'With fists and heels'. According to Beamish's excellent biographer, Doug Stokes, in *Wings Aflame* (1985), the secret of his success – not counting his leadership skills and Irish charm – was his peerless skill as a fighter ace: 'The ability to snap-shoot on the turn in the confusion of a dogfight was often the only way to get out of trouble – or at least take your opponent down with you. Beamish was very good at this and it probably saved his life on numerous occasions.'

On the morning of 11 November, 249 were scrambled to patrol the Thames Estuary on convoy protection duties, keeping to a height of 6,070 m (20,000 ft). Beamish set off with his detail, but because of poor weather only seven Hurricanes reached the location. Stokes describes what happened next:

> Possibly because of the weather, but more likely because he wanted some freelance action, Beamish headed out east on his own, flying through mist and cloud towards where the Italians were reported by the North Weald controller. Picking up the coastline through the murk east of Harwich he joined the melee. Beamish closed to 100 yards [90 m] on two CR.42s and raked them with three-second bursts drawing smoke from the second biplane which half rolled into a vertical dive in the haze over the sea, looking to Beamish 'as if he went straight in,' some 20–30 miles [30–50 km] east of Southwold. He searched unsuccessfully for more prey and returned to North Weald to claim the CR.42 as probably destroyed.

Although the wing commander is the only member of 249 to be credited with combating the Italian force that day, another of the squadron's pilots also diverted to the area over Harwich on his own initiative and later claimed to have shot down an enemy aircraft. The man's name was Flight Lieutenant Robert A Barton.

Barton was another of the ubiquitous Canadians who had crossed the Atlantic to join up with the RAF in June 1940. His summer had been one long round of successful convoy patrols and dogfights until the afternoon of 5 September. At 15.30 hours he engaged in a scrap with a Bf 109 while flying over Shell Haven on the coast of Essex and 'got the worst of it', to use his own words. He had to crash-land, but fortunately escaped with no serious injuries.

There is no doubt that the flight lieutenant *was* in the vicinity of Harwich during the Italian raid and he *did* shoot down an enemy aircraft. His logbook is quite specific about the attack, complete with his verdict that the plane 'went into the sea like a torch'. Because he could not be absolutely certain as to the identity of his prey, though, Barton added that it might possibly have been a Junkers Ju 86.

The truth of the incident had to wait until after the war to be finally resolved when the records of the British, German and Italian air forces became available for inspection. Then it became evident that Barton's victim was certainly not a CAI plane and was in all probability a German aircraft dispatched to the English coast on a mercy mission that went horribly wrong.

Indeed, all the facts point to the machine being a Focke-Wulf Fw 58, flown by *Unteroffizier* [Leading Aircraftsman] Karl Nispel, who had been sent to try to rescue three fighter pilots shot down in the Thames Estuary during a raid a few hours earlier. Matching the details of the disappearance of Nispel's plane No. 3551 of *Jagdegeschwader* 51 Squadron to those of Flight Lieutenant Barton's destruction of an enemy aircraft – which coincide in time and place – answers the mystery of this particular kill.

This is not the end of the mystery kills associated with the 'Chianti Raiders', though – because a number of the Italian pilots flew back to Belgium claiming successes of their own. I shall return to this controversial element of the battle between the *Corpo Aereo Italiano* and the RAF later, after we have examined the next phase of the Italian raids that continued throughout November and into the dark days leading up to Christmas 1940.

THE BATTLE OF FOLKESTONE

9

Winston Churchill was, as usual, busy reading the daily pile of war reports and action memos that had arrived on his desk in the Cabinet War Room deep under King Charles Street in Whitehall early on the morning of Tuesday, 12 November. The cramped underground rooms were the headquarters from which the Prime Minister, his cabinet and chiefs of staff had been controlling strategy ever since the outbreak of the war. Equipped with 21 small suites including a meeting room, map room and even a bedroom for Churchill, it was the nation's 'nerve centre' and believed to be the safest and most secret place in London.

The foresight in creating the War Rooms had been evident ever since Hitler had begun his aerial campaign to bomb Britain into submission. From this sanctuary, Churchill was able to direct operations throughout the crucial days of the Battle of Britain and, naturally enough, he always took a special interest in the Air Precaution Reports. On this particular morning, the information from that source – neatly typed, brief and to the point, as the PM liked it – described a raid on the east coast the previous day that had been beaten off without loss by the RAF. For once, the contents actually brought a hint of a smile to his face. He shifted his first cigar of the day from one side of his mouth to the other and read the final paragraph again: 'Following enemy aircraft reported to have crashed at about 14.10 hours: one in sea off Orford Ness, one Italian fighter on beach at Orford, one Italian bomber at Bromeswell, east of Woodbridge, and at 14.17 hours, one Italian fighter at Corton, north of Lowestoft.'

Churchill initialled the sheet of paper, decided it required no direct response, but allowed himself a typical pithy comment: 'They might have found better employment defending their fleet in Taranto.'

Even such mild sarcasm from the Prime Minister did not disguise the fact that neither he nor his advisers believed they had seen the last of Mussolini's airmen. They knew the dictator's vanity and desire to impress his Axis co-partner would not allow a setback or two to stop Italian involvement in the Battle of Britain. Indeed, while Churchill was reading the report in his subterranean HQ, the CAI was already counting its losses and Air Marshal Fougier was preparing new plans.

Apart from the aircraft that had been lost in the action over the east coast, others trying to return to base had also found themselves in trouble as a result of the attacks by the RAF. Four more bombers that had been hit had to make forced landings as soon as they crossed the Channel. Three were so damaged and short of fuel their pilots put them down on the coast at beaches between Dunkirk and Antwerp. A fourth, flown by Lieutenant Luigi Gnechi of 242 *Squadriglia* from Chièvres, crash-landed and broke in half at Bray-Dunes, killing the radio-operator.

The fighter pilots, however, fared far worse. Reports indicate that at least nineteen CR.42s were unable to make it back to their base at Ursel because of damage or lack of fuel. Notable among these was Lieutenant Franco Bordoni-Bisleri, who had a brush with death on landing that could have prematurely ended his career as one of Italy's leading combat aces.

Bordoni-Bisleri was a charismatic personality and a scion of the Milan family that manufactured the famous digestive liquor, *Ferro-China Bisleri*. He had been privately educated, proved himself a talented racing car driver, and developed a passion for flying. When told he was unfit to join the *Regia Aeronautica* in 1936 because of a breathing problem, Bordoni-Bisleri was so affronted that he paid for his own flying lessons and obtained a civil pilot's licence. In June 1940 when Italy entered the war, however, he was welcomed with open arms into the air force. Assigned to 95 *Squadriglia* as a newly appointed lieutenant, he saw action in France before moving on to Belgium. At Ursel, he soon became a familiar figure, the fuselage of his CR.42 embossed with the symbol of a lion and the word 'Robur' ('Strength', in Latin) that he had copied from the label of his family's familiar liquor bottles. The combative and extrovert flyer also earned the nickname 'Robur' among his contemporaries.

After surviving the forced landing in Belgium that wrecked his fighter, Bordoni-Bisleri remained with the squadron until January 1941, when he was transferred to North Africa. His successes here, and in later missions in other theatres of the war before Italy's defeat, earned him several awards – including the first *Medaglia D'Argento al Valore* of several and a German Iron Cross – along with the status of an ace credited with nineteen 'kills'.

Another of 95 *Squadriglia*'s fighter pilots, Lieutenant Ramolo Artina, also had a lucky escape that November day. He managed to nurse his battered biplane back to the vicinity of Ursel and almost achieved a successful landing in a field before his machine cartwheeled. Although the aircraft was wrecked, Artina escaped with only slight bruising. The same fate also awaited Pilot Officer Peppo Re of 85 *Squadriglia*, who turned his CR.42 over when forced down near Dunderlewe.

An even more spectacular return to earth awaited Sergeant Mario Sandini of 83 *Squadriglia*. Flying back from the English coast, his plane damaged and short of fuel, he lost height while crossing over Amsterdam and crashed into a public square. The CR.42 was destroyed, several inhabitants unfortunate enough to be in the vicinity were badly injured, but Sandini remarkably escaped from the wreck with only slight injuries.

* * * * *

A week was to pass while the CAI debriefed its pilots, considered the lessons to be learned from the attack – in particular the complaint by the fighter pilots that the changing of the two 12.7 mm guns to one 12.7 mm and one 7.7 mm on their aircraft, which was supposed to make them lighter and more manoeuvrable, had instead lessened their effectiveness – and planned the next raids. With the port of Harwich still high on the priority list, a series of half a dozen bombing raids were scheduled between 17 November and 22 December. These enjoyed varying degrees of success in terms of damage – though no injuries or death – and according to Julian Foynes the bombs dropped during the 20 November raid, 'were largely dispersed onto other areas… falling around the Blackwater and some later salvoes as far away as Grimsby'. This claim is rather improbable, though.

Certainly, the aim of the Italian bombers was rather more accurate when they decided to hit the adjacent port of Felixstowe on the evening of Sunday, 17 November. They hoped the British would be at church on this particular day and perhaps a little less wary than on other nights of the week. Six BR.20Ms from 43 *Stormo* at Chièvres were detailed for the operation, accompanied by the same number of Bf 109s, 'because the Germans now feared for their allies,' according to Michael Bowyer. Both the Axis powers believed the port to be an important naval base with a long tradition in warfare. They were correct on both counts.

The history books showed that the port had been regarded as a valuable prize for invaders ever since the days of the Romans and the Saxons. The sixteenth-century Landguard Fort on a narrow spit of land had withstood a raid by more than two thousand Dutchmen in 1667 – the last attempted invasion of England by a foreign force – and the Martello towers nearby proved strong enough to thwart any plans Napoleon might have had for taking the country. With the advent of the Second World War, the harbour had become a haven for trawlers, drifters and all kinds of small boats – many of which took part in the evacuation of Dunkirk – as well as Royal Navy corvettes, minesweepers, patrol ships, motor torpedo boats, high-speed rescue launches and tenders for three Fokker TVIII twin-engine seaplanes brought to England to escape the Nazis by their pilots of Netherlands Marine Air Force. Not forgetting, of course, the two thousand or so men and women required to run the port.

The residents of Felixstowe – those who had not been evacuated for safety reasons – lived in one of the closest points on the mainland to Europe and were only too conscious of the threat from across the North Sea that had been posed ever since the Nazi occupation of the Low Countries and France. As R Douglas Brown explained in *East Anglia at War* (1981), 'As they had walked to church on Sunday mornings, people along the coast, as far north as Felixstowe, heard the continuous, distant rumbling of gunfire drifting across the water from Belgium and France.'

For these people, the spring and summer days of 1940 had regularly been torn apart by German bombing raids. Some of those living in houses close to the front had even seen a number of enemy seaplanes land on the sea not more than 2 miles off Felixstowe to lay mines. Others had been perilously close to the first bombs to fall on the town in May – which 'caused a great deal of noise, but little damage' to quote R Douglas Brown again – but after several more raids the spirits of the townspeople had risen at the sight of the first Dornier being brought down on 31 August. None of them, though, was quite prepared for the Italian air force to join the fray.

Felixstowe, naturally, had its own defences. Apart from offshore mines laid to catch out the audacious Nazi seaplanes, there were anti-aircraft guns in the port and pillboxes all along the coast. There were also two 12-in howitzers on railway trucks permanently stationed in a special siding on the town's branch line that could be hauled out at a moment's notice by the men of the No. 9 Super Heavy Battery of the Royal Artillery to engage the enemy.

The whole town lay under a blanket of darkness when the CAI's bombers flew overhead on the Sunday evening. They came in low from the south, passing over the gaunt mass of Landguard Fort, and releasing their bombs among the cluster of vessels and service buildings in the harbour. A soldier on duty was killed, along with a civilian employed as a net maker, who was working overtime in one of the yards.

In some accounts of this raid, it has been suggested that the Italian raid killed and injured a dozen people, but this is confusing the event with another attack on 18 November by a *Luftwaffe* squadron of Me 109s on Lowestoft. Julian Foynes has set the record straight: 'Next day, nine men from HMS *Europa* were wounded while three soldiers and three civilians simultaneously perished outside. This was the first of only two occasions when the Patrol Service Depot, with its hordes of personnel a fine target, was hit.'

The pilots of the six BR.20Ms returned to their base at Chièvres as soon as they had dropped their bombs, apparently unseen and certainly not intercepted by the RAF. Perhaps they had been right about the British being at church. Certainly, it was a far more satisfactory result for them than the debacle a week earlier.

* * * * *

Encouraged by this success, Fougier pored over his maps at his HQ at Petite Espinette and decided on another mission farther afield. On his desk was a copy of a guidebook to Britain that had been given to him on his arrival in Belgium by Field Marshal Kesselring. The German commander had told him it was full of data about the country and had already proved invaluable to the *Luftwaffe* in planning their air attacks on England.

The book was one of the famous Baedeker guides for tourists, published ever since 1872 by the German company founded by Karl Baedeker, which produced regularly updated editions to all the European countries. They were packed with information about the towns and cities as well as maps and a star system for the best hotels. Used in conjunction with the aerial reconnaissance photographs taken by the *Luftwaffe*, the guides were said to be as useful for airmen as they had been to tourists.*

Fougier studied the area of East Anglia that he had been directed to attack and concluded that Norwich, the county town of Norfolk, met his criteria as a substantial target as well as being far enough inland to test the efficiency and strike power of his men. Other

* The use of the Baedeker Guides in German military planning was not, in fact, known to the British until 24 April 1942 when Baron Gustav von Stumm, Deputy of the German Foreign Office Press Department, announced a series of *Vergeltungsangriffe* [retaliation raids] ordered by Hitler as a result of the RAF bombing of places of 'religious, historical and aesthetic value' such as Lubeck and Rostock. 'We shall go all out to bomb every building in Britain marked with three stars in the Baedeker Guide,' he said. Unfortunately, nobody picked up the significance of this in Exeter, Bath or Norwich, which were all devastated in the next week – although the Baron actually got his facts wrong, for the guides never awarded more than *two* stars to any building!

items among his collection of documents revealed that the Germans had already made several unsuccessful attempts to bring the city to its knees.

In fact, five sets of photographs of Norwich had been taken by a German plane on 3 September 1939. These focused primarily on important targets including the great Norman cathedral with its 315-ft-high (96-m) spire, the *Flugzeugfabrik* [engineering works] of Bolton & Paul and the *Hauptkraftwerk* [power station] at Thorpe. The pictures had evidently been used in briefing the *Luftwaffe* crews who dropped bombs and incendiary devices on the city on 27 April, destroying or seriously damaging twenty factories and many houses in the old quarter. After the bombers returned again on 8 May a Nazi radio broadcast ludicrously claimed they had reduced Norwich to an 'enormous heap of ruins'. A third raid on 26 June caused some further damage, but nothing to prevent life going on in the usual resilient British way.

Air Marshal Fougier, who read English and spoke the language well, sensed the accolade to be won from successfully attacking Norwich. He ordered another group of six bombers be prepared to carry out a surprise mission under the command of Group Captain di Capoa of 13 *Stormo*. At 10.10 on 20 November, the BR.20Ms, each armed with ten 110-lb [50-kg] bombs, flew off from Melsbroech for Norfolk.

There are conflicting reports about the outcome of this challenging mission. One account by aeronautical historian Thomas Potts says, simply, that the mission was aborted 'due to unsuitable weather' and the bombers were recalled. It gives no indication as to whether the aircraft crossed the North Sea or got anywhere near Norwich.

The second account maintains the aircraft did cross to England at virtually their maximum ceiling and headed across East Anglia in the direction of the cathedral city. A some point on their journey, around midday, they ran into a storm and turned back, dropping their bombs in the vicinity of Wetheringsett and Grundisburgh, two places on their flight path home. Certainly both locations reported bomb damage on that date, though no deaths or injuries occurred.

I am inclined to believe the force reached the county town that day. Partly because the time scale would have allowed them to do so, but also because there is a strong local tradition to that effect. This is reflected in a saying that originated at the time and is still recalled by some of the older residents, 'You could tell Italian bombers by the sound.' If asked to expound, people say the noise resembled tin cans being rattled together...

* * * * *

It seems probable that as part of the CAI's strategy at this time, the high command decided in conjunction with the *Luftwaffe* to target Ipswich, the county town of neighbouring Suffolk, which had also been photographed by the Germans and attacked half a dozen times.

Situated 10 miles up the River Orwell from the coast, the town was serving as a naval base codenamed HMS *Bunting*. This entailed a considerable number of troops being stationed in and around the town for defence against air attacks. One particular group bivouacked in tents at Nacton became something of a local legend for naming their encampment 'Fairyland'. Many of Ipswich's more vulnerable buildings were covered in camouflaging paint, although this did not entirely prevent them from being damaged by enemy attacks.

Ipswich was raided for the first time just after midnight on 22 June when ten German high-explosive bombs fell with a 'weird, whistling noise', killing an elderly couple and their maid in Dale Hall Lane. The town was also one of the first targets when the Battle of Britain began on 10 July. A group of *Luftwaffe* bombers swooped across and dropped eighteen high explosives along the edge of Martlesham airfield, although there was little damage and no casualties. On 21 August, after another German attack, five Dorniers were brought down by the RAF, one crashing in Gippeswyk Park in Ipswich. It is, therefore, no real surprise to find a Mass Observation correspondent writing after a visit to the town:

> The siren goes nearly every night, often twice a night, and has done so continually ever since the blitz raids started. There has never been a lull in the sort of air war that Ipswich has experienced. The fact of the war has been kept in people's minds all the time, and they have very much a frontline mentality, with people evacuated, previously

unheard-of numbers of troops in the town and surrounding countryside, and bombers passing overhead every night, to the accompaniment of sirens.

Now it was the turn of the Italian air force to add to Ipswich's troubles. For this operation, Fougier decided to double the size of the attacking force and sent off twelve BR.20Ms from Melsbroech, led by Squadron Leader Gino Mini, a long-service pilot who had commanded bombing raids in Spain and France and had flown a number of practice missions over Belgium. The aircraft, all fully laden with 250-kg (551-lb) and 100-kg (200-lb) bombs, took off some twelve hours after the Norwich raid between 23.30 hours and 00.45 hours to rendezvous over Ostend.

The bombers dropped to a ceiling of 5,000 m (16,400 ft) as they flew to the north of Felixstowe and set their sights on Ipswich, still and silent in the darkness. The tranquil scene changed almost instantly when a radar report of 'intruders' was received at Martlesham at the same time as a sighting by an anti-aircraft battery at Nacton that reported, 'many fighters at 4,000–5,000 feet'. Despite mistaking the type of plane, the gunners were soon firing at the Italians as they dipped towards the town. In all, seven of the 250-kg bombs were released on target and a scattering of seventy of the smaller 100-kg version fell in and around Ipswich. Then the BR.20Ms turned tail and headed back for Belgium.

On their return journey, several night fighters from Martlesham apparently caught up with the bombers a few miles off the coast. Three of the Italians are believed to have been damaged and one, from No. 5 *Squadriglia* piloted by Lieutenant S Paoli, was hit and last seen descending rapidly into the North Sea. No sign of the plane was ever found, although two days later, the bodies of Lieutenant Paoli and his co-pilot, Sergeant G Rildani, were washed ashore at Wassenaar. The men were not wearing parachutes, but still had on their life jackets. Of the three other members of the crew there was no trace.

The damage inflicted on Ipswich encouraged the CAI to launch a number of reconnaissance flights and repeat raids during the following weeks. The first attack was four days later on 25 November – 'to little effect', according to R Douglas Brown – but was followed by a more effective operation two days later when another group of bombers from 13 *Stormo* blasted a couple of small industrial complexes and returned home without loss. A strike on the 29th was hindered by bad weather and those bombs that were launched landed in the Orwell or on pastureland between Woodbridge and Shotley.

The following month, on 5 December, twelve more BR.20Ms from Melsbroech returned around midnight, again inflicting damage to several properties in Ipswich. Before Christmas, two more raids – on the 14th and 21st – were carried out, the second of which has been recorded in painful detail by Michael J F Bowyer, utilising local records:

> At Ipswich on 21 December four HE's were dropped at 17.55, also seven 43 lb [19.5 kg] incendiaries with semi-armour piercing noses, revealing the Italian connection. Unusual was the penetrating capability of the bombs for at No. 109, Bixley Road, a UX buried itself 30 inches deep in the garden and at No. 85 one burst into flames even though it was buried 3 ft deep. At No. 62, Bixley Road one fell 6 ft from a lady holding a linen basket. After lying flat for a few minutes, she hurried to the front of the house as the bomb burst. She soon put it out with handfuls of soil. At No. 60, Princethorpe Road, a bomb bounced off a kitchen dresser and on to the floor. Others fell in the garden of No. 22, Princethorpe Road and outside No. 20, by No. 45, Cheltenham Road and the school playing fields in Cobblestone Road where high explosives were also dropped. At Ness Farm near Ipswich two large incendiaries burnt for 28 minutes.

Despite this blitz, life went on as resolutely in Ipswich as it was doing everywhere else in East Anglia.

* * * * *

The surviving logbooks of the pilots of the *Corpo Aereo Italiano* indicate that throughout November and December 1940 – as long as the weather was favourable – training flights, reconnaissance duties, bomber and fighter operations and even the occasional nuisance raid went on from the bases in Belgium almost every day. Hundreds of journeys in all, sometimes taking the navigators way off course and often to very little effect. Whatever damage was being done to the men's dreams of success, the airmen and ground crews persevered with their duties in the face of setback after setback. Each day they all shivered through what was proving to be a long, cold winter, dreaming of the warmer climes of home – as a few surviving letters to wives and sweethearts in Italy make poignantly clear.

On 23 November, the CAI began a new series of fighter operations, or 'sweeps', against targets along the south coast. As always planned and operated in conjunction with the *Luftwaffe*, these missions were flown by some of the best Italian pilots and were designed to challenge what their commanders hoped were the depleted ranks of the RAF over their own territory.

The most critical of these missions later became known colourfully as 'The Battle of Folkestone' after it had been fought out high over the coast of southern England. In the aftermath, the RAF registered seven 'kills' and two 'probables', while the CAI claimed five enemy fighters. Both totals are open to dispute.

The fighter sweep was set for Saturday, 23 November and consisted of 29 CR.42s hand-picked from the pilots of 18 *Gruppo* at Ursel. Leading the wing was the brilliant and resourceful Squadron Leader Feruccio Vosilla, with the charismatic Lieutenant 'Robur' Bordoni-Bisleri – now fully recovered from his 'prang' on 11 November – as his wingman. The group were to sweep along the English coast while up above, 24 of the newer G.50s of 20 *Gruppo* commanded by Squadron Leader Mario Bonzano would fly cover. Both forces planned to share in the 'kills' they hoped would occur when the RAF put up its planes and found themselves caught between the fire of not one, but two packs of enemy fighters.

The flight plan had been carefully prepared. Departing from base at 11.30, the Italians would fly to Dunkirk, then cross the 21 miles of the English Channel to Margate. There they would turn directly south to Ramsgate and on to Deal. Finally, they would pass over Dover and Folkestone before heading back across the sea to the French coast and the safety of Calais.

It was intended to be a surprise mission, but was actually fatally flawed. The CAI had not expected the RAF to already have aircraft in the air as they approached England. But one squadron, 603, was on patrol, the planes having left their base at Hornchurch at 11.40. The wing was travelling south when they received a 'bandits heading west' message over the r/t.

There was something singularly appropriate that it was pilots from 603 who would spoil the Italians' plan. They rejoiced in the motto *Gin ye daur* – 'If you dare' – and had been responsible for inter-cepting the very first German air raid on Britain in October 1939. They were also based at the same airfield where Pilot Officer 'Hawkeye' Wells had scored the very first success against the CAI.

No. 603 Squadron had been formed in October 1925 at Turnhouse in Scotland as a day bomber unit of the Auxiliary Air Force. The pilots flew a variety of aircraft – including Avro 504Ks, Wapitis and Harts – until October 1938, when it was re-designated a fighter unit. The squadron was re-equipped with Gloster Gladiators until shortly after the outbreak of the Second World War, when these were exchanged again for the new wonder plane, the Spitfire.

The eager pilots of 603 wasted no time in becoming proficient with the Spitfires and were operational in time to destroy the first German aircraft to be shot down over Britain in the Second World War on 16 October 1939. They remained on defensive duties in Scotland until August 1940, when they were moved south to Hornchurch and performed a vital role in the remainder of the Battle of Britain.

The pilots were, in fact, on what would prove to be one of their last patrols in England – they returned to Scotland at the end of December – when they spotted the CR.42s off Folkestone, hurrying west. They needed no invitation to take offensive action.

According to a later account of the battle in the sky in the *Folkestone and Hythe Gazette*, the Spitfires of 603 Squadron hit the Italians suddenly – and hard – from the rear, emerging from cloud cover. Gun bursts from the RAF planes raked several of the CR.42s before they could take avoiding action and the rest scattered at the onrush of the defending aircraft. Two CAI planes were seen plummeting down into the Channel, smoke streaming from their shattered engines. They were not, though, to be the last victims in the minutes of intensive action that followed – each one seeming to the combatants to go on for hours.

The dogfight over Folkestone proved once again to be one-sided from the start – the element of surprise being extremely difficult for the Italians to counter. Most of the CAI veterans did fight back, though, and several of them got in bursts of damaging return fire as they scrapped valiantly with the faster and better-armed Spitfires. All this time, there was no sign of the G.50s, who were supposed to be 'riding shotgun'.

Seven of the 603 pilots in the thick of the action were able to claim hits when they disengaged and returned to Hornchurch. Pilot Officer Archie Winskill registered two 'kills', as did Sergeant Archie Darling. Pilot Officer Ronald Berry, then the squadron's leading Battle of Britain ace, who had already claimed eight victims during the summer, added a ninth. Another officer who had also been on constant duty for the past four months, Flying Officer Colin Pinkney, added a third claim to his total for the year. Pilot Officer Brian Macnamara put in for the seventh 'kill' of the day's bag. Pilot Officer Berry also registered a 'probable', as did Flying Officer John Boulter. Boulter's claim would later come to be remembered with some sadness by his colleagues, as it proved to be his last before his death in a tragic accident on 17 January 1941.

A head-count of the Italian pilots later in the day revealed a bloody cost for the 'sweep'. The two aces, Vosilla and Bordoni-Bisleri, had returned safely, but Lieutenant Guido Mazza of 83 *Squadriglia* and Sergeant Guido Grillo of 95 *Squadriglia* were both reported to have been shot down in the sea and were now presumed dead. Two other of 83 *Squadriglia*'s experienced pilots, Flight Sergeant Franco Campanile and Sergeant Paolo Melano, were initially reported missing, but both were subsequently found to have force-landed in Belgium while on their way back to Ursel. The men were slightly injured, but Campanile had amazingly escaped death when it was found that his parachute pack had absorbed several machine-gun bullets from one of the Spitfires during the battle!

Perhaps an even more remarkable escape was reported by Warrant Officer Felice Sozzi, another member of the redoubtable 83 *Squadriglia*. He had seen a Spitfire on the tail of his friend Flight

Sergeant Luigi Gorrini's CR.42, who was himself in the process of attacking an RAF fighter. In attempting to help Gorrini, Sozzi had come under fire from behind by two more Spitfires. He suffered three bullet wounds in the lungs, but still managed to fly his crippled biplane back across the North Sea and ditch on a Belgian beach. He survived this trauma and was later awarded the *Medaglia d'Argento al Valore.*

The records of the CAI indicate that 18 *Gruppo* claimed five enemy 'kills' that day. As it was not *Regia Aeronautica* policy to credit individual achievements, the only name that can be definitely linked with a claim is Flying Officer Giulio Giuntella of 85 *Squadriglia.* His CR.42 was apparently hit several times during the dogfight, but he flew the damaged fighter back to Ursel and noted the kill in his logbook. His claim will be examined in detail later.

The story of 'The Battle of Folkestone' does not quite end there. Before 603 Squadron left the English coast, another wing was sent into action against the Italians by Fighter Command, who had just tracked further enemy aircraft. This was 92 Squadron, who were scrambled from their base at Biggin Hill at 12.25.

The new pilots on the scene were also the possessors of a formidable reputation, as their badge of a cobra and motto *Aut pugna aut morere* – 'Either fight or die' – bore witness. Formed in London in September 1917 as a fighter unit, 92 had been assigned to attacking duties over the Western Front in France until the end of the war. Reformed at Tangmere in October 1939, the wing had initially been equipped with Blenheims, but this all changed the following May when they were replaced by Spitfires and pushed into the frontline of defence against the *Luftwaffe.* The squadron's efficiency at offensive operations and Biggin Hill's proximity to the scene of the action made them an ideal call-up unit.

According to the records of 92 Squadron, when the flight reached a position several miles south of Dover they reported a group of aircraft identified as Messerschmitt Bf 109s. The planes were apparently flying high and fast in the direction of France. To their dismay, the RAF pilots were unable to engage the enemy and had to return to base.

Subsequent investigation suggests that 92 Squadron wrongly identified the fleeing aircraft. They were in all probability the Fiat

G.50s of 20 *Gruppo* who had been sent to cover the main band of CR.42s sweeping the English coast and arrived to find the dogfight over and their surviving colleagues limping back to base. Indeed, this is confirmed by the records of the CAI, which state that the latecomers, 'saw a formation of British fighters, but did not engage them'.

* * * * *

The CAI evidently learned another hard lesson from 'The Battle of Folkestone' and after a week of bad weather – which caused at least two sorties planned for Margate and Eastbourne to be aborted – sent an offensive patrol over the south coast to Kent at 12.00 on 28 November. This time it was 23 of the faster G.50s that spearheaded the operation, accompanied by the same number of CR.42s and a small formation of Bf 109s for additional protection.

Once again the lack of documentation makes it difficult to state what happened. The Italians claim to have swept in high over Dover, skirted Ashford and continued inland until they had sighted the town of Maidstone, almost 30 miles from the coast, before turning back. They returned to base across the Romney Marshes and Dungeness, 'without engaging any enemy fighters'.

Weather records for that Thursday indicate the cloud base was low and visibility was poor, which may account for neither side having spotted the other. Sounds of aircraft passing overhead were reported at Lydd, though, and the description of them as 'rattling' seems to confirm the Italian presence. It was to prove the last occasion on record when the CAI targeted the south coast.

That weekend, Air Marshal Fougier decided to shift his focus back to East Anglia, where his efforts had been most successful. A Friday night raid was scheduled against the ports of Lowestoft and Great Yarmouth on the Suffolk/Norfolk border. Prior to the attack, a single BR.20M was dispatched to reconnoitre the two localities.

Lowestoft is famous as the first town in Great Britain to see the morning sunlight – as is evidenced by its motto, *Point du Jour* ('Break of Day'). For years a busy port for herring and trawl fisheries, its trade was considerably enhanced by the creation of a navigation route linking it to Norwich. The town's prosperity increased with the development of a thriving shipbuilding industry – but this also made it a prime target for Germany when the First World War broke out. On 3 November 1914, a Zeppelin dropped six bombs on Kimberley Road, the Maconochie Estate and Latten's Timber Yard, causing extensive damage, but mercifully no fatalities.

However, the raider did not stop at Lowestoft, but moved on to Great Yarmouth to carry out a second attack. This port, built on a narrow sandbank, also had a long history as a centre for fishermen, sailors, merchant adventurers and even pirates. The growth of a shipbuilding industry and allied trades similarly turned it into a thriving community – and irresistible to the Germans, who proceeded to bomb Crown Road and St Peter's Plain. A large number of houses were wrecked, a church badly damaged and two people killed. Curiously, one of the bombs that fell on Great Yarmouth failed to explode and photographs of it appeared in the next day's edition of the *Norfolk News* under a banner headline: 'FIENDISH BEHAVIOUR OF HUNS – Innocent Civilians and Children Bombed'.

There was probably no one in either Lowestoft or Great Yarmouth who did not expect the two ports to once more become the focus of enemy attention when the Second World War broke out. Indeed, the skippers of the trawlers and drifters who sailed out to feed the population quickly found themselves with extra duties sweeping the sea lanes, where the Germans were forever laying minefields. While at work, of course, these vessels proved to be ideal targets for the *Luftwaffe* who dive-bombed and machine-gunned them to deadly effect. And if this was not bad enough, there were also U-boats and E-boats lurking to attack the unwary – although the Hurricanes from Martlesham and Coltishall did their best to provide protection.

German bombers dropping thousands of incendiary and high-explosive bombs also regularly attacked both ports. In one raid in February 1940, a whole street in Lowestoft was destroyed, and on 9 April – in what would prove to be the worst raid of the year – 22 people were killed and 39 injured. Two days earlier, an attack on Yarmouth had resulted in more property being destroyed than in any other wartime raid on East Anglia. A total of 17 people died during the night and a further 68 were injured.

Because of evacuation, both ports had lost at least half of their populations and one resident's description of day-to-day existence given to a Mass Observation correspondent serves equally well for both: 'It's a life of continual apprehension. The raids so sudden that they are almost over before the noise of battle has begun. The roar of hostile planes unseen in low cloud, the thud of bombs, bursts of machine-gun fire, and it's all over.'

Lowestoft and Great Yarmouth were, though, protected with pillboxes and barricades at strategic points, as well as anti-tank defences and miles of barbed wire. Both also possessed fixed artillery defences including four 6-in and two 12-lb guns, which were constantly manned.

Still, though, the enemy got through to attack both ports. In common with the other places in East Anglia and along the south coast, however, no one had been expecting Italians to add to the toll already being inflicted by the *Luftwaffe*. No one, that is, except the Royal Navy officers manning the important naval base in Lowestoft known as HMS *Europa*. This 'stone frigate' was the cover name for the Royal Navy Patrol Service and it had the dubious distinction of being the closest British military establishment to the enemy. The men working there had already been informed of the CAI's presence in Belgium and circulated with details of the raids on Harwich and elsewhere.

The base was located in what had previously been the Sparrow's Nest Theatre under the command of Commodore B H Piercey. However, its existence was evidently known to the Germans because of radio broadcasts by the traitor, William Joyce – 'Lord Haw-Haw' – in which he had made a number of derogatory references to the 'sparrows in the nest'. Commenting on the significance of the base, Charles Goodey and Jack Rose have written in their history, *The Story of HMS. Europa*:

> The Luftwaffe made several attempts to blitz the little birds out of their nest [but] so well arranged were these dug-outs that the whole place could be cleared in a matter of seconds and although the Nest remained an inviting target for the German bombers between the cliffs and the beach on the

most easterly point of Britain the raiders always missed it – at
the expense, more often than not, of the civilian population.

Perhaps the CAI thought they might break this record when
ten bombers from 13 *Stormo* took off from Melsbroech at 17.45 on
29 November. They were armed with 100-kg (220-lb) and 50-kg
(110-lb) bombs and after a rendezvous over Zeebrugge set course for
the two English ports.

The Italians reached their destination undisturbed, splitting their
force in half for separate attacks. But even as the leading bomber
began its approach to the nearer harbour at Lowestoft, crossing the
partly destroyed section of Claremont Pier that had been blown up
as an anti-invasion measure, the probing beams of two searchlights
lit up the sky and were followed by a fierce burst of anti-aircraft fire.

The combination of blinding light and accurate AA fire clearly
affected the bomber pilots and they were only partly successful in
releasing their loads from heights of between 5,700 m and 5,000 m
(18,700 and 16,400 ft). Still, a cluster of six fell on the CWS Canning
Factory in Waveney Drive, Lowestoft, causing the death of three
civilians and leaving six others injured. The adjoining Richards
Shipyard was also damaged and a coaster in the harbour, the *Empire
Sound*, received a number of splinter holes in one side.

The five other Italian bombers that rattled noisily over the South
Quay at Great Yarmouth a few minutes later received a similar
hot reception. Their bombs caused damage, but no casualties, and
their contribution to the night resulted in a total of 41 of the
heavier bombs and 20 of the smaller variety being dropped on the
two bases. The remainder of their payloads fell between Lound,
Hopton and Bradwell, causing damage to a few properties, but no
loss of life.

Despite the well-practised expertise of the defence forces in
Lowestoft and Great Yarmouth – and the arrival of RAF night
fighters as the raiders were turning for home – only three of the
BR.20Ms were damaged, though one was quite badly damaged. This
aircraft, piloted by Lieutenant T Rebuscini, had a difficult return
flight with one engine damaged and its control system failing
gradually every mile of the way back.

The bomber did make it over the North Sea, but was losing height as it crossed the coast of Belgium. By the time it neared Melsbroech it was flying only a few hundred feet off the ground. Within sight of the runway, the bomber suddenly lurched downwards and struck the roof of a farm building at Zavantern. Plunging on to the ground, the aircraft turned into an inferno of flames, killing the entire crew. Posthumous recognition for their bravery was given to Lieutenant Rebuscini, his co-pilot, Lieutenant Dal Forn, and aircrew, E Romito, G Columbano, G Maruelli and M Cini.

* * * * *

The bad weather that had caused so many operations to be cancelled or aborted no sooner had the CAI planes taken to the skies – if they had even left the ground – got still worse in December 1940. The records are confusing as to what operations did take place. One document for the night of 6 December indicates that twelve bombers from 13 *Stormo* 'attacked' Ipswich, but the evidence suggests that the mission was called off over Belgium.

It is more likely that a group of seventeen bombers from 13 and 43 *Stormo* carried out a 'nuisance' raid on Harwich on 13 December. It appears that the Italians had ambiguous feelings about Friday the 13th being lucky or unlucky; three of the planes developed engine problems and had to return to base soon after taking off. The remainder made it to the Essex port, where several were hit by anti-aircraft fire. The pilots' logs state that a total of 36 bombs were dropped on the harbour and in the vicinity of Trimley and Upper Dovercourt. These included two 249-kg (550-lb) explosives, fourteen of the 100-kg (220-lb) bombs, twelve of the 220-lb incendiaries and eight 50-kg (110-lb) incendiaries.

The bombers returned to Harwich twice more before Christmas – making it, ultimately, the location most bombed by the Italians. On the evening of 21 December at 17.47 hours, four BR.20s from 13 *Stormo* appeared over the port and dropped twenty 220-lb bombs and twenty incendiaries. Several high explosives fell in the Market Street area, causing ten casualties and seriously damaging fifteen houses and shops. Julian Foynes, who has collected the data, adds:

> The bombs on Harwich that night were fairly well concentrated, falling just outside the harbour boom, near Shotley Barracks, near Upper Dovercourt, and on Harwich Town, where the International Stores in Kings Head Street were demolished and one civilian lost a leg. That these were Italian raiders was confirmed by the bomb fragments examined by C.M.F. Bernard, the Harwich Civil Defence Controller, after the raid.

Curiously, one of the Italian aircraft on this raid is stated by CAI records to have returned with damage to its wings and fuselage, which had apparently been caused 'by an attack by a British night fighter'. Yet an exhaustive search of RAF reports makes clear that no squadron in East Anglia took part in any combat that night. The defender's flack, or possibly even one of his own colleagues trying to fire in retaliation, must have hit the unfortunate pilot.

The last strike of the year took place in the early hours of Monday, 23 December, when six bombers from 43 *Gruppo* were dispatched to Harwich. Once more the only reported damage that night occurred some distance away on the Shotley Peninsula between the little villages of Erwarton and Chelmondiston. All the aircraft returned safely to Belgium.

There are two more footnotes to end the account of the year. On 19 December, the RAF carried out its one and only retaliatory raid on the CAI. A single Bristol Blenheim light bomber belonging to No. 107 Squadron based at Wattisham in Suffolk flew across the Channel and unleashed four 113-kg (250-lb) high-explosive bombs across the runway at Ursel Airfield. The personnel on the base were evidently so surprised when the Blenheim ran in at around 30 m (100 ft), that no one thought to organise a pursuit until it had disappeared into the gathering gloom, leaving a trail of wrecked aircraft and damaged hangars.

If that solo effort was a surprise, then the CAI's last 'operation' before Christmas can be described as almost ridiculous. On Tuesday, 24 December, a solitary BR.20M piloted by Squadron Leader Giuseppe Tenti headed off from Chièvres, apparently with the intention of bombing London. Whether the veteran pilot was on an actual mission – or had decided to take a little direct action to demonstrate that Italian pilots lacked none of the courage and spirit of adventure of their RAF contemporaries – there are now no documents to explain, though solo missions were not altogether out of the ordinary, as Michael J F Bowyer has written:

> That there were lone daylight cloud cover ventures is certain, a Fiat BR.20M being seen over Ipswich by Mr. D.F. Brock. Clacton, too, was probably a target on 27 November; a dusk raid was attempted off Southwold; and there remain strong suspicions of night penetrations to Bedford and Huntingdonshire. Certainly, some very strange-sounding engines were heard overhead at this time.

What *is* beyond dispute is that Squadron Leader Tenti became hopelessly lost on that dank, mist-shrouded day and wandered around the Belgian countryside vainly looking for a familiar landmark until he ran out of fuel. Fortunately, the embarrassed officer and his crew were able to bale out safely as their plane dropped to earth in a field near the town of Abbeville. According to legend, the five men stayed in the town over the Christmas period before showing their faces again in Chièvres.

Perhaps predictably, neither this episode nor the bombing of Ursel by the RAF found their way into the media back home in Italy. There, the press and radio had been busy sensationalising the CAI's activities against the British and wildly overstating the achievements of its pilots ever since the day they had landed in Belgium. And, in some instances, even earlier…

THE MYSTERY OF THE ITALIAN 'KILLS' 10

On the morning of Friday, 25 October 1940, Italians awoke to hear their radios broadcasting the news that during the previous day the *Corpo Aereo Italiano* had been busy raiding towns and cities of their hated enemy, the British. The morning newspapers, too, were full of stories about the success of Italian aircraft bombing England. One of the biggest-selling titles, *Il Giornale D'Italia*, ran a front-page story under the headline 'British Aggression Answered by Italian Might', which stated:

> By boldly executing attacks and well-aimed bombs, Italian aircraft have obtained great successes against harbour works in the east of England. This marks the beginning of action against the metropolitan territories of Great Britain as a reprisal and severe warning against the aggression of the RAF over the territories of northern Italy.

The *Corriere della Sera* – one of the oldest papers in the country – carried a similar front-page story, informing its readers that their leader had taken 'a personal decision' to create a special Italian air corps of 'an impressive size'. The war now in progress had been caused 'wholly by British intervention' and *Il Duce* was 'grateful that Germany had accepted the offer of Italian participation'. The newspaper added, 'The air force is now collaborating with the *Luftwaffe* and has successfully bombed London.'

In none of the broadcasts or reports, however, was there any specific information provided about the achievements of the new force. There were no details about the locations, other than it was London that had been raided, or whether any casualties had occurred. Even a rather reserved quote from the German high command that they welcomed Italian involvement said no more than the aircraft had 'taken part in raids on England from their starting point in France' – a clear indication that both sides wanted the fact the Italians were actually based in Belgium kept secret for as long as possible. One of the newspapers even managed to mis-spell the name of the air marshal in charge of the operation as 'Pougier'.

Ever since Mussolini and the Fascists had come to power, the Italian media had, of course, been under their control. *Il Duce* had already been demonstrating a mastery of 'spin' long before the term had been coined. As a former journalist, he knew very well the value of propaganda as a tool to influence the population, and the press and radio were both carefully supervised to create the illusion that Fascism was the only true doctrine of the twentieth century and would replace liberalism and democracy wherever it existed. He knew, too, that one of the most potent ways of delivering this to the masses was to show the success of Italian forces now that they were fully committed to the war.

From the day that Mussolini announced from the Palazzo Venezia, his fifteenth-century headquarters in the centre of Rome, that Italian airmen were taking part in the Battle of Britain, the media had 'reported nothing but victorious engagements for the Corps fighter squadrons over the Hurricanes and Spitfires of Fighter Command', to quote Gordon Kinsey in his book, *Martlesham Heath: The Story of the RAF Station, 1917–1973* (1975).

At the forefront of this propaganda push were the formerly independent papers such as *Il Giornale d'Italia, Corriere della Sera, La Stampa* and *La Tribuna* – all now run by hand-picked Fascist editors –

and *Il Popolo d'Italia,* the daily paper that Mussolini himself had founded in 1913 to promote the pro-war group, the *Fasci d'Arzione Rivoluzionaria.* Its pages particularly favoured highly coloured accounts of the *Regia Aeronautica* pilots who had been posted to the strike force now apparently streaming across the Channel to wreak terrible destruction on the enemy, his homes and factories, and especially his defences.

Reports such as these had, in fact, begun to appear as early as the second week of October, when the CAI was not even fully in place in Belgium. By the time the first tentative flights to 'spy out the lie of the land' (Kinsey) were taking place, they had almost reached a frenzy. The 'success' of these non-events could be judged, the papers claimed, by the fact that the RAF had such depleted numbers as to be almost impotent and no Italian pilots had been lost. *That,* of course, would not occur until the CAI began suffering the accidents of its own making at the end of the month.

The lack of any photographs of these 'courageous missions over the English Channel' did not deter the wartime spin doctors. The newspapers instead carried a mixture of drawings, cartoons and a powerful campaign of advertisements and posters emblazoned with the single word 'LONDRA!' and showing the ancient Roman gesture of a giant down-turned thumb – signifying 'kill' – hovering over the capital city. The Tower of London, Tower Bridge and various church spires and tall buildings were all depicted as flaming ruins. To further spur the population, Mussolini also delivered a speech about the importance of the link with Hitler and Germany: 'Nothing can better make the lasting relations between peoples animated by common ideas than bloodshed in the common cause and sacrifices shared. I am sure that Italian airmen and Italian submarine crews are being an honour to their flag.'

Denis Mack Smith, the Senior Research Fellow at All Souls College, Oxford, has gone to some pains in his excellent political biography *Mussolini* to show how the dictator had learned all about the artifices of journalism, beginning with his very first stint on a newspaper in 1909 while he was living in the Austrian province of Trentino:

> His experience of working on a daily paper was excellent
> training. He remembered how it taught him many tricks of

the trade, including how to invent a news story and how to write a whole article about some non-event without arousing disbelief. Few other lessons in his life were to be more useful.

Mussolini also used this experience to promote Fascism – notably in an article that appeared in the *Enciclopedia Italiana* in 1932 – and that same year supervised the publication of the official booklet for a great exhibition designed to be a monument to the 'Fascist Age' that described the festival as embodying, 'the will of *Il Duce* in whom all the mysterious forces of the race converge'. Just to make sure there were no 'misunderstandings', Mussolini personally selected every newspaper editor and decreed that no one would be allowed to work as a journalist unless they possessed a certificate of approval from the Fascist Party. There was one outcome of this state control that he probably did not anticipate, however, as Denis Mack Smith has pointed out:

> It was his [Mussolini's] frequent boast that he continued to read hundreds of newspapers a day; as many as 350, he once said. He liked to impress journalists by telling them that he followed them all individually and was carefully watching out for their peccadilloes. It was his belief that by studying the newspapers each day he could keep his finger on the pulse of public opinion. But this was a dangerous piece of self-deceit – he forgot that the news and comments on the news were increasingly being manufactured in his own press office.

Small wonder, then, that such unpleasant events in early November as the successful British raids against Italian troops in North Africa and the battering of the Italian fleet at Taranto by the Fairy Swordfish 'stringbags' received no space, while so-called aerial 'triumphs' over England were celebrated with large headlines. Readers were probably not as surprised or cynical about such achievements by their air force as they might have been, however. For had they not just been hearing all about Italy developing the world's first *jet* aircraft?

Once again, Mussolini had taken full advantage of his control of the media to herald the first flight of the Campini Caproni CC.2, or 'Thermojet', in Milan on 27 August. It was a triumph of Fascist engineering, his papers claimed, and if anything would ensure the future strength of the air force and turn the *Regia Aeronautica* into the greatest in the world – as *Il Duce* planned – it was this machine, designed by the Bologna engineer, Secondo Campini. As early as 1931, Campini had submitted a report on the potential of jet propulsion to the Italian Air Ministry and three years later been given approval to start experiments.

Campini's engine was, in fact, not like the modern jet engine at all, but a conventional piston-engine that drove a compressor that forced compressed air into a combustion chamber, where it was mixed with fuel and ignited. The exhaust drove forward the prototype aircraft – known as the N-1 – which had a wingspan of 14.6 m (47 ft 10 ⅔ in), a wing area of 36 m (388 ft) and was 12.1 m (39 ft 8in) long. It was estimated that the 'jet' could achieve a top speed of 360 km/h (224 mph) and would be able to climb to an altitude of 4,000 m (13,123 ft). Its armament had not yet been decided.

According to the media, test pilot Mario de Bernardt carried out the first flight of the N-1 on a Tuesday morning in August at the Caproni factory at Vizzola Ticino near Milan. Details of the success were released at once, along with the news that the *Fédération Aéronautique Internationale* had 'recognised the flight as the first by a jet aeroplane'. Mussolini took time off from his duties to congratulate the designer and pilot and place himself firmly centre-stage at the propaganda coup.

Not for the first – or last – time, the dictator's claims were to prove ill founded. A jet plane driven by a true turbojet had, in fact, already flown on 24 August 1939, a whole year earlier. It was the Heinkel He 178, a 7.3-m-long (24-ft) barrel-shaped, single-seat monoplane, designed by a brilliant young German scientist, Pabst von Ohain, and piloted by *Luftwaffe* Captain Erich Warsitz. Powered by Ohain's tiny engine producing just 838 lb/sq ft (4,090 kg/sq m) of static thrust, it was capable of reaching speeds in excess of 644 km/h (400 mph). If the He 178 had actually been developed – its potential was, it appears, virtually dismissed by the German air force – it might well have changed the course of the subsequent war and, with it, history. Certainly, it ushered in the jet age.

Whatever Mussolini may have felt about the subsequent revelation of this achievement by his Axis partner, he kept to himself. But development of the CC.2 certainly went no further and only a single prototype survived the war and was subsequently taken to Britain to the Royal Aircraft Establishment at Farnborough for study.

Mystery surrounds what happened to the 'Thermojet' after that. The prototype disappeared and, by all accounts, was probably broken up for scrap. It was to prove another of the grandiose dreams that Mussolini had for his air force that turned to nothing.

* * * * *

The reader should be aware that although Mussolini obsessively controlled and often sensationalised the news that was released to the public, the high command of the *Regia Aeronautica* did try to keep a particular type of record of their pilots and their achievements, as Chris Dunning has noted in his exhaustive study, *Courage Alone: The Italian Air Force 1940–1943*:

> The high command frowned upon individual achievements, preferring to note successes as joint results by the unit – 'a result from the combined action of many other pilots.' The idea was to prevent loss of morale by less able pilots and crews. Individual pilots were allowed to note their claims in their personal logbooks, but the claims were officially credited to their units.

This was certainly the position throughout the Italian conflict with Britain. Later, however, in 1943, when Italy began to lose the war, the *Regia Aeronautica* had second thoughts and – probably anxious to encourage morale – offered a bonus scheme to pilots for every 'kill' claimed and witnessed. According to surviving documents, the going rate for a single or twin-engine enemy was 5,000 lire, which would be trebled for a four-engine aircraft. Even ships were included in the list, with the unlikely offer of a quarter of a million lire for sinking a warship!

This method of 'accounting' is just one of the problems the researcher faces when investigating the combat successes of Italian pilots during the Second World War. It is also a fact that the major reference book, *Stralcio dell'Opera Aeronautica Italiana nella Seconda Guerra Mondiale* by General Giuseppe Santoro, published in 1953, is notoriously unreliable. The general's two-volume work is certainly based on copious research, but also contains a lot of guesswork because of the *Regia Aeronautica*'s ad hoc method of recording and the 'rewards' for claims by pilots. The result is a book that several historians, notably Gordon Kinsey and Julian Foynes, have described as containing 'more raids and victories than were in actual fact'.

In volume one of his book, for example, which includes details of the CAI raids from Belgium against England, Santoro makes the first claim for a 'kill' on 8 November. During the afternoon, he says, 22 G.50s of 20 *Gruppo* carried out an offensive patrol between Dungeness and Margate and later reported a dogfight with four RAF fighters. One of the pilots – not named, as per CAI custom – claimed to have hit a Spitfire that veered away sharply and was last seen trailing smoke as it disappeared into low cloud.

This report does coincide with the account of Squadron Leader Brian 'Sandy' Lane of No. 19 Spitfire Squadron based at Duxford, who was struck by enemy fire while in the vicinity. The reformed First World War squadron – motto 'They can because they think they can' – had achieved its first 'kill', a Junkers Ju 88, on 11 May. By September, Lane was the leader of No. 19 and had his first shared kill, a Bf 110, shot down over Hornchurch.

On the date quoted by Santoro, 8 November, Lane was involved in a dogfight and had to make an emergency landing at Manston, where his Spitfire was found to have suffered 'category 2' damage. This certainly does not amount to a 'kill' – and the general's claim is further deflated by *Luftwaffe* records found after the war that the damage was in all probability caused by a Messerschmitt pilot, *Hauptmann* [Flight Lieutenant] Hans 'Assi' Hahn, whose claim to have damaged a Spitfire at this same time stands up to much closer scrutiny.

Hahn, a German army officer turned fighter pilot, was a member of JG 2 based at Zerbst during the Battle of Britain, and claimed five victories – including three Spitfires – which earned him an Iron Cross. Just a week before the fateful encounter over Margate when he damaged Squadron Leader Lane's Spitfire, Hahn had been promoted – and by the end of the year had amassed a total of 22 'kills'.

Santoro is on much firmer ground when he reports the shooting down of a Hurricane during the CAI raid on Felixstowe docks on 17 November. There is no question the plane crashed; it is the issue of whether the attacker was actually Italian or German that is open to dispute. The RAF pilot was Flying Officer Count Manfred Czernin, a remarkable character and member of the Austrian aristocracy, who had joined the force in 1939 and was a fully fledged fighter pilot with No. 17 Squadron at Martlesham Heath when war broke out. A fearless and ruthless pilot, Czernin was a man with a mission against the Nazis for seizing his homeland, and destroyed his first enemy, a Dornier Do.172, off Orfordness on 12 July. Before the end of the year, he would claim nine 'kills' and be awarded a Distinguished Flying Cross (DFC).

On 17 November, Czernin took off in his Hurricane to intercept a large formation approaching the Suffolk coast. Audaciously flying into the heart of the attackers, his fighter came under repeated fire and was badly damaged, forcing him to bale out. Czernin eventually parachuted down at Ufford, escaping with only slight injuries. His Hurricane went into a vertical dive and buried itself in a field in the village of Bredfield near Woodbridge.

According to General Santoro's book, Czernin's aircraft was destroyed by one of the BR.20Ms that raided the south coast that day. However, the evidence suggests he has confused the superficial resemblance between the Italian bombers and German Me 110s. By way of confirmation of this error, *Luftwaffe* sources claim that Czernin's plane, No. V.7500, was shot down by an opponent whom there was no mistaking: the formidable fighter ace, Major Adolf Galland, of JG 26 *Gruppe*, who was commanding a covering flight of Me 109s that morning. This fact might have been of some consolation to the fearless Austrian nobleman, but did nothing to deter his single-minded pursuit of the enemy – a pursuit that would ultimately leave him with the credit for thirteen destroyed, five shared and three 'probables'.

It is when Santoro's history of the CAI reaches that extraordinary day of 11 November that distortion really sets in, with a 'claim' for the destruction of a total of nine RAF fighters. The Italian loss of three fighters and three bombers is recorded simply as statistics. The facts are that two Hurricanes suffered damage from the BR.20M gunners and just one Italian fighter pilot has the evidence to claim to have shot down a Hurricane. The man in question was *Maresciallo* [Warrant Officer] Giuseppe Ruzzin, whose career makes interesting reading.

Ruzzin was born in April 1916 at Spresiano in the province of Treviso, one of the most beautiful parts of Italy, where the waterways are a constant reminder of nearby Venice. They were troubled times for the people of the area with the First World War rumbling on and in the autumn of 1917 the Ruzzin family fled from their home across the country to Genoa. There, in the ancient city made famous by trade and piracy in almost equal measure and with a reputation for harbouring political refugees and radical thought, young Giuseppe grew up with dreams of becoming a pilot and seeing the world.

In 1936, Ruzzin joined the *Regia Aeronautica* and worked hard to become a skilful airman. That September, after completing only 110 hours of flying time, he volunteered to join the pilots being sent to Spain to help the Nationalist cause. There he was assigned to a squadron of the *Aviacion del Tercio* based at Tablada. In the next three months he gained invaluable experience on the CR.32, which he later said was 'the best fighter in the world, easy to fly and very manoeuvrable'.

Ruzzin scored his first 'kill' while flying over Torrijos on 7 December. The plane was a Russian single-engine monoplane, the Polikarpov I-16, which looked like a 'stumpy racer' and was reckoned to be around 100 km/h (62 mph) faster than any contemporary fighter. It was newly in service and known as a 'Young Eagle' by its pilots and a *Rata* [rat] by Ruzzin and the other Nationalists who fought it. The young Italian took great pride in out-thinking and out-shooting his enemy and seeing him fall in flames on to the scorched terrain of the Iberian Peninsula.

On Saturday, 13 February, while returning from another mission with fifteen colleagues, forty *Rata*s bounced Ruzzin's flight. The situation could not have been worse for the Italian, as his guns had jammed during the operation and resisted all his efforts to free them. However, the sudden appearance of the Polikarpov I-16s caused him to take violent evading action – which, amazingly, freed his guns. Without hesitation, he turned into the fray and managed to shoot down one of the enemy with his last remaining bullets. The dogfight caused extensive damage to his CR.32, though – about 150 bullet holes were later counted in his fuselage – and he was forced to make an emergency landing at Getafe. His squadron had, nevertheless, achieved a total of nine 'kills' during the day.

In the months that followed, Giuseppe Ruzzin earned a notable reputation for his tactics and skill in the aerial warfare that continued over Madrid, Guadalajara, Aragona and Avila. In fourteen months he spent over 300 hours in the air, took part in 234 missions, and was credited with four 'kills' and six shared destructions.

On his return to Italy, Ruzzin was posted to 85 *Squadriglia*, then based at Mondovis airfield at Cuneo, where his expertise was put to good use training new pilots. When *Il Duce* declared war in June 1940, Ruzzin was posted to Cervere airfield in Piedmont on the Italian border to take part in the assaults on French airfields in Provence. During this brief campaign, Ruzzin, now flying the newer CR.42, was involved in several combats and was one of a quartet that claimed to have shot down three of the French single-engine Bloch MB.152 monoplanes over Beau Champ on 15 June. There is, however, no record of this fact in any French source.

The next destination for Warrant Officer Ruzzin was Ursel in Belgium as part of 18 *Gruppo*. The missions to England were to prove something of a disappointment after his previous experiences, although the bad weather and poor visibility did not help flying. The attack on 11 November led by Squadron Leader Ciccu was to be the only memorable combat of the posting.

The failure of the G.50s and the German Bf 109s to reach the CAI's destination at Harwich left Ruzzin and the other CR.42s as the only escort for the bombers when the RAF fighters appeared on the horizon. His account of what follows is terse and to the point:

> I was near the bombers when the attack developed. I was having trouble with my oxygen. I noted a small convoy of four ships beneath and the next thing to happen was that the British attacked from astern. The melee was fast and furious. I fought against Spitfires and Hurricanes. Gunned 4. Certainly killed one. Landed at St. Denis (Ghent).

Elaborating on this claim later, Ruzzin said that the Hurricane 'fell away with a long trail of smoke'. He also believed that between them, he and the other CAI pilots had accounted for a total of nine RAF fighters and 'probably' four more during the dogfight. Ruzzin said he added the success to his log and would have been quite prepared to fly against the RAF again. However, on 18 November he was reassigned to night fighter and reconnaissance duties at Vlissingen and in January 1941 ordered home with the rest of 18 *Gruppo*. A new posting to 154 *Squadriglia* saw him escorting convoys in the Mediterranean before he was relocated to Sicily for raids on British-held Malta. One engagement with a Spitfire provided another moment he never forgot:

> It was shortly before midday on 29 June, 1943, that several Spitfires from Malta attacked Comiso airfield [on Sicily]. I was sent up and engaged with one of them until I had exhausted all of my ammunition. Then I flew alongside a Spitfire because it seemed he also had no means of continuing the fight. We both gave friendly waves to one another before I turned back to Comiso.

The gesture was also to signal the ending of Giuseppe Ruzzin's war. He would fly half a dozen more missions, the last on 7 July, before a shortage of aircraft and the end of Mussolini's dictatorship confined him to *terra firma*. Ruzzin received several decorations for his bravery in combat – including two *Medaglie D'Argento al Valore*, one *Croce di Guerra al Valore* and from his erstwhile allies, the Iron Cross, 2nd Class. But for him, one of the most satisfying memories of the war remained that November day when he matched the RAF in their own skies in a biplane and scored what he believed to be a notable 'kill'.

* * * * *

General Santoro's next major claim is that Squadron Leader Feruccio Vosilla's 18 *Gruppo* shot down five enemy aircraft in the fighter sweep they carried out across the English coast from Margate to Folkestone on 23 November. Again there is no evidence in RAF records to substantiate this number, although the British certainly did suffer one badly damaged Spitfire. The man in the cockpit, Pilot Officer Archie Winskill of 603 Squadron, managed to land safely with the satisfaction of being able to lodge two CR.42 'kills' in return.

The Italian responsible for the damage was Flying Officer Giulio Giuntella, who had earlier shared action in France with Warrant Officer Ruzzin. As a young man, Giuntella had been caught up in the excitement surrounding the exploits of Air Marshal Balbo and signed on with the *Regia Aeronautica* in 1938. After earning his 'wings', he joined 85 *Squadriglia* and was flying CR.42s when war was declared.

Giuntella first saw action after being posted to Villanova D'Albenga airfield on the French border, where his squadron was assigned to attacking the enemy airfields of Cuers Pierrefeu and Hyères just to the east of Toulon. On 15 June, as one of a flight of 25 CR.42s commanded by Squadron Leader Vosilla, he was cruising over Beau Champ, when a squadron of Bloch 152s intercepted them. In the dogfight that followed, three of the French aircraft were shot down along with two of the Italians.

In *Regia Aeronautica* tradition, the three 'kills' were credited to 18 *Gruppo*, but Santoro gave four pilots a share: Giuntella, Ruzzin, Pilot Officer Felice Squassoni and Captain Giulio Anelli. He omits to mention that two of the triumphant Italian forces were badly damaged when trying to land at Villanova D'Albenga, which had been flooded by heavy rain in their absence.

By the time 18 *Gruppo* was sent northwards to join the CAI at Ursel, Giuntella had developed his skills considerably. Both he and

Ruzzin took part in several of the missions, but it was not until 23 November that he had something to match his colleague's claim of a 'kill'. Giuntella, though, went into this fighter sweep better prepared as a result of the events twelve days earlier, as he later explained:

> I engaged one of the British fighters from a range of between 40 to 50 metres [130–165 ft]. Then I saw a Spitfire, which was chasing another CR.42, and I got in a shot at a range of 150 metres [500 ft]. I realised that in a manoeuvred flight the CR.42 could win or survive against Hurricanes and Spitfires, though we had to be careful of a sweep from behind. It was the twenty minutes delay while the fighters and bombers joined up over the French coast and the failure of the G.50s to appear that proved fatal. In my opinion, the English .303 bullet was not very effective. Italian aircraft received many hits which did no material damage and one pilot even found that his parachute pack had stopped a bullet.

The mission on 23 November took Giuntella and the other pilots across the French coast at Dunkirk and on to Margate. As they swept over the south-east coast with Canterbury to the west, the CR.42s were suddenly hit from behind by a group of Spitfires. It was precisely what the lieutenant had feared and two of the Italian planes were almost immediately shot down. Bravely, though, he hauled around on his attackers and though hit several times got in a number of bursts on one particular Spitfire. The RAF plane began to lose height, he said, and on his return to Ursel he claimed a 'kill' to put alongside the four claims of the other pilots.

Consulting the records, however, indicates that only Giuntella's claim stands up to examination and the safe return of his 'kill', Pilot Officer Winskill consigns it to the 'damaged' category or, as the Italians would describe such an outcome, *Riparabile in Ditta – R.D. –* 'Repairable only in the builder's workshop'.

Like Ruzzin before him, Flying Officer Giuntella was reassigned in January 1941 and happily left the harsh winter of northern Europe for the warmer temperatures of Libya. In May 1941, he was appointed commander of 85 *Squadriglia* and served in Greece, before a second term in Libya in 1943 brought an end to his war.

* * * * *

The last of the CAI claims described by General Santoro is attributed to Flight Sergeant Luigi Gorrini, a protégé of Giuseppe Ruzzin. A handsome, forthright man, Gorrini was destined to survive the war as one of the country's top aces with 15 'kills' and a *Medaglia d'Oro al Valor.* Born in July 1917 in Alseno, a small town not far from Piacenza, Gorrini left this rather unassuming area of Italy, which is often passed over in favour of Parma or Modena, while in his late teens to join the *Regia Aeronautica.* He began training as a pilot in 1937 at the Fighter School at Castiglione del Lagos in Perugia and flew his first CR.32 in May 1939.

After graduating to the new CR.42 fighter in November, Gorrini was sent to join 85 *Squadriglia* at Mondovis airfield in Cuneo. Here he met Ruzzin, who had just returned from the Spanish Civil War and had been put in charge of training promising pilots. The warrant officer immediately spotted Gorrini's potential, and his tutelage saw the young man soon made up to the rank of sergeant. By the time the French campaign began, the two pilots had become good friends, though Gorrini saw little of the action.

In October 1940, Ruzzin and Gorrini flew together to Ursel and on 11 November set out in the same wing for England. It was not, however, the kind of experience Gorrini had been anticipating, as he was under specific instructions that prevented him from joining the action. He explained later:

> My orders were simply to stick with the bombers. That made me unhappy because I wanted to see what the CR.42 was capable off against the RAF fighters. I was also not very happy because I could not intervene when one of my friends was attacked and shot down. That created a very bad impression.

On 23 November, Sergeant Gorrini finally had a chance to get in the action in the big fighter sweep. He tangled with a Spitfire and later reported hitting the enemy with a burst of fire. He thought it unlikely he had caused any serious damage, but Santoro's book credits him with an 'R.D.'

The following January, 18 *Gruppo* was withdrawn from Belgium and sent to Libya. There, on 16 April 1941, Gorrini became the first Italian to shoot down an RAF Bristol Beaufighter, the formidable two-seat, four-cannon, long-range fighter that had only just arrived in North Africa. Further action over Benghasi, Sirte and Tunisia – including a close-call encounter with the RAF ace Flying Officer Neville Duke, later to become a leading British test pilot – helped Gorrini achieve the rank of Warrant Officer and to amass a total of fifteen kills by 1943.

After the war, Gorrini was to become one of the strongest advocates of the bravery and courage of his fellow pilots during the CAI's campaign in Belgium. He believed the reason for their lack of success over England had been the inferiority of their machines compared to the RAF's Spitfires and Hurricanes as well as the wintry conditions in which they had been forced to operate. He also pointed out that radio messages from the Belgium bases invariably seemed to be intercepted by the British, providing their squadrons with plenty of warning of the approaching CAI forces. Worse still, many of the Italian aircraft sent on the raids did not even have radios. Gorrini added: 'Of course, the RAF also had this system of radio location. It enabled them to locate our forces before we reached the English coast and attack us from directions we least expected.'

According to Luigi Gorrini, no one at the time seemed to know anything about the secret weapon called radar. He may, though, be mistaken in this assumption. For the fact is that the centre of the British radar network was a well-known landmark used by both German and Italian pilots. There is evidence, too, that some of their senior commanders perhaps knew more about the development of the 'magic eye' than is generally acknowledged...

THE SECRET OF BAWDSEY MANOR

11

The January morning was bitterly cold and the soldiers lying in sandbagged trenches behind barbed wire shivered in the pre-dawn light, shifting uncomfortably on the frozen earth and blowing on their hands to keep warm. A few yards away, the North Sea heaved and tossed great white breakers on to the beach at Upper Dovercourt, while to their left, vessels could be seen leaving the port of Harwich, already stirring with activity around the dockyards.

The men were members of the 10th Battalion of the 15th Division Cameronians (Scottish Rifles), who had been posted to the area to guard against a German attack and were now about to take part in a mock-invasion exercise. The famous old regiment that had been formed in Lancashire in 1881 and performed heroic service in the First World War – particularly during the horrifying battle at Ypres – was renowned for its hardy infantrymen, although these latest recruits were finding it difficult to live up to their reputation on such a freezing day. The men all knew, though, that their commanding officer, Major General Robert Money, was anxious that they should impress all those involved in the exercise with their training and dedication to duty.

For once, the Nazis who had been threatening to cross the English Channel since the summer were not to be the villains of the piece. Much to the surprise of the men of the 10th Battalion, the mock enemy on this occasion would be Italians. An entry in the Battalion's War Diary for that month explains the concept in rather atypical military fashion: 'England is a portion of the globe of which Italy is in temporary possession. The population is unarmed, but loathes the Wop [a slang term for Italian men] and is pro-British in its sympathies.'

Quite what quirk of the military imagination – or sense of humour – had inspired the organisers to dream up such a scenario there is now no way of knowing. Could *someone* have thought that perhaps the raids by the CAI on the district might presage an Italian invasion? Certainly, the soldiers of the 10th Battalion had heard about the raids and on several occasions in the past couple of months, they had formed working parties to go to Harwich and Ipswich to help clear up the debris from wrecked houses and buildings. This day, again, they would be working alongside some of the same groups – including the Local Defence Volunteers (Home Guard), Civil Defence and a few of the public services – in order to stop the 'invaders' making their supposed possession of the area permanent.

The 10th Battalion had taken part in mock-invasion exercises before and its troops were familiar with the drill. The intention was to make the soldiers and those civilians involved fully aware of the dangers – and, hopefully, to become more proficient in dealing with them. A report in the *Harwich & Manningtree Standard* after one such exercise in November is just as pertinent about what was going to happen again:

> The increase in importance of the effect which the behaviour of the civilian population can have upon the success of military operations under invasion conditions was empha-sised by a large combined exercise which took place on Sunday. There were air raid incidents, attacks by parachutists, attacks from the sea, gas attacks and all incidental problems of providing for the wounded and the homeless. In addition organising emergency hospitals,

> keeping the public informed of the situation and giving them
> instructions, the failure of the main services and the blocking
> of roads by bomb craters, all of which have to be overcome.

The *Standard*'s report finished on a slightly reproving note that the men crouching along the coast that morning knew had not gone down well with their superior officers: 'On the whole,' the paper said, 'it was a successful day.' This new exercise would not be on such a grand scale, so they knew they were expected to do even better.

Unlike some of the earlier mock-invasion exercises in the spring and summer of 1940 – which had not all been strong on realism – a good deal of ingenuity had been invested in creating a tenable framework for beating the Italian 'occupiers'. A team of umpire-observers would be on hand to decide the consequences of each move as the fighting progressed. They would rule on the number of casualties on each side, which positions had been overrun, and finally decide how many prisoners had been taken.

A group of the 10th Battalion men had been selected to play the enemy and were already dressed up in imitation Italian uniforms. They had strict instructions to stay clear of the real anti-invasion mines already in place on the desolate shingle beaches, although they could erect roadblocks at any suitable point to stop traffic and set up sniper nests in trees to catch out unwary foot soldiers.

No live ammunition was to be used by either group of men, they had been told by the officer in charge during the previous day's briefing. Furthermore, a red band around an enemy rifle meant it was a Bren gun, with a blue one signifying an anti-tank rifle – a somewhat idiosyncratic idea that had prompted a good deal of banter between the 'combatants'. There were also the usual jibes flung backwards and forwards between the two factions as they set off for their positions. The LDV veterans were the object of some fun, too, being teased by the soldiers that their initials stood for 'Look, Duck, Vanish.'

On this particular morning, however, the well-trained men of the 10th Battalion set about capturing or 'killing' their adversaries with enthusiasm, driven on by an equally strong desire to keep warm. The Civil Defence made short work of 'extinguishing' bombs, while the

Home Guard and police efficiently arrested some 'fifth columnists' that had been planted in the operation, at the same time moving local people out of danger.

The result of 'Operation Wop', as those who took part always remembered it, was a comprehensive defeat for the 'Italians'. Indeed, within a matter of hours 'friends' and 'foes' were all sharing mugs of steaming hot tea and sandwiches in Harwich.

As far as the real Italians in Belgium were concerned, however, the aerial battle against Britain was not yet over – but it was undoubtedly nearing a climax....

* * * * *

The weather records for the first month of 1941 reveal that it was the second coldest January since the beginning of the century. The strict imposition of the blackout, which made any kind of travel at night difficult, provided a stark contrast with the whiteout conditions of the daytime. For a time, parts of East Anglia were under drifts 4 to 5 feet deep, and around Lowestoft and Great Yarmouth bus services were interrupted and cars abandoned in deep drifts along a number of roads. It was said that any optimism among the people about an early end to the war – the belief that had kept them going a year earlier – had now gone. Still the question uppermost in most minds was the same: when would the Nazis invade?

The snow that blanketed the airfields as thoroughly as the roads left the eastern half of the country at the mercy of aerial attack from across the North Sea. Every day, the RAF ground staff battled gamely to keep the stations open – though morning after morning the same snowy wastes greeted their eyes.

Air Marshal Fougier and his staff in Belgium had no such problems, however, as their airfields were free of ice and snow. When reconnaissance flights by CR.50s from Ursel brought news of the conditions in England, they decided to take advantage of the enemy's plight. The CAI's only problem was the effect they knew the intense cold would have on their aircrews – not to mention keeping from them the bad news of what was happening in the war back home. During the opening days of the new year, the RAF had bombed Naples and

Italian bases in North Africa, while British and Commonwealth troops in Libya had captured 25,000 Italian soldiers at Bardia and, two days later, seized Tobruk. The only good news for the Italians was that the *Regia Aeronautica* and the *Luftwaffe* were now retaliating, pounding British bases on Malta with bombs and high explosives.

There was to be no let-up from Belgium, either, Mussolini had decreed. On January 2, four BR.20M bombers from Melsbroech flew a night mission against Harwich. Snow flurries caused two of the planes to turn back before they reached the coast, but the remaining pair continued and dropped ten 100-kg (220-lb) incendiaries on the port, causing considerable damage in the harbour area.

A week later, with the bad weather still gripping East Anglia, another four aircraft flew to Harwich in broad daylight on the morning of Tuesday, 7 January. The snowbound port provided the pilots with a dazzling vista, but the battery of fire that opened up from the AA guns drove them away before they could drop their bombs. The incendiaries were apparently off-loaded between Ramsey and Bradfield, but caused no injuries or real damage to property.

On Tuesday, 21 January, the port that had withstood everything the Italians could drop on it was the target of what would prove to be its last visit from the CAI. It took the form of a solitary BR.20M bomber which, according to the *Harwich & Manningtree Standard*, dropped a number of bombs and incendiaries on the centre of the town. The report continued: 'One of the bombs severely damaged the shop which a Mr. and Mrs. Bateman owned. Mr. Bateman was in hospital at the time and died a few hours after the attack without knowing that his home and business had been destroyed.'

Tragic as this news was, the people of Harwich would probably have been cheered to know that the Italian bombers were about to be removed from operations and would never darken their town again. The BR.20Ms made just two more strikes against England, on 23 January and 7 February, before Fougier decided to send what remained of his two *Stormi* back to Italy. It had become painfully obvious, despite the courage and determination of the pilots, that the bombers were too outdated for this theatre of war and too costly in terms of men and machines.

The first of the raids – both on Ipswich – occurred on Thursday, 23 January at breakfast time with snow once again falling. The bombers caused damage to houses in Till Road, Stanley Street and Summer Road, injuring fourteen people. The second attack, on Friday, 7 February, was hampered by poor visibility, but the pilots still managed to drop a number of bombs and incendiaries around the harbour and train station, badly injuring several railwaymen.

All of the raiders made it safely back to Belgium and, within a matter of days, their relieved crews were heading south for Italy. However, the men had no idea there would little respite for them and the other aircrews in the two wings. Within days, they would be on the move again to take part in the Italian operations against Greece and Yugoslavia.

Simultaneously, the decision was taken that the remaining out-fought and out-manoeuvred CR.42s of 18 *Gruppo* should be flown back to Italy. Squadron Leader Feruccio Vosilla and his squadrons would also soon be on the move, too, thrust again into another fierce conflict with the RAF – this time in the skies over Libya.

Only the newer G.50s, which had put up better opposition to the Hurricanes and Spitfires, were to remain and continue operations in conjunction with the *Luftwaffe*. The fighters were divided between two units, 352 and 353 *Squadriglia* of 20 *Gruppo* under the command of Squadron Leader Mario Bonzano. On 10 January, they transferred from Ursel to Maldegem, a military airfield in East Flanders not far from Bruges. The grass runway here had only been laid in 1939, but was fully operational when seized by the invading German army. Closer to the coast than any of the other bases occupied by the CAI, Maldegem was to witness the last act in the Italians' battle with England – a very unsatisfactory one, as several aeronautical historians have described. Chris Dunning is typical of these, writing in *Courage Alone*:

> Low range capability and lack of radios kept them from being more active in this theatre and several pilots suffered from severe frostbite due to the lack of cockpit heating. Escorts and sweeps were, however, carried out over Ramsgate and Harwich, but without much opposition. After

the main CAI units had left for Italy, 352 and 353 Squadrons remained for patrols along the Dutch, Belgian and French coasts as far as Calais until 15 April.

Nicola Malizia in her account, *20 Gruppo in Belgium* (2002), is even more unequivocal. She describes what happened to the squadrons after they were incorporated into the *Luftwaffe* as 20 *Jagdegeschwader* 56:

> The unit retained on the sides of their Fiat G.50s, the 'untouchable' Black Cat emblem, although the little grey mouse became more the colour of green. The operation base was Maldegem, which, in truth, did not fit into the context of the war on that difficult front. Not one of the pilots from the unit ever succeeded in firing even a shot from their machine guns against an enemy aircraft. Their mission patrolling the Flemish coast facing the Manica [English] Channel had its rewards, but they sustained some losses. Two pilots died and one was gravely wounded and could not fly again.

This said, there was some compensation for an elite group of Squadron Leader Bonzano's top pilots during their time at Maldegem when the *Luftwaffe* offered them the chance to fly the superb Messerschmitt Bf 109E fighters. Another smaller group was given the same opportunity at the *Jagdegeschwader's* training unit at Cazaux, just across the border in France. Being 'checked out' – the aeronautical term for learning to fly a new type of aircraft – during February and March 1941 remained for many of these men the happiest time of their stay in Belgium.

There were several of these happy few who argued that if they had been able to fly an aircraft as proficient and deadly as the Bf 109E, the outcome of the battle with Britain might just have been different. One of these men was Captain Furio Doglio. He had flown with the *Regia Aeronautica* for several years before the war and joined 353 *Squadriglia* in August 1940. During his time in Belgium, Doglio had flown several missions in CR.42s and been engaged in two close encounters with the RAF, escaping on both occasions without injury to himself or damage to his aircraft. The captain was so impressed by the Bf 109E that he helped draw up a list of pilots who urged Air Marshal Fougier to order some for the CAI.

According to papers in the archives of the *Regia Aeronautica*, a request for one hundred of the fighters was formally put to the German high command on 25 March. For a week nothing was heard from Berlin – then news came that the application had been turned down. They were asking for too many planes, the Italians were told; the *Luftwaffe* now needed every aircraft it could get for the invasion of Russia. An offer to supply a dozen Bf 109Es for one of the units was rejected with very little grace.

Captain Doglio was no doubt as disappointed at this outcome as anyone. In April he returned to Italy and was reassigned to North Africa, where he continued to fly the G.50 with great success and claimed seven victories against the RAF. His luck held good until the morning of 27 July 1942, when he was shot down over Malta. His adversary was the Canadian-born Spitfire 'ace' Flight Lieutenant George 'Screwball' Beurling. Obsessed with flying from his childhood, Beurling had joined the RAF in September 1940 and after achieving several 'kills' during the Battle of Britain was transferred to Malta – which he liked to refer to as 'The Fighter Pilot's Paradise' – and ended the war with a total of 31 victories.

Despite Nicola Malizia's insistence that none of the G.50 pilots ever fired a shot against the enemy, two more incidents occurred before the group was recalled to Ciampino on 16 April that bear the hallmarks of encounters with RAF fighters. The first took place on 3 April over the village of Cremarest in France, when Sergeant Remo Meneghini of 353 *Squadriglia* died after what was described as a 'flight accident'. A group of Spitfires are known to have attacked the nearby German airfield at Desvres that same day.

More significant is the story of Lieutenant Mario Roncalli of 352 *Squadriglia*, a 30-year-old veteran from Bergamo, who had been flying with the *Regia Aeronautica* since 1930 and served in the Spanish Civil War. On Sunday 13 April, Roncalli was scrambled to intercept an 'enemy aircraft' flying at around 300 m (980 ft) over Western Flanders. According to one version of events, Roncalli aborted the mission because of bad visibility and while returning to Maldegem lost control of his plane near the town of Steenbrugge, some 37 km (23 miles) south of Bruges, and crashed to his death.

A second version of events, from Steenbrugge itself, claims the Italian's plane was seen flying over the town's famous abbey – known for its founder, St Arnold, the patron saint of brewers – and had just crossed the canal when another plane appeared from out of low clouds. In this account, the plane fired a short burst at Roncalli's aircraft, which almost at once plummeted to the ground. In the opinion of eyewitnesses, the attacker could only have been British.

Whatever the truth of this crash – and the G.50 was so badly wrecked that an inspection to find the cause of the crash proved impossible – Lieutenant Mario Roncalli was given a military funeral and his body laid to rest in the municipal cemetery. It lies in the same spot today, a marker to the last, sad death suffered by the 'Chianti Raiders'.

* * * * *

Probably the most difficult question to resolve about the Italian airforce raids on England is what, if anything, they knew about the British secret weapon: radar. Thomas Potts, in his history of the time, has no doubts and describes a lack of this knowledge as one of the contributing factors to the *Corpo Aereo Italiano*'s defeat: 'Their bombers lacked adequate navigational aids and the Germans revealed nothing of their advanced systems. The Italians were told absolutely nothing about radar, either British or German.'

However, the CAI certainly regularly targeted the locality where the all-seeing 'eye' was developed. Equally, their pilots used the most visible signs of its existence as landmarks when carrying out raids inland.

The exact location was Bawdsey Manor, a Gothic-looking mansion on the Suffolk coast, just 11 km (7 miles) north of Harwich. CAI documents contain several references to the imposing building on the headland with its eight giant towers in the grounds that must have seemed from the air almost like pointers to the three major centres in the area: Harwich, Felixstowe and Ipswich.

German aircraft that raided this part of the Suffolk coast in the winter of 1939 were the first to make deliberate turns around the site, an action that understandably unsettled the scientists working beneath them. The appearance of Italian bombers in the autumn of 1940 only compounded their anxiety. When some bombs actually fell on the shore during one of the CAI raids on Harwich in November, the fears of those in Bawdsey Manor that the enemy must know of their existence seemed to be all too real.

Certainly, at that time no one could be quite sure what the Axis powers knew about radar – and it would not be until after the war that any kind of answers could be found. As far as the British public were concerned, of course, there had been suspicions about a secret weapon for years, but it was not until 1945 that the remarkable invention came off the secret list, thanks initially to an article in *The Aeroplane Spotter*, a weekly journal for air enthusiasts and organisations such as the Royal Observer Corp and the Air Training Corps. On 19 April, the *Spotter* lifted the veil a fraction with this revelation:

> Radar, as Radar Location is known, is a contraction of the words Radar Detection and Ranging, which form the same word forwards or backwards. It is the 'Magic Eye' with which the RAF has been able to spot the approach of enemy planes and track the paths of our own aircraft.

It would not, in fact, be until June of that same year that the organ of the establishment, *The Times*, explained the phenomenon in full, complete with technical details for the benefit of lay readers and experts alike. The article revealed just why the RAF had been so keen to keep under wraps one of the main reasons for its success in the Battle of Britain. It may even have caused an embarrassed grin on the faces of the millions of readers who, in the meantime, had been taken in by the claims of the Ministry of Information that the reason for the pilots' successes at night had been because they ate lots of carrots.

One of the first pointers that the Italians might have known something about radar arose in 1944 after the successful invasion of France and the Low Countries by Allied forces. At a number of the Belgian airfields from which the enemy had hastily fled – including two occupied by the CAI at Maldegem and Melsbroech – the troops discovered hundreds of sets of the *Luftwaffe* target photographs similar to those of Norwich that Air Marshal Fougier had found so useful. These pictures had obviously been used by both of the Axis powers and among them were some very significant sets relating to the east coast, as Christopher Elliott explained in another of his wartime articles, 'Death To East Anglia' published in the *East Anglian Magazine*, May 1967:

> About a year ago, I made enquiries in Belgium about an unsorted hoard of German Air Force target sets for the British Isles. Cast aside by Allied troops in 1944, these sets – 1,190 in all, made up of rather less than 40,000 separate documents – were rescued in September of that year and carefully put away in their original khaki and red folders. Only recently, however, was the job of sorting them completed and a list compiled after over 20 years. Among these were some 60 sets relating to civil and military targets. Mostly, in East Anglia, the Germans were interested in airfields and experimental establishments – *especially Bawdsey Manor [which] saw the birth in the 1930s of British radar.* [My italics.]

Elliott listed the various places covered by the sets – including Martlesham, Lowestoft, Great Yarmouth, Woodbridge and even Boxford with its 'dummy' airfield – and explained how the Italians had used them in planning their raids. Is it not possible then, as Elliott suggested, that the Italian high command might have dismissed the local rumours of 'death ray' at Bawdsey Manor or the German opinion it was a 'De Te Station' (standing for 'Decimetre Telegraph' for radio communications) and speculated that something less mysterious and more technologically advanced was providing a warning every time their planes appeared on the horizon? Certainly, the swift arrival of the RAF could not always be put down to luck or sheer coincidence.

The object of this interest was isolated and strange enough to make almost anything seem possible. The manor house had originally been a rich man's dream, incorporating early Dutch, Elizabethan and Oriental architecture, which had taken fifteen years and a fortune to complete after work began in 1890. Perched on a secluded headland with two waterfronts – one overlooking Hollesley Bay and the North Sea, and the other across the estuary of the River Deben towards Felixstowe – Bawdsey Manor had been laid out over 68 hectares (168 acres) and included a pig farm, large fruit and vegetable gardens and, significantly, a 'beautiful Italian garden', too grand and picturesque for anyone to miss.

The locality had, in fact, formed a part of the east coast's defence system since Norman times, with the spire of the nearby church of St Andrew in use for centuries as a landmark for shipping. In the First World War, the Devonshire Regiment had requisitioned the manor and there was no denying the foresight of the Air Ministry when they purchased the estate in 1936 with the Nazi threat gaining momentum in Europe. There, in conditions of great secrecy, the Scottish physicist Robert Watson-Watt and his team of scientists and radio technicians had developed radar. With the coming of war, the strategic importance of the place was emphasised again, as Gordon Kinsey has explained in his definitive study, *Bawdsey – Birth of the Beam* (1983):

> One of the five operational stations guarding the air approaches to London, it carried out to the full its wartime duties. As new types of radar were developed most stations specialised in one type of equipment, but Bawdsey Manor possessed them all and was by far the most important British radar station of the war. Several times it served as the site of the prototype for new systems which were success-fully brought to operational status, and although it was the oldest radar station in the world, it was also always the most up-to-date.

It is probably true that neither the unprepossessing T [for 'Transmission'] Block, where many of the early experiments were conducted, or the ring of recessed concrete pillboxes around the estate would have attracted much attention from passing aircraft. No one could possibly miss the eight huge towers standing in two rows, like giant sentinels, however. These were, in fact, the transmitting and receiving towers that enabled those operating the system to 'see' the coming and going of all aircraft across the North Sea.

The four larger towers were the 'transmitters': 110 m (360 ft) tall, constructed of steel, with aerials weighing two and a half tons slung between them. The 'receivers' were smaller: 73 m (240 ft) high, made of timber with metal ties, each having cross-shaped copper aerials situated at three levels. In time, these towers would become the standard pattern for all radar stations – or Chain Home Stations, as they were known – that ultimately stretched from Angus in Scotland to the Isle of Wight. In an example of chance at its most perverse, the first fifteen stations in this system went on air as the vanguard of the country's defence systems on Good Friday, 1939 – the very day that Mussolini invaded Albania.

Operating the radar was the preserve of the 'boffins', but running Bawdsey itself was the responsibility of the resourceful and highly efficient Wing Commander David Turnbull. It was a very different task from those he was used to, such as operating an RAF station, as he later confessed in an interview with *The Times*. Not the least of these risks was the likelihood of attack by enemy aircraft:

> All sorts of emergencies presented themselves, especially during the Battle of Britain. There were five officers and around 50 other ranks occupying a prime invasion area – half a mile of cliffs was the only high ground – with an arsenal of five revolvers and about fifteen rifles, hardly any ammunition, and with the scattered Beds and Herts men to the north and south of us. A desperate call on the 'scrambler' to Headquarters, Fighter Command, brought an immediate response. A thorough inspection of Bawdsey's cliffs and riverbanks followed and our position was quickly assessed. Within 24 hours, contractors were in and Bawdsey's expansive lawns were scarred with a deep trench through the middle and an extensive barricade of poles and barbed wire was erected to repel parachutists. Guns were placed at strategic cliff-top positions and a fairly powerful

naval gun sited to cover the Point on the Deben estuary. In
less than a week we felt a little more secure.

The wing commander knew that although he was now better
prepared, it was essential not to draw attention to Bawdsey for fear
of alerting the enemy to its importance. Turnbull recalled silently
watching with some of his men while enemy aircraft passed
overhead – including, on several occasions, the 'old-fashioned Italian
planes which looked and sounded to some of us like a bit of a joke'
– but with all of them hoping for the swift arrival of the RAF. They
were rarely disappointed.

According to Gordon Kinsey, the Bawdsey 'radio location
operators' – to give them their correct title – tracked down all the
CAI aircraft that raided the East Anglian coast and towns, passing on
the information to Fighter Command and the Observer Corps. On
two occasions, he writes, 'the Manor was the target of air raids, but
on both occasions it escaped damage, and on the second occasion
three bombs dropped harmlessly in the sea.'

On hearing about these attacks, Winston Churchill, who had
himself visited Bawdsey in early 1940 to see radar in operation,
expressed concern for the safety of the Women's Auxiliary Air Force
(WAAFs), who had been installed in the Manor to monitor the
system. He advised that the girls should be removed from 'such an
exposed and vital station'. The WAAFs, it seems, would hear nothing
of such chauvinist remarks and voted to stay put. Among those who
remained was Gwen Reading from Hampshire, who recalled her
time there to Gordon Kinsey:

> Radar was still very secret – we did not dare breathe a word
> of it or our work to anyone outside. Even the locals still
> speculated about 'death rays'. The site was always very
> busy, except during very poor weather conditions. Bawdsey
> was frequently complimented by the RAF Stanmore
> Headquarters on its general performance and accurate
> estimation of numbers of aircraft. Sometimes we would be
> asked by Stanmore to concentrate on certain aircraft, leaving
> the nearby stations to cope with the remaining activity.

Often these aircraft limped in at a painfully slow speed, getting lower and lower and sometimes finally disappearing while still over the sea.

The CAI aircraft were also monitored by another covert operation employing women as its 'ears' rather than eyes. This was the 'Y' Service, a group of Wireless Units deployed along the eastern and southern coasts of England to listen in to enemy transmissions – especially between pilots and their bases in Belgium. One of their operators was an Ipswich-born WAAF, Aileen Clayton, who spent countless hours of the day and night listening in to conversations of the 'Chianti Raiders' with very mixed emotions, as she later related in her book, *The Enemy Is Listening* (1980).

Aileen belonged to the No. 63 Wireless Unit of the 'Y' Service, stationed at Kingsdown, a small town on the Kent coast near Deal. Her group was based in the exotically named 'Hollywood Manor', which was actually a rambling old Victorian house standing on the highest point of the Kentish Downs with views directly across the Straits of Dover to France. Here, her job was to track down 'Bogeys' – the RAF slang for unidentified aircraft – by listening in to their r/t transmissions. Her administration officer was the formidable Jean Conan Doyle, daughter of Sir Arthur Conan Doyle, creator of that most famous of all snoops, Sherlock Holmes. In Aileen's book, she recalls that one of the most unusual episodes of her life as an eavesdropper occurred when the Italians joined in the war:

> The 'Y' Service, in the United Kingdom and overseas, had been assiduously monitoring Italian wireless traffic for some considerable time. Much of this material was sent straight to Station X for decoding and after collation it was signalled back to Cairo or Malta or East Africa for use by Intelligence in those theatres of operation. In the autumn of 1940, the German Air Force decided to let their newly acquired allies participate in the action on the Western European Front. We were not unduly surprised in Kingsdown when we started to intercept Italian Air Force r/t which apparently came from fighter aircraft based in Belgium.

After a short period of training, there came the initiation of the Italian Air Force in offensive operations against the United Kingdom. Their efforts could hardly be described as a roaring success. Nobody could have told them about a band of young women who were listening in to the enemy r/t and whose conscientious monitoring would be largely responsible for British fighters being so well placed they were able to effect a crushing defeat on the first Italian sortie of note made on 11 November.

More significantly for our story, Aileen Clayton reveals that 'Y' Service intercepted a number of enigmatic conversations that suggested the Italians were investigating the use of radio technology in tracking enemy aircraft:

It seemed as if they might be aware of the work of Watson-Watt and his team and their 'fly-bys' of the receivers and transmitters at Bawdsey Manor anything but a matter of chance. However, the Italians' withdrawal from Belgium the next spring left such speculation unresolved, although the mystery itself remained.

During her time at Kingsdown, Aileen Clayton said she listened in to hundreds of conversations between CAI aircrews – making note of the informative ones, the indiscreet ones and the tragic ones when the usually happy Italian tones were replaced by fear. Among those that particularly stuck in her mind were transmissions from pilots over the North Sea who used the 'clock-code' when they suddenly became aware of the presence of RAF fighters: *'Numero ventuno a Numero ventidue. Rumore di velivoli. Otto. Otto. Cappa, Cappa'* ['Number 21 to Number 22. Noise of aircraft at 8 o'clock. Over to you, over']. Or the unmistakable voice of an Italian bomber pilot as he was being attacked by a Spitfire or Hurricane: *'Numero dieci a Numero uno. Rumore di velivoli. Rumore di velivoli. O Mamma mia! – zero, zero. Rumore di velivoli zero!'* ['Number 10 to Number 1. Noise of Aircraft. O my dear mother! – zero, zero!']

Aileen says that it was not unusual for some of the female operators to claim to have actually heard over the r/t the sound of machine guns being fired or bombs being dropped. This never happened to her, she said, and she was rather inclined to believe they were cases of wishful thinking. What she did hear on a number of occasions were the agonised voices of Italian pilots screaming they had been hit or shouting they were about to bale out. She relayed these transmissions to Fighter Command, too, but usually with a feeling there was nothing that could be done for those in the crashing aircraft. In many cases, Aileen and her colleagues were the last people to hear the doomed airmen before they died.

It is true, though, that a few of the CAI fighter and bomber pilots and airmen shot down by the RAF survived. Some were taken prisoner after they had crash-landed; others were rescued from the sea. All were arrested, interrogated and finally put in prisoner of war camps. Their stories – in particular those who made new lives for themselves inside *and* outside these camps – are told in the final chapter of this book.

THE GODFATHER OF ASHFORD LODGE

12

The search for information about the fate of the 'Chianti Raiders' shot down over East Anglia begins not in England but in Italy, with a relative of one of the pilots determined to find out what had happened to the missing group of men. Antonio Bianchi was a small boy when his cousin, Ernesto, left home to fight the British and, like thousands of other relatives across the nation who lost people close them, Antonio was still very much in the dark about what had happened to his cousin when Mussolini's ill-conceived war came to its disastrous end three years later.

Had Ernesto Bianchi, a bomber pilot with 243 *Squadriglia*, been killed or taken prisoner after he had flown off from Chièvres on the bombing raid of 11 November 1940? The family had heard nothing beyond a simple message received two weeks later that Pilot Officer Bianchi and his crew of five on BR.20M 243-10-MM22620 were 'missing'. There was no indication as to the fate of the bomber or the airman – and it would take Antonio Bianchi almost a quarter of a century to find out the truth. A truth with a finale more extraordinary than he could possibly have imagined.

Events in this long quest, which would take Bianchi on a search through archives in Italy, Belgium and England, began in the little town of Gurro in the far north of Italy. It was here that he had grown up in the heart of the beautiful Cannobina valley, with its spectacular views across Lake Maggiore. With hindsight, it was partly the town's unusual origins and its centuries-old links with Britain that had prompted Bianchi's interest in history and later inspired him to find out what had happened to his cousin – and, perhaps, those others who had flown with him and had been lost in action.

The first hint of Gurro's connection with the country that *Il Duce* had declared war upon in June 1940 lies in the strange local intonation of its language, which has been studied by generations of historians of ethnic groups and scholars of glottology. The second lies in the restaurant in Fiume Street called 'Scotch', where whisky is a more popular drink than wine. And, thirdly, there are the names of certain local people that tradition says have been Italianised – such as *Patritti*, from Patrick, and *Bianchi*, from White.

To some visitors, Gurro seems a bit like a small outpost of Britain – most obviously the Highlands of Scotland – and the reason is not hard to discover. The story goes back to the year 1525 when the Holy Roman Emperor, Charles V, and his bitter rival, Francis I of France, were again disputing territory. This time it was land in what is now the mountainous border region between Italy and Switzerland. Among the French troops were a group of mercenaries, consisting of two or three nationalities, but predominantly Scots.

Wearied, though, from years of fighting for little reward, the mercenaries decided to pull out and took refuge in the ruins of a Roman village in the Cannobina valley, known in local tradition as 'at the ends of the earth'. It was a particularly isolated spot that was difficult to reach, easy to defend and would in time become known as Gurro, derived from the word *guardare*, meaning 'to watch or look over'.

After repairing the walls and roofing the houses, the men went in search of the one thing they were missing: women. Legend has it that some of the mercenaries intermarried with girls from local villages, but others went out under the cover of darkness to kidnap their females. The infants from these unions took the names of their fathers and preserved a bloodline – and a legend – that would flourish into the twentieth century. When Mussolini joined sides with Hitler, Gurro had a population of over six hundred.

The evidence of the town's origins was all around for young Antonio Bianchi to see and hear. In some of the oldest buildings, such as the church of St Andrea, there was a framework of crossbeams typical of those to be found in sixteenth-century Scotland. Tartan-style patterns were noticeable in some of the skirts and scarves worn by the women and a few of the men even wore kilts on special occasions, such as the annual festival on 25 August to commemorate the founders of Gurro. Ancient bagpipes would occasionally be produced to enliven the occasion.

As the years passed and stories of the festival spread, Scottish tourists began to turn up in the village and share tales of their homeland. Friendships were made and invitations were extended to those Italians with obvious connections to visit the birthplace of their founders. As Antonio Bianchi would admit later, it was an invitation he dreamed of accepting – and finally had a chance to pursue when he qualified as an engineer and went to live in Rome. He thought it might also enable him to solve the mystery of his lost cousin.

Antonio's search took him first to the city archives to consult the records of the *Regia Aeronautica,* in particular those documents that related to the CAI. The trail led from there to Belgium, where he found more details of 243 *Squadriglia's* time in Chièvres. There were tantalising references to the bombing raid scheduled for Harwich, which he knew had been the last on which Ernesto Bianchi had flown. From all this information, it was evident that any final answer lay in England.

Correspondence with the Italian Embassy in London informed Bianchi that he would need to consult the Public Records Office in Kew (now the National Archives), which housed all the records of the RAF and Air Intelligence from the Second World War. Although Bianchi spoke good English, he suspected his problem would be finding his way around the vast collections of data. Then, quite unexpectedly, fate intervened.

In 1965, Bianchi was sent to England on an exchange visit to the Zenith Carburettor Company in London. His contact was another engineer, W O G 'Bill' Lofts, and the two men soon discovered they shared a passion for recondite research. Indeed, when Lofts retired three years later, he spent the next 29 years reinforcing his reputation as one of the century's great researchers – a fact colourfully emphasised in his obituary in the *Independent* in July 1997:

> He was assiduous in his explorations and excavations, almost pedantically so. If you mentioned in passing that you had trouble in tracking down the death certificate of a certain obscure person, a week or so later he would present you with the information, together with the colour of the coffin he was shuffled off in and the wood it was made of.

This is a verdict with which I totally agree. Not only was Bill Lofts a great help for over twenty years with my own research, but on his death he bequeathed me his archives. The fifteen boxes proved to be an eclectic mix of information he had gathered on all manner of topics, from the identity of the pseudonymous authors of juvenile fiction to untold stories of the Second World War – in which he, it transpired, had served with the Royal Artillery in Burma. It was among these papers that for the first time I came across the story of the Italian air force's raids on Britain and Bill's part in helping Antonio Bianchi to solve the family mystery.

It seems that following their meeting at the Zenith works, Lofts invited his new Italian friend to his cramped little flat in Sheringham House, Lisson Street – appropriately situated just behind Baker Street, the home of one of his literary heroes, Sherlock Holmes, whose tireless style of enquiry he emulated. There, intrigued by Bianchi's story of his cousin, he promised to see what he could discover. As with everyone for whom he took on research, Lofts did not disappoint the Italian – a fact the files that ultimately came into my possession made abundantly clear.

Not only did Lofts solve the mystery of Ernesto Bianchi, but as a direct result of his many hours of studying documents in the Public Records Office, British Museum, British Newspaper Library, not forgetting the births and deaths ledgers at Somerset House, he discovered what had happened to all the other CAI pilots shot down over England. These facts, which Bill pursued very much for his own gratification – as well as to please his friend, Antonio Bianchi – have also enabled me to complete the story of the 'Chianti Raiders'.

Antonio Bianchi made several more trips to Britain – visiting Scotland twice – as well as corresponding with Bill Lofts for another fifteen years. Apart from the facts he unearthed, Bill also came up with another surprise for the Italian – the opportunity to see one of the Italian aircraft that had survived being shot down in England. The two men travelled to the Battle of Britain Museum in Hendon and stood there admiring, in their very different ways, a Fiat CR.42 fighter.

The little aircraft, resplendent in its original camouflage of sand shade mottled green with a silvery blue underside and repainted white numbers 13/95, was somehow symbolic for them of the end of a successful quest. Conversely, it also provides an ideal starting point for the story of the group of Italian airmen who fought in the Battle of Britain, were shot down *and* survived for their stories to be told.

* * * * *

The CR.42 in the Battle of Britain Museum is actually the fighter plane that crashed on the shingle at Orfordness during the dogfight watched in astonishment by young Harry Hawes. The fact that it is still in one piece makes it a unique artefact in the story of the Italian role in the Battle of Britain.

There were actually several other people on the Suffolk coast that day who saw the plane fall. Gordon Kinsey, who talked to several of these eyewitnesses years later, used their collective recollections for his account of events in *Orfordness – Secret Site* (1981):

> Spiralling out of the autumn sky, the CR.42 fighter flattened out and landed on the shingle beach, a quarter of a mile north of the lighthouse, ran for a while and then slowly tipped onto its nose as the wheels ground into the loose shingle. RAF personnel from the [Orfordness] Island were soon on the scene and captured the young airman who had been forced to land by a severed oil pipe.

One of the first on the scene was PC Norman Middleton, who was stationed on the island and had been on patrol when the battle between the Italians and the RAF broke out. His notes, which were filed at Ipswich Police Station, describe the outcome of the dogfight and provide the first personal details about the Italian pilot.

> Suddenly the clear autumn sky above Orfordness was filled with planes twisting and diving on each other, the sun glittering on their wings. One blazing bomber, it is believed, fell into the sea off the lighthouse. Two fighters followed, their pilots being killed when their parachutes failed to open. There were other splashes in the sea, too. Then the sound of battle died away.

The pilot of the fighter plane that crashed on the shingle climbed out and was sitting on the beach, dazed and confused, according to PC Middleton. The upended aircraft had 'a broken propeller and minor engine trouble'. A bystander – who may well have been Harry Hawes' father – told the policeman that the Italian was 'convinced he had come down in the desert and was doomed to die of thirst, so bare and desolate was the area where he had landed'.

Once the pilot realised he was safe and would be accorded the treatment of a prisoner of war, the policeman had no difficulty in obtaining his details. The man's name was Pietro Salvadori, he was a sergeant in 95 *Squadriglia* based at Ursel. He was formally arrested and taken to Ipswich Police Station. On the journey, PC Middleton found the pilot 'aggrieved at the fate which had brought about his crash and indignant about the war in general'.

Salvadori's statement says that he was born in Turin in 1917. He had been a reservist in the *Regia Aeronautica* for several years and learned to fly on seaplanes. In 1938, he was called up and flew 100 hours at various flying schools, before joining 95 *Squadriglia* at Novi Ligure in June 1940. Salvadori had completed almost another 100 hours when his squadron was transferred to Belgium. The fateful mission on 11 November was the tenth he had taken part in. PC Middleton's account elaborates the story from the moment of Salvadori's arrest on the beach:

Speaking loquaciously, the prisoner pointed out to sea where planes could be seen streaking homewards at great speed. He said that the *Luftwaffe* escort, which should have been patrolling above the Italian formation, had fled at the crucial moment leaving the bombers to their protection alone. Even before the combat started, he said his aircraft had got a broken oil duct that made it impossible for him to stay in formation. The engine then began to overheat and he was forced to make an emergency landing on the beach. The landing was successful and the aircraft did not sustain any large damage. Shortly after landing, a Hurricane flew over him and he waved at it, at which the Hurricane responded by waggling his wings.

The file on Sergeant Pietro Salvadori that Bill Lofts examined also contained a copy of an intelligence officer's report on the Italian and his character. It read:

The morale of this pilot was very poor. He was dissatisfied with his officers, loathed the climate in Belgium and could not stand the food or the Germans. He did not want to fight any more and was really happy to have left the war.

Salvadori's plane did not remain on the beach at Orfordness for long, either. It was collected by the RAF and taken to Duxford Airdrome in Cambridgeshire. Here, RAF mechanics made it serviceable again. All identification marks were painted out and it was re-registered as BT474 with RAF roundels in place of the Italian axes. Subsequently the little biplane was flown on a series of evaluation trials, although to be on the safe side, a pair of Hurricanes flew as escorts to avoid any inadvertent attack over home soil.

The test pilot was Captain Eric Brown, who reported that the CR.42 was 'remarkably fast' for a biplane, with a top speed of 434 km/h (270 mph) at 3,810 m (12,500 ft) and 'a marginal stability which is the mark of a good fighter'. The captain also thought it was 'brilliantly manoeuvrable, an acrobatic gem, but under-gunned and very vulnerable to enemy fire'.

Thomas Potts, who also investigated the fate of CR.42 M5701, claims that it was used in a propaganda coup to help demoralise the Italians. He explains: 'A few days after it was forced down, the RAF attacked the Fiat works in Turin. They dropped photos of the machine suitably inscribed. One was picked up by the pilot's fiancée and sent to Belgium. Thus the Italians learned the fate of their aircraft.'

Sergeant Salvadori also survived the war as a POW in England. He returned to Italy and in 1950 rejoined the *Regia Aeronautica* with 51 *Stormo*. According to Lofts' enquiries, Salvadori planned to write about his wartime experiences, but died tragically in April 1953 while flying a new-generation fighter that must have seemed light years ahead of the little CR.42 biplane – an American F-84G Thunderjet.

* * * * *

A second Italian fighter, which crashed farther up the Suffolk coast at Corton, was in no condition for restoration after it ploughed into farmer Bob Wright's field. The pilot, Sergeant Antonio Lazzari, was also lucky to be able to get out of the wrecked aircraft under his own strength. He was, though, still shaking from his madcap flight and at a complete loss as to where he might be.

Lieutenant Way of the 5th Battalion, King's Own Rifles, formally arrested the pilot. A report by the 514 Coastal Regiment, who had first observed the approach of the intruder coming in over the Pakefield Cliffs at Corton, describes the events:

> At 14.17 hours, an aircraft with queer markings flew over the Fire Command Post and made a forced-landing nearby in a ploughed field just north of the LNER Station at Corton. The plane ran over the railway embankment as it landed, tearing off the fixed undercarriage. It bore the markings 85/16 and the number MM6976. There were several .303 bullet holes in the tail plane. The pilot, *Sergente Pilota* Antonio Lazzari, aged 23, of 85 Squadron based at Ursel, was unhurt and later taken to Lowestoft Police Station in Regent Road.

Lazzari proved as talkative as his colleague from 95 *Squadriglia*. His command of English was, though, somewhat better and he insisted on retelling his flight along what he now realised was the East Anglian coast to several members of the station. As far as personal details were concerned, the Sergeant said in his statement that he came from Bologna and claimed to be a relative of the famous Italian composer, Ferdinando Antonio Lazzari. He had been called up in 1940 and assigned to the air force, although he said that he would have preferred the navy. Lazzari revealed that he had been trying to find his way back to base when the crash occurred. The police report added: 'The pilot claimed he had been forced to land because the variable pitch mechanism of the propeller had failed. This had left one blade at a different angle and caused severe vibration.'

The talkative man from Bologna had fully recovered from his experience by the time he was escorted from Lowestoft Police Station to Ipswich Railway Station two days later. Here he was put into one of five specially reserved compartments in a train bound for London. In the adjacent compartment sat Pietro Salvadori and in the others, the survivors of the BR.2OM bomber that had crashed in the forest near Woodbridge.

Though none of the men knew it, they were all destined for an interrogation centre in the heart of the nation's capital – one with a fearsome reputation, and which was known as 'The London Cage'.

* * * * *

A number of people had been in the vicinity when the bomber numbered 243/MM22621 crashed at Bromeswell. This was to be the only Italian plane to fall on English territory in which crewmembers would be logged as 'Killed in Action' (KIA). One of the crew had, of course, died in the air and another would die of his wounds in a local hospital. However, the first reaction of Les Dunnett when he reached the scene was one of amusement, as he later recalled:

> I had a good laugh because one or two farm workers were standing near the aircraft with pitchforks and the crew were sitting inside apparently not daring to move. The crew

wore tin hats and carried bayonets. They were also carrying a bottle of champagne, a bottle of Chianti and a block of cheese. There was even a cheese grater beside one of the gunner's seats.

PC Thurston Clarke, who arrived at the scene on his bicycle, had some difficulty in getting the basic details about the crew. They appeared to be convinced they would be shot, he said later, and all were deeply disturbed by the death of one of their colleagues, who was still inside the wrecked fuselage. The pilot gave his name as Lieutenant Pietro Affiani, and named the dead man as the radio-operator, Aircraftsman Armando Paolini. His co-pilot, Sergeant Giuliano Ripolini, was badly wounded and Aircraftsman Emanuele Degasperi had also suffered injuries during the RAF attack. Only the unit photographer, Aircraftsman Mario Pensa, who had the misfortune to have been assigned to this aircraft to photograph the raid, escaped relatively unharmed.

Records at Ipswich Police Station, where the crew were taken, indicate that Sergeant Ripolini was too weak to answer questions and transferred to Ipswich Hospital that afternoon. He died of his wounds during the night. Lieutenant Affiani appears to have been the only man to have been questioned in detail about the mission before the three survivors were put on the train to London. The report of their time in police custody adds:

> The men were observed in the force headquarters at Ipswich. They were apprehensive of the treatment they might get. There was an officer, *Tenente* P Affiani in a very smart uniform, while the dress of the others varied. The officer, who spoke English, said he had flown his aircraft at 14,000 feet and the effect of the lack of oxygen had made them partly lose their senses. They had been told before flying that the biplanes sent to protect them could manoeuvre, while the Hurricanes could not.

There was no longer any doubt in the minds of the men that their bombers were no match for the RAF – and they would probably have been surprised at the care their hosts took with the wreckage of their machine. Bill Lofts discovered that the aircraft was lifted from the scrubland on to a trailer and transported across the Eastern Counties to the Royal Aircraft Establishment at Farnborough. Although the identification insignia from the two tail fins had been removed by Squadron Leader Tuck and his men, the unusual-looking plane caught the attention of many people – even those grown blasé at the sight of wrecked aircraft – as the trailer trundled across the countryside. At Farnborough, the bomber was examined for several weeks by RAF technicians, who apparently found nothing that might further British aircraft development and the plane was unceremoniously scrapped.

The journey of the CAI airmen from Ipswich to London also caused a stir of interest. Each of the five men travelled in a separate compartment with a guard, the bomber crew as yet unaware of the two fighter pilots travelling in the same carriage. The surprise, when it came, proved to be greatest for Mario Pensa, the unit photographer, who suddenly found himself on the receiving end of a photographer's lens. Showing the kind of persistence a member of today's paparazzi might have envied, a cameraman from the London *News Chronicle*, who received a tip-off about the Italian prisoners, boarded the train at Chelmsford and proceeded to photograph all five. For once the censor must have had no objection to pictures of a clutch of Britain's enemies in custody, and a striking series of photographs appeared the following day, complete with the caption:

> Italian airmen who were brought down by the RAF in a battle over Britain were brought to London on their way to a prison camp. These exclusive *News Chronicle* pictures were taken on the train. They are shown eating sandwiches and smoking. One man, surlier than the rest, scowled at the photographer and turned away as he took his picture. But the pilot [censored] smiled as he was photographed.

For the record, the uncooperative airman was the photographer Mario Pensa and the smiling pilot, Lieutenant Pietro Affiani.

* * * * *

The train journey was to prove the last relaxing time the five captured airmen would enjoy before the next week while they were being interrogated by men from 'The London Cage'. The organisation occupied a former stately home at 6, Kensington Palace Gardens. It had been set up in the immediate aftermath of Dunkirk and was known officially as the headquarters of the Prisoner of War Interrogation Section (PWIS). The 'cage' was commanded by Lieutenant Colonel Alexander Scotland and served as the nerve centre for a group of POW camps in which captured Germans could be cross-examined for information about Nazi war plans.

Lieutenant Colonel Scotland, generally referred to by his initials 'A P', already had a reputation as a 'rough-diamond interrogator'. He had become an intelligence officer in the First World War after being arrested in South Africa in 1914 by the Germans, who kept him a prisoner for almost a year. On his return to the UK, the British Intelligence Service – anxious to make use of his inside knowledge of German methods – recruited him to cross-examine German prisoners. For a time he was also sent to do espionage work behind enemy lines.

The call came again in 1940, when it became evident to the War Office that numbers of Hitler's soldiers, sailors and airmen would be falling into their hands with valuable information. Scotland immediately began recruiting intelligence officers and setting up the 'cages' where the POWs could be held for questioning – in solitary confinement, if necessary.

From his HQ overlooking the architectural opulence of Kensington Palace Gardens – which also had a number of deep cellars for 'difficult' cases – the lieutenant colonel organised camps in such diverse locations as Prees Heath, Shropshire, at a football ground in Preston, the winter quarters of Bertram Mills Circus at Ascot, a partly built housing estate at Huyton, Lancashire, and several racecourses ranging from Catterick to Doncaster, which were ideal for the purpose as they provided plenty of space and accommodation for prisoners and staff. Captured Germans believed to have the most vital information, especially *Luftwaffe* flying crews in the Battle of Britain, were kept closest to base at a very secure camp in Cockfosters, north London. As Scotland explained later in his autobiography, *The London Cage* (1957): 'It was a full-time job, travelling, organising, interrogating, clearing up disciplinary troubles, watching for signs of escape plans, and for ever hunting those precious pieces of information from prisoners to aid the efforts of Britain and our allies.'

The lieutenant colonel went to great lengths to ensure that the interrogation methods were thorough and utilised a variety of techniques. One tried-and-trusted method was to 'plant' an under-cover soldier who spoke fluent German – usually a Pole – to glean as much as possible from the prisoners. Scotland also comments on this aspect of his work:

> Among German air force prisoners, for example, there were some nicely varied types of character. There were the *Luftwaffe* men who were shot down; and there were those – quite a number in the early part of the war – who calmly landed their planes on British soil in order to escape the rigours of Hitler's war.

There were, of course, equally varied characteristics to be observed among the Italian airmen brought up to London on Wednesday, 13 November. Scotland and his interrogators were naturally intrigued about cross-examining these men, as they were the first CAI aircrews to have fallen into their hands in England.

There are no surviving documents of the interrogation of the five airmen in the 'London Cage', but Bill Lofts was able to discover details about their imprisonment and subsequent incarceration in a POW camp from a series of files in the old Public Records Office, numbered WO 199/407. From these it was evident that each man was grilled on military matters and the role of the CAI in Belgium. As the men were new participants in the aerial war, the lieutenant colonel's team wanted to know about the distribution of the Italian forces across the country, the numbers of pilots, crew members and ground staff at the various bases, and any operational plans they might be aware of for the future. As the five men had experience of both the fighter squadrons at Ursel and the bomber base at Chièvres, their information was invaluable in augmenting the details that reconnaissance flights had already supplied to Air Intelligence.

The interrogators were especially interested in anything the Italians could tell them about the numbers of German pilots and aircraft in the *Jagdegeschwaders* sharing their bases. The declining numbers of planes on the airfields that November was a clear sign of the *Luftwaffe's* inability to win the Battle of Britain. It was evident, too, from the men's bitterness, that they felt they were being left to do the 'dirty work' with inferior aircraft and had grown thoroughly disillusioned with their allies. It seemed to Scotland that they would not pose a threat as prisoners of war and could be sent to one or other of the two POW camps that had been earmarked for Italian prisoners.

Interestingly, although Scotland only mentions the Italian prisoners in passing in his book, he devotes several pages to Field Marshal Kesselring, at that time still the German commander in Belgium. Later, the field marshal would become supreme commander of German troops in Italy and, after the country's defeat by the Allies, would be accused of committing 'barbarous reprisals' against the local population. In fact, the lieutenant colonel interrogated Kesselring in the 'Cage' in 1946 and reached the conclusion that '[He] had not been responsible for the brutalities of which he was accused.'

After the cross-questioning of the five Italian airmen was complete, they were dispatched by train to Cambridge and from there in an army truck to Barton Field POW Camp at Ely. On the journey, the men were put together for the first time and apparently spent the two hours eating sandwiches, smoking and swapping stories of their experiences and lives back in Italy.

Barton Field – designated Camp No. 26 – was one of two camps that had been set up only a few weeks earlier to accommodate Italian prisoners captured in the battle for North Africa. The other was No. 29, based at Royston in Hertfordshire. Barton Field was located in an isolated spot within sight of the magnificent Ely Cathedral, towering over the Fens. It was the larger of the two Italian camps, equipped with barbed-wire fences and guard posts and had been designed for an initial intake of five hundred men. Royston, by comparison, could house three hundred. In both cases, it was intended that a fifth of the

POWs would be put to work building the Nissen huts and outbuildings in which they were to live, while the rest would be sent out to work on local farms.

Although the name Ely had been derived from *Elig*, meaning 'island of eels' – a name given to it by St Dunstan, who had apparently been offended by the 'lack of celibacy' of the local monks and turned them into slimy eels – the Italians proved much less inclined to try to slip away from custody than their German counterparts. As far as celibacy was concerned, however, the hot-blooded Italians who had been away from their women for months, wasted no opportunity to pursue local girls, as the local historian R Douglas Brown has reported:

> The authorities ruled that there must be no fraternisation between these Italians and local residents, but these proved extremely difficult to impose and up to a point the authorities turned a blind eye… Despite this official attitude, there was little ill-feeling towards the Italians and their ready smiles and relaxed attitudes earned them a good deal of sympathy, especially among the women, many of whose men had been called into the services.

The five CAI airmen found the conditions in the camp much better than they had been led to expect from the horror stories they had been told in Belgium. However, they did feel that living on the Fens was 'rather like being on a desert', to quote Sergeant Peter Jordan, a guard who later gave his reminiscences of life in the camp to the *Cambridge Daily News*. He told the paper that both prisoners and guards received the same amount of rations – their weekly allowance was 42 oz of meat, 8 oz of bacon, 5 ½ lb of bread, 10 ½ oz of margarine, as well as vegetables, cheese, cake, jam and tea – which meant they were actually better fed than the British civilian population.

The working day for the prisoners began with a wake-up call at 5.30 a.m., followed by breakfast and a roll call in time for those who had been designated for farm work to reach their destinations. The working day finished at 6 p.m., when they would have tea and then be free to do what they liked until lights out.

It was not hard for the five men to settle into this new existence after the dangers of life in the air force. For the next six years, in fact, the time would pass uneventfully for them in Cambridge until, when the war ended, they were able to return home.

However, for two of their fellow countrymen who also crashed on the east coast that same day and were taken prisoner, the years that followed would be anything but uneventful. One of them was Antonio Bianchi's missing cousin.

* * * * *

It has proved impossible to establish just how many men of the *Corpo Aereo Italiano* were killed or taken prisoner as a result of their attacks on England. The records would suggest the number is at least 21 dead and perhaps double that number when the names of known POWs are included. Several more are believed to have crashed into the North Sea, their bodies never recovered. Out of a total of almost a thousand missions of all types flown from the Belgian bases, this figure does credit to the skill and bravery of the CAI pilots, no matter what their achievements may have amounted to.

The records of the British lifeboat crews along the Norfolk, Suffolk and Essex coast during the autumn and winter period of 1940 contain a number of instances where attempts were made to rescue the occupants of shot-down aircraft. Derek E Johnson in his book, *East Anglia at War*, cities several examples:

> During the Battle of Britain, the lifeboats rescued both Allied and enemy airmen. The Walton and Frinton boat, *Emed*, was called out five times in 1940 and seven in 1941 to crashed aircraft. In one incident they found a dead German pilot floating upright supported by his lifejacket and in another the decomposing body of an Italian airman who had been washed up onto a sandbank.

Robert Malster, a specialist in the maritime history of the East Anglian coast, made an exhaustive study of the crews of the lifeboats during the Second World War and wrote about them with great feeling in his book, *Saved from the Sea* (1968):

> Those days of 1940 were busy ones for East Coast lifeboat men, though many of their trips were without any result. Reports of explosions, of flares seen at sea, of crashed aircraft, all had to be investigated, but time after time the same note appears in the records: 'Nothing found.' Occasionally the lifeboat men found a big patch of oil, some wreckage, or an empty boat; often their search was not even rewarded by that.

Malster makes particular reference to the record of the Aldeburgh RNLI motor lifeboat, *Abdy Beauclerk*. Launched in 1931, it carried out the first recorded lifeboat rescue of the Second World War on 10 September when racing to the 8,640-ton liner *Magdapur*, sunk by a German mine, and saving 74 of the 80 passengers and crew. The *Abdy Beauclerk* was to slide out across the town's shingle beach dozens of times during 1940, he says, to answer reports of aircraft crashed in the sea, airmen descending by parachute, or rubber dinghies reported drifting. The 'sterling service' of this boat would see it launched over fifty times in all weathers during the war years and save 107 lives in all.

The day of the major Italian raid on 11 November was to be one of the busiest for the Aldeburgh crew, according to Malster. Just after lunchtime, a large, unusual aircraft was seen to fall in the sea not far from the coast. The boat went out, but of the plane and crew there was no sight. Only a solitary parachute floated on the surface. The author continues:

> Markings on the parachute enabled it to be identified as Italian and probably from one of the BR.20M bombers known to have been operational that day. A little later another BR.20M also landed in the sea, but again the lifeboat was unable to find the bodies of the crew. Another two Italian bombers crashed further south and two airmen were rescued by the Walton and Frinton boat, *Emed*.

* * * * *

The lack of more specific information about the loss of Italian aircraft would probably have discouraged any researcher except Bill Lofts. But his painstaking scouring of the records in the Public Records Office and matching these to the lists that Ernesto Bianchi had provided him from CAI records, finally enabled him to establish that the two airmen rescued by the *Emed* tallied with a report from Squadron Leader Ciccu's 99 *Gruppo* that had lost two BR.20Ms on the 11 November raid. Flying 242-3, number MM22267, had been Pilot Officer Enzio Squazzini, while 243-10, numbered MM22620, had been commanded by Pilot Officer Ernesto Bianchi. Both were reported Missing in Action (MIA) with the proviso 'fate unknown, presumably POW'. Finding the second name convinced Lofts that he was getting closer to solving the mystery of what had happened to his friend's cousin.

In the records of the Essex County Police Force at Chelmsford, Lofts found that a 'Sottotenente Squarrini' and 'Sottotenente Biancho' had been brought to the police station on the evening of 11 November after being rescued at sea. Despite the mis-spelling, the names were too close to be anything other than those of the men posted as missing and their places of birth, given as Milan and Cannobina, matched CAI records. After being interviewed, both were dispatched under guard to London the following day. It   seems likely that the pair were interrogated at Cockfosters, but were probably not able to add a great deal to what Lieutenant Colonel Scotland had already learned from their predecessors. Finally, Squazzini and Bianchi were transported to POW Camp 29 at Royston.

This camp, on Therfield Heath to the west of Royston, was very different to Barton Field. Situated in the middle of 420 acres (170 hectares) of picturesque Hertfordshire grassland, the area derived its name from the old English words for 'dry place' – reflecting the free-draining nature of the underlying chalk – and had been used for farming ever since the Neolithic age. The Italian prisoners who came to the camp in their hundreds travelled into Royston on the Old North Road, which closely followed the line of Ermine Street built by their Roman forebears.

The first POWs at Camp 29 were responsible for constructing the living quarters on the site, which had first been used almost 150 years before by volunteers preparing to repel Napoleon and from 1855 for training by the Herts Militia. A large paddling pool built nearby in the 1930s for the children of Royston had, sadly, suffered from vandalism and any hopes the men from the Mediterranean might have nursed about using it to swim in the summer months were dashed when it was drained and used for the storage of coal.

Squazzini and Bianchi remained at Therfield Heath working in the camp and on local farms until the following year when they were moved in a party of fifty prisoners some 35 miles across country to another camp predominantly filled by Italians, Ashford Lodge. This camp – No. 129 – had also only recently been opened to cope with the increasing tide of prisoners resulting from the gains by British forces throughout 1942. The first months of their occupation were taken up with further construction work, followed by labouring in the fields of rural Essex.

The two former pilots were evidently not happy with the 'uniforms' that replaced their CAI flying clothes. They now wore a kit that somewhat resembled the British battledress, though it was chocolate brown in colour with large circles of red cloth stitched on to the back of the jacket and left trouser leg. To Enzio Squazzini with his Milanese fashion sense and 'hot-headed nature', the suits were almost an insult and he began to grow more aggressive towards the other prisoners and even some of the guards.

According to Bill Lofts' research, Squazzini became increasingly assertive when working outside the camp. He would take every opportunity to avoid any form of labour and used his dark good looks and easy charm to try to seduce any local female or land girl (member of the Women's Land Army, WLA) who crossed his path.

A fascinating study of this element of the war, *Prisoners of England* by Miriam Kochan (1980), has described how the POWs in England proved irresistible to many married and single women starved of male company with their men away at war. There were frequent prosecutions, the author says, attempting to discourage close relationships. In a number of instances, girls were fined for 'fraternising with Italian prisoners-of-war, thereby committing acts likely to prejudice discipline'. One excuse that was frequently given by women was that they would not have known the man in question, 'if he had not worked on the same farm as me'. Such fraternisation was particularly prevalent in Essex where, for example, two land girls were brought before a court for 'unlawfully dispatching letters to two prisoners-of-war at Finchingfield'.

These situations prompted some furious reactions in the press. Condemning one case, the *Essex Weekly News* thought it was shocking that there should be conduct of this kind: 'The national enemy is the private enemy, and these men with whom there were these intimate friendships are men whose purpose it has been to destroy everything these women enjoyed, and to kill our own flesh and blood.' Another paper, the *East Anglian Daily Times*, was also angered by lazy Italians: 'Everywhere there are complaints about their indolence – cannot some steps be taken to make them earn their keep?'

Each of these charges could have been levelled at Enzio Squazzini. He had affairs with women at both of the nearby villages of Pebmarsh and Colne Engaine where he was sent to work. On many occasions, too, it was said he made other prisoners who were afraid of him do his share of the work in the fields. Bill Lofts' notes continue: 'He behaved a bit like a Mafia Godfather. He intimated the other POWs into doing his labouring and took his pick of the prettiest girls. He even organised a strike in 1944 which nearly ruined the harvest.'

Local historian R Douglas Brown, confirms the facts of this event in his book, *East Anglia at War 1944*:

> In the summer of 1944, Ashford Lodge became the headquarters of the 129 Italian Labour Battalion. Five hundred prisoners-of-war lived in 50 huts. There gradually built up an outcry about the performance of some of the Italians, powerfully stimulated when they went on strike during the harvest period. Farmers who had been promised their services were immediately up in arms, one asserting that Fascists had stirred up the trouble. The strikers were put in strict confinement and part of their punishment was some meals of only bread and water.

This piece of troublemaking was in all probability the last incident in which Enzio Squazzini was involved and the details of his subsequent life are unknown. It has been suggested that he eventually left the country in August 1945 in the RAF's curiously named 'Operation Dodge' flying Italian prisoners home, but there is no evidence to substantiate the fact. Be that as it may, the Allied victories all across the world the previous year pointed to an end to the war and a consequent easing of the restraints on POWs (though not on the Germans, who still aroused strong emotions), as Brown also noted:

> Italians who had opted to collaborate with their captors were enjoying a large measure of freedom by the later months of 1944. They were allowed to talk to civilians and to visit private houses if invited, to visit cinemas at the discretion of their officer in charge and to make purchases in local shops; but they could not enter public houses or use public conveniences, except when on duty.

Despite these constraints, however, the last of the 'Chianti Raiders', Ernesto Bianchi, had actually been enjoying all of these freedoms and more for considerably longer – as far back, in fact, as 1942.

* * * * *

Antonio Bianchi told Bill Lofts that his cousin, Ernesto, was known to have been, 'headstrong, clever and self-sufficient'. A strapping, handsome young man with curly brown hair, he had learned to speak English at school where, for some unknown reason, he had earned the nickname Bruno. Called up into the *Regia Aeronautica*, he had proved to be a better-than-average bomber pilot – obtaining his wings in under 100 hours of flying – and risen to the rank of Pilot Officer before he and the crew of MM22620 had been posted to Chièvres. According to Antonio Bianchi, Ernesto was just 25 when he had flown off on the November mission that ended in tragedy off Harwich and from which he was the only survivor.

The young POW made the best of his situation in England and soon became friends with Enzio Squazzini. The pair moved from

Therfield Heath to Ashford Lodge, where Bianchi began to share his friend's dissatisfaction with a life of farm labouring. As the camp guards became more relaxed, he made up his mind. Early one morning in May 1942, Bianchi calmly swapped his chocolate-brown uniform for the long coat of a farm labourer and walked 10 miles to the railway station at Colchester. There he used his command of English and some of the pay he had saved from his farm work to board a train for London... and was never heard of again.

These were the facts that Bill Lofts knew were indisputable about the Italian with Scottish blood whose family name had originally been White. The rest of Ernesto Bianchi's subsequent life story he deduced from enquiries in London and with the help of John Gosling, a recently retired detective superintendent of the Metropolitan Police.

Lofts turned to Gosling because of the policeman's intimate knowledge of the Italian community in wartime London. Meeting the amiable and helpful DS proved a double bonus when he discovered that Gosling lived in Suffolk at Brantham, just across the estuary from Harwich, and knew all about the CAI raids. During his police work, he had even heard stories of an Italian pilot rumoured to be hiding in the London underworld.

Gosling had begun his career as a city copper in 1929 and ten years later had been promoted to Detective Sergeant. In 1939 he became a member of the famous Flying Squad and was plunged into another kind of war against the local criminals who were continuing to break the law and flourishing despite – or perhaps because of – all the upheaval of war. Soon Gosling had built up an intimate knowledge of the gangs operating in various areas of London. Among the most notorious of these were the Sabini family in the section of Clerkenwell known as 'Little Italy' and the White family of Islington and King's Cross who controlled much of Soho. Italian and Maltese pimps ran prostitution, while the protection racket was in the hands of two Soho gangs, the Messina and Vassalo families.

When Mussolini declared war on England, Special Branch officers had immediately rounded up seven hundred Italians in London in what was described as one of the biggest swoops on enemy aliens ever made in the country. According to a report in the *Daily Sketch* of 11 June:

> The Special Branch for a long time had under observation a
> large number of Italians who might have proved dangerous
> to this country. Last night's round up was almost a routine
> job to the detectives who knew exactly where to go. There
> are 50,000 Italians in London and throughout 'Little Italy' –
> the small streets in the neighbourhood of Gray's Inn Road
> and Mount Pleasant – and in the more famous Soho, there
> were many police raids. Among the Italian centres raided
> were the Italian Club in Charing Cross Road and the Littorio
> Club in Soho. Shortly after blackout, a stone was thrown
> through the window of an Italian café in Crompton Street,
> Paddington. The smashing of other café windows followed
> and police were rushed to the district.

The initial public antipathy against Italians – some of whom had
lived in the city for generations and whose families had seen
husbands, sons and brothers go off to join the British services – began
to subside as the months passed. City life, clothed in blackout at
night and under the constant threat of bombing raids by day,
continued as best it could. There was now, though, an even larger
floating population when the criminals were joined by deserters and
runaways.

In the restless, shadowy atmosphere, many of these men could be
found trying to make some cash by dealing in cigarettes, drink and
any other saleable commodity – always with one eye open for the law.
Alongside men like Detective Sergeant Gosling, officers of the Military
Police, naval pickets and RAF Special Police carried out routine
searches for men who had gone Absent Without Leave (AWOL). In the
warren of narrow streets with their cheap hotels, squalid boarding
houses, seedy restaurants and cafés and hundreds of illegal, basement
drinking clubs, it was easy enough for a determined 'absentee' to lead
an undetected life. As Donald Thomas has written with the benefit of
hindsight in his *An Underworld at War* (2003):

> Deserters divided into two groups: those who sought
> refuge with family or friends, and those who took to crime,

through force of habit or desperation. Defendants who had sheltered deserters were on the whole lightly dealt with... Public reactions to deserters and those who harboured them lacked the high moral indignation which the authorities encouraged.

Bill Lofts became increasingly convinced that Ernesto Bianchi had joined the ranks of these displaced persons – there were said to be as many as 18,000 in London at one time – and John Gosling shared his view. The pilot's namesakes, the White family, were known to have sheltered a number of British-born Italians who avoided call-up, notably the criminal Joey Mazzini, who was eventually arrested and charged with complicity in a series of big robberies of railway goods. The Whites also put a number of other burly Italians into jobs as doormen and bouncers, where they were never slow to use their fists or knives to keep their domains – and those inside – inviolate. One of these men, Antonio 'Babe' Mancini, doorman of the Palm Beach Bottle Party in Soho, who killed a clubber, had the dubious distinction of being the first gang member to be executed in wartime. Writing of this aspect of London underworld life in 1942, John Gosling says in his autobiography, *The Ghost Squad* (1959):

> The Italians always looked after their own. They controlled some of the darkest and most dismal streets in London, a veritable 'Crooks' Dormitory'... There were investigations by the military authorities into a number of reports of Italians avoiding the services. One family was rumoured to have sheltered an Italian airman who had ended up in London.

Although the Flying Squad had more important things to investigate than an enemy alien on the run, Gosling believed the man was probably not involved in crime. He agreed, though, that men with no criminal record or no file in the Criminal Records Office were always welcomed by the underworld. It was not difficult for gangsters to obtain the essential identity card and ration book – which had been introduced in September and December 1939, respectively – and to the Whites, no problem at all.

There is also the possibility that Ernesto Bianchi might have contacted one of the 'Bianchis' listed in the London phone book – although his cousin had never heard of any direct relative living in the city. He might even have picked up a contact listening to BBC Radio's Italian service, which had been on the airwaves of Europe since 1941. In particular, the programme, *Parla Londra!* (London Calling) hosted by the influential émigré, Massimo Coen, who broadcast the latest news and provided contact between Italians at home and abroad, 'gathering an immense following,' according to an account of his life by *The Times*.

In his excellent study *Crime in Wartime* (1982), Edward Smithies points out that an alternative for those on the run to being concealed among family or friends was to work anywhere that people might be prepared to turn a blind eye in return for cheap labour. He cites several instances in the city of London, all based on court proceedings. Among the examples he quotes is one of particular interest:

> *An Italian café proprietor* [my italics] in the Commercial Road
> was sent to prison for four months in 1943 for harbouring a
> deserter, who committed ration offences on his behalf for
> two years, and also for harbouring a girl who had run away
> from an approved school.

A coincidence – or the last twist of fate in the extraordinary story of the 'Chianti Raiders'? Certainly, there is nothing further known about Ernesto Bianchi after this year. But consult the records of Thames Magistrates Court for 13 July 1943 concerning the case in question and be prepared for a real surprise – just as the two 'detectives', Bill Lofts and John Gosling, were surprised back in the Sixties.

For the name of the proprietor is stated to have been Bruno Bianchi ...

EPILOGUE

In the second week of June 1970, England was gearing up for a general election. Labour Prime Minister Harold Wilson was expressing confidence about gaining a mandate for another term and despite the industrial strife that had plagued his administration was dismissing his opponent Edward Heath and the Conservative Party as 'Yesterday's Men'. He could hardly have imagined that the sudden overthrow of the Argentine president Juan Carlos Ongania by an army coup on 8 June would prove an omen for the fate that awaited him at the hands of the voters just ten days later.

That week would also see a remarkable incident that harked back to the years of the Second World War and one of the most famous periods of its history, the Battle of Britain. It was a reminder of certain enemy aircraft that had once planned to bomb the capital city into submission – and some elements of the story still remain a mystery today.

The event began on the morning of Wednesday, 10 June over the Thames Estuary, then basking in the sunlight of another warm summer's day. Two aluminium-coloured jet aircraft were seen heading in low towards London at a height of about 700 feet. The sound of their engines was loud enough to be heard over the bustle of London and one after another men and women in the streets looked upwards as the pair of aircraft screamed overhead. They were gone within moments, leaving a city full of puzzled people, only the older inhabitants having seen anything like this before. Within minutes, the Metropolitan Police were receiving dozens of agitated calls about the 'Buzzing of London' as it became known.

It would not be until weeks later – the news media in the interim full of the Conservative Party's surprise election victory on 19 June – that the facts of the incident, such as they were, came to light. The flight of the jets so low over the city was clearly an embarrassment to the Civil Aviation Authority and the RAF, both of whom said they had no record of it on their radar. What amusement there was to be had came from an unexpected source – the pilots of the jets were revealed to be members of the Italian air force who, by flying unchecked over the city, had achieved a feat their predecessors had so signally failed to do thirty years earlier.

The story – like that of the *Corpo Aereo Italiano* – began in Belgium: on this occasion at Beauvechain Airbase, a station some 30 miles south-east of Brussels, which had formerly been occupied by the *Luftwaffe* and by 1970 was a training base for NATO air forces. Originally opened in 1936 by the Belgian military, it had been bombed by the *Luftwaffe* on 10 May 1940, causing extensive damage to the buildings and aircraft on the ground. Beauvechain was shortly afterwards occupied by the Germans who remained there until October 1944 when the Americans recaptured the base. In the aftermath of the war, the airfield served as home to 160 Wing of the Belgian Air Force, flying Spitfires.

In 1955, Beauvechain was renamed *Base Charles Roman* after the wing commander who had died in action while in command of six squadrons. It became a fighter station and was made infinitely more effective by the arrival of the outstanding new supersonic combat plane, the Lockheed F-104 Starfighter. On 18 May 1958, one of the aircraft set a world speed record of 2,259.82 km/h (1,404.19 mph) and the following year, on 14 December, notched up a world altitude record of 31,514 m (103,395 ft) – making the Starfighter the first aircraft to hold both records simultaneously.

With its tremendous speed and armament of a six-barrel, M-61 20 mm Vulcan cannon, the F-104 proved to be a brilliant tactical fighter and soon many versions were being built in the USA and other countries for their military programmes including, appropriately, the Low Countries, Germany and Italy. It was two Italian pilots taking part in a training programme on Starfighters who flew to London on 10 June. Taking off from Beauvechain, they sped across the North Sea and up the Thames, before swinging south and heading back across Surrey and Kent to Belgium.

Legend has played a considerable part in elaborating the Italian 'raid'. One story states that the pilots – who have never been named – may have been related to a couple of the CAI airmen who attacked England in 1940. Another tale – which is far less likely – maintains the pilots were just out on a joy ride and knew they could outrun and outclimb anything that might pursue them. There have also been a number of conspiracy theorists busy with the 'facts': they maintain that the pilots were actually chasing a UFO that had been sighted over Belgium and was heading for England!

No doubt the story of the Italian 'Buzzing of London' in 1970 still has far to run.

* * * * *

The end of the 'Chianti Raiders' that came with the formal withdrawal of the CAI from Belgium on 15 April 1941 was, by any standards, a failure after all the grand plans that had sent them to the Channel coast. Air Marshal Fougier, who had done his best under the restrictions imposed on him, returned to Italy to continue Mussolini's ill-advised war. In November 1941, he was made Undersecretary of Aeronautics, and a year later promoted to the rank of General. The veteran airman was removed from office by the fall of Fascism in July 1943. He died on 24 April 1963.

The air force that Fougier had commanded in the Battle of Britain was soon forgotten in Italy and became the briefest of footnotes in the British history of that momentous year. Its men, though, still formed part of the grim statistics of the *Regia Aeronautica*'s losses up to the Armistice on 8 September 1943: over 5,700 were killed, with almost 10,000 taken prisoner. These same statistics also show that the force lost more than 5,200 aircraft, but claimed to have shot down over 4,500, although these figures must, of course, be treated with caution.

The reasons for the failure of the CAI mission have, I am sure, become obvious in these pages: they were unprepared, ill equipped and fatally lacking in resources. Indeed, these flaws were clear enough to certain observers as early as the end of 1940, though no one – least of all Mussolini – would take heed. On 7 December of that year the Aeronautical Correspondent of *The Times*, himself a former pilot, wrote what was virtually the finale on the CAI in a column entitled 'Italian Defeats in the Air':

> It is becoming increasingly clear that neither in men nor machines can the Italian Air Force compete on anything like equal terms with the RAF. The poor show which the force has put up is probably attributable to three things: first, the mediocrity of their aircraft; secondly, their lack of adequate training facilities; and, thirdly, to the fact that most of the pilots and crews have little heart for the war.

The prescient journalist could not resist a final jibe at the role of the Italians' erstwhile partners in the mix of skill, bravery and farce. He spotlighted a similar flaw in their leadership that would ultimately bring about a similar crushing defeat, but on a world scale:

> It was the Germans themselves who first commented on Italy's lack of first-class aircraft and on the inadequacy of her flying facilities. This was, of course, said some time before the war.

BIBLIOGRAPHY

Anonymous, *R.A.F: The Second Year* (A & C Black, 1942)
—*Winged Words: Our Airmen Speak for Themselves* (Heinemann, 1941)
Bacon, Jean & Stuart, *The Suffolk Shoreline* (Segment Publications, 1984)
Bekker, C, *Luftwaffe War Diaries* (Transworld Publishers, 1964)
Benham, Harvey, *Essex at War* (Essex County Standard, 1945)
Bickers, Richard Townshend, *The Battle of Britain* (Salamander, 1990)
Blond, Georges, *Born to Fly* (Souvenir Press, 1956)
Bonciana, Carlo, *F Squadron* (Dent, 1948)
Bosworth, R J B, *Mussolini* (Arnold, 2002)
Bowen, E G, *Radar Days* (Hilger, 1987)
Bowyer, Michael J F, *Air Raid! The Enemy Air Offensive Against East Anglia
1939–1945* (Patrick Stephens, 1986)
Box, C G, *Great Yarmouth – Frontline Town* (Great Yarmouth Corporation, 1945)
Brown, R Douglas, *East Anglia at War 1940* (Terence Dalton, 1981)
Bullock, Alan, *Hitler: A Study in Tyranny* (Odhams Press, 1952)
Churchill, Winston S, *The Second World War: Volume 1* (Cassell, 1952)
Collier, Basil, *Defence of the United Kingdom* (HMSO, 1957)
Deighton, Len, *Fighter* (Jonathan Cape, 1977)
Dobinson, Colin, *Fields of Deception: Britain's Bombing Decoys of the Second
World War* (Methuen, 2000)
Dunning, Chris, *Courage Alone: The Italian Air Force 1940–1943* (Air
Research Publications, 1988)
Farrell, Nicholas, *Mussolini: A New Life* (Weidenfeld & Nicolson, 2003)
Forrester, Larry, *Fly For Your Life* (Frederick Muller, 1956)
Foynes, Julian, *The Battle of the East Coast 1939–1945* (Foynes, 1992)
Garnett, David, *War in the Air: September 1939 to May 1941* (Chatto &
Windus, 1941)
Gillman, Peter & Leni, *'Collar The Lot!' Refugees and Aliens in World War II*
(Quartet, 1980)
Goodey, Charles, & Rose, Jack, *The Story of HMS Europa* (Royal Naval
Patrol Association, 1977)
Gosling, John, *The Ghost Squad* (W H Allen, 1959)
Hitchman, Harry G, & Driver, Philip, *Harwich: Five Years in the Front Line*
(Harwich, 1985)
Jackson, Robert, *Air War Over France* (Ian Allan, 1974)

Jenkins, Ford, *Lowestoft: Port War* (W S Cowell Ltd, 1946)

Johnson, Derek E, *East Anglia at War 1939–1945* (Jarrold's, 1978)

Jones, Professor R V, *Most Secret War* (Hamish Hamilton, 1978)

Kinsey, Gordon, *Aviation: Flight Over Eastern Counties Since 1937* (Dalton, 1977)

—*Bawdsey – Birth of the Beam* (Dalton, 1983)

—*Martlesham Heath: The Story of the RAF Station, 1917–1973 (1975)* (Dalton, 1975)

Kochan, Miriam, *Prisoners of England* (Macmillan, 1980)

Malster, Robert, *Saved from the Sea* (David & Charles, 1968)

Mason, F K, *Battle Over Britain* (McWhirter, 1969)

Masters, David, *'So Few': The Immortal Record of the Royal Air Force* (Eyre & Spottiswoode, 1941)

Middleton, Drew, *The Sky Suspended* (Secker & Warburg, 1987)

Moen, Lars, *Under the Iron Heel* (Robert Hale, 1941)

Monks, Noel, *Squadrons Up* (Gollancz, 1940)

Moore, Bob, & Fedorowich, Kent, *British Empire and its Italian Prisoners of War, 1940–1947* (Palgrave Macmillan, 1996)

Overy, Richard, & Wheatcroft, Andrew, *The Road to War* (Macmillan, 1989)

Price, Alfred, *Blitz on Britain* (Ian Allan, 1976)

Richards, Denis, *The Royal Air Force 1939–1945* (HMSO, 1953)

Rootes, A. *Frontline County* (Robert Hale, 1980)

Santoro, General G, *Stralcio dell'Opera Aeronautica Italiana nella Seconda Guerra Mondiale* (Mondadori, 1953)

Scotland, Lt Col. A P, *The London Cage* (Evans Brothers, 1957)

Segre, Claudio G, *Italo Balbo: A Fascist Life* (University of California Press, 1990)

Sgarlato, N, *Italian Aircraft of World War Two* (Delta, 1979)

Shores, Christopher, *Regia Aeronautica: A Pictorial History of the Italian Air Force 1940–1943* (Squadron, 1976)

Smith, Denis Mack, *Mussolini* (Weidenfeld & Nicolson, 1981)

Smith, Graham, *Suffolk Airfields in the Second World War* (Countryside Books, 1995)

Smithies, Edward, *Crime in Wartime* (Allen & Unwin, 1982)

Spaight, J M, *The Battle of Britain* (Chatto & Windus, 1941)

Stokes, Doug, *Wings Aflame* (William Kimber, 1985)

Thomas, Donald, *An Underworld at War* (John Murray, 2003)

Thompson, J, *Italian Civil and Military Aircraft 1930–1945* (Aero, 1963)

Townsend, Peter, *Duel of Eagles* (Cassell, 1970)

Vergnano, P, *Fiat Fighters 1930–1945* (Intyrama, 1969)

Walbank, F Alan, *Wings of War* (Batsford, 1942)

Weaver, Leonard T, *The Harwich Story* (Harwich, 1975)

ACKNOWLEDGEMENTS

Once again I am very happy to acknowledge the debt I owe to a number of people for making this book possible. In particular, my late friend, W O G 'Bill' Lofts, whose initial research provided me with the impetus to tell the story; also his friend, Antonio Bianchi, who helped to fill in many of the gaps from the Italian side. Marella Wise was a great help while I was fact-finding in Italy and John and Margaret Kent have been a valuable source of information on translating Italian texts. Among the others who generously provided information were Harry Hawes, Michael Soanes, Thomas Potts, Peter Jordan, Doug Patrick and Christopher Elliott, as well as Mark Bentinck, the Royal Marines Records Officer, and Matthew O'Sullivan of the Royal New Zealand Air Force. The staff at the RAF Museum in Hendon and the Battle of Britain Historical Society answered many of my technical questions about both the British and Italian aircraft involved in the conflict.

I must also acknowledge the National Archives at Kew, who hold a series of relevant military reports from the Second World War (classified from AIR22 to AIR27) and those of the Ministry of Home Security from the same period (HO198–HO202). The Department of Documents in the Imperial War Museum proved a major source of Italian Air Force files from the period. When seeking more local information about the CAI attacks on East Anglia, I received a great deal of assistance from the staffs of the Public Libraries in Hadleigh, Sudbury and Colchester, as well as the archivists at the two Country Records Offices for Suffolk, based at Bury St Edmunds and Ipswich, where some invaluable police reports of the time are lodged – plus the Essex Records Office at Chelmsford and the Norfolk Records Office in Norwich.

Finally, I would like to thank the following newspapers, magazines and publishers for permission to quote from their publications: the *East Anglian Daily Times*, the *Eastern Daily Press*, *East Anglian Magazine*, *The Times*, BBC Sound Archives, *Air International*, *Air Pictorial*, *Interconair Aviazione e Marina*, *Aerospace Historian*, *Fly Past*, *Flight*, *Illustrated London News*, *Punch* and the publishers Random House, Orion Publishing Group and Pan Macmillan. Thanks, also, to my publisher Jeremy Robson, my dedicated editor, Jane Donovan, Rob Dimery for copy-editing the manuscript and Sarah Barlow for proofreading the pages. 'The Chianti Raiders' now have their place in the history of the Battle of Britain, thanks to them all.

INDEX